ONE WEEK LOAN

6/5/08

Culture and Politics in the Information Age

How are new social movements making use of the latest information and communication technologies? How is the internet reshaping forms of political mobilisation, protest and communication?

Have we entered an era of 'new politics'? New Labour in Britain may be one aspect of the 'new politics', alongside the emergence of 'lifestyle' and 'identity' politics where matters such as equal rights, environmental justice and world poverty take centre stage. Add to this new media – and the internet – and the idea that things really are new seems compelling. *Culture and Politics in the Information Age* looks at the claims for a new politics, often with a quizzical eye.

It is not only new technologies that are reshaping the context of politics today, but also the apparent decline in the salience of traditional political organisation and debate. Globalisation, the decline of the nation state, global media and post-ideological politics all contribute to a 'new politics', where conventional distinctions between parties on the grounds of class, are now replaced by 'lifestyle' issues, and cultural politics have emerged in the form of social movements such as animal- and human-rights activism, the environment and gender issues.

Highly regarded contributors from both sides of the Atlantic address key aspects of our changed situation, applying empirical case studies alongside challenging social theory on issues such as digital democracy, cultural politics and transnational communities. This highly topical book will be invaluable reading for students of politics, communications and IT, sociology and cultural studies.

Frank Webster is one of Britain's best-known analysts of the 'information society'. He has been researching information trends since the 1970s. His many publications include the best-selling *Theories of the Information Society*, and (with Kevin Robins) *Times of the Technoculture* (also published by Routledge). He is Professor of Sociology at the University of Birmingham.

Transnationalism
Series Editor: Steven Vertovec, *University of Oxford*

'Transnationalism' broadly refers to multiple ties and interactions linking people or institutions across the borders of nation-states. Today myriad systems of relationship, exchange and mobility function intensively and in real time while being spread across the world. New technologies, especially involving telecommunications, serve to connect such networks. Despite great distances and notwithstanding the presence of international borders (and all the laws, regulations and national narratives they represent), many forms of association have been globally intensified and now take place paradoxically in a planet-spanning yet common arena of activity. In some instances transnational forms and processes serve to speed up or exacerbate historical patterns of activity, in others they represent arguably new forms of human interaction. Transnational practices and their consequent configurations of power are shaping the world of the twenty-first century.

This book forms part of a series of volumes concerned with describing and analysing a range of phenomena surrounding this field. Serving to ground theory and research on 'globalisation', the Routledge book series on 'Transnationalism' offers the latest empirical studies and ground-breaking theoretical works on contemporary socio-economic, political and cultural processes which span international boundaries. Contributions to the series are drawn from Sociology, Economics, Anthropology, Politics, Geography, International Relations, Business Studies and Cultural Studies.

The series is associated with the Transnational Communities Research Programme of the Economic and Social Research Council (see http://www.transcomm.ox.ac.uk).

The series consists of two strands:

Transnationalism aims to address the needs of students and teachers and these titles will be published in hardback and paperback. Titles include:

Culture and Politics in the Information Age
A New Politics?
Edited by Frank Webster

Routledge Research in Transnationalism is a forum for innovative new research intended for a high-level specialist readership, and the titles will be available in hardback only. Titles include:

1 New Transnational Social Spaces
International Migration and Transnational Companies
in the Early 21st Century
Edited by Ludger Pries

2 Transnational Muslim Politics
Reimagining the Umma
Peter G. Mandaville

Culture and Politics in the Information Age

A new politics?

Edited by
Frank Webster

London and New York

First published 2001
by Routledge
11 New Fetter Lane, London EC4P 4EE

Simultaneously published in the USA and Canada
by Routledge
29 West 35th Street, New York, NY 10001

Routledge is an imprint of the Taylor & Francis Group

Typeset in Baskerville by
Keystroke, Jacaranda Lodge, Wolverhampton
Printed and bound in Great Britain by
MPG Books Ltd, Bodmin

British Library Cataloguing in Publication Data
A catalogue record for this book is available from the British Library

Library of Congress Cataloging in Publication Data
Webster, Frank.
    Culture and politics in the information age : a new politics? / Frank Webster.
        p. cm. – (Transnationalism)
    Includes bibliographical references and index.
    1. Information society. 2. Information technology–Social aspects. 3. Information
technology–Political aspects. 4. Internet–Social aspects. 5. Internet–Political aspects.
6. Politics and culture. 7. Social movements. I. Title. II. Series

HM851 .W43 2001
303.48′33–dc21   00–068996

ISBN 0–415–24635–0 (hbk)
ISBN 0–415–24636–9 (pbk)

Contents

Acknowledgements

Most of these papers were presented originally at a conference at the University of Birmingham on 16 and 17 September 1999. This was hosted by the Centre for Cultural Studies and Sociology. I should like to thank staff in the Department of Cultural Studies and Sociology at Birmingham who helped in diverse ways.

Funding for the conference was supplied by the ESRC (Economic and Social Research Council) through the agency of Steve Vertovec, director of the Transnational Communities Programme, and Professor Robin Cohen of the University of Warwick. Versions of some of the papers later appeared in the pages of the journal *Information, Communication and Society*. For help with this I thank *iCS*'s excellent editor, Brian Loader of Teesside University.

Thanks also to Brian Tomlin of *Canadian Foreign Policy* for permission to use the article 'Globalisation, Citizenship and Technology: The MAI Meets the Internet' (*Canadian Foreign Policy* 7(2): 83–105) by Peter Jay Smith and Elizabeth Smythe. This was presented at the International Studies Association conference in Los Angeles in March 2000.

Barrie Axford of Oxford Brookes University, an old friend, generously shared his thoughts on the topic with me.

Finally, thanks to my family. Living and working in two places – Oxford and Birmingham – certainly has its strains. Liz, Isabelle and Frankie are (usually) balms to the tensions of living in such a fraught and frenetic manner.

F.W.
Headington / Edgbaston
October 2000

Contributors

Mario Diani is Professor of Sociology and Head of the Department of Government in the University of Strathclyde in Glasgow. Major publications in English include *Social Movements* (1999), *Green Networks* (1995) and *Studying Collective Action* (1992). He is the European Editor of *Mobilization: The International Journal of Theory and Research in Social Movements*. Current research projects include studies of networks of civic organisations in Britain, in the context of the ESRC Democracy and Participation Programme, of transformations of environmental action in Italy, and of applications of network analysis to the study of collective action.

Alan Dordoy is Principal Lecturer in the School of Social, Political and Economic Sciences and Programme Director for undergraduate courses at Northumbria University, Newcastle-upon-Tyne. His teaching interests are in sociological theory, modern social and political thought, and IT applications in the social sciences. Recent research is in the area of environmentalism and political theory and a paper on 'Ecological socialism – a feminist materialist perspective' (with M. Mellor) is in *Capitalism, Nature, Socialism* (2000). He also has an interest in the development of teaching and learning in the social sciences, including being director of an FDTL project on Sociologists in Placement.

Mary Mellor is Chair of the Sustainable Cities Research Institute and Professor in the School of Social, Political and Economic Sciences at the University of Northumbria. She has published extensively on the links between socialist, feminist and ecological thought. Her most recent book is *Feminism and Ecology* (1997). She is at present working on radical economic theory in relation to social equality and ecological sustainability.

Kate Nash is currently Lecturer in Sociology at Goldsmiths College, London. She is the author of *Universal Difference: Feminism and the Undecidability of 'Women'* (1998) and *Contemporary Political Sociology: Globalization, Politics and Power* (2000). She has also edited *Readings in Contemporary Political Sociology* (2000) and co-edited (with Alan Scott) *The Blackwell Companion to Political Sociology* (forthcoming).

Jenny Pickerill's research focuses upon the use of computer-mediated communication technologies, in particular its use by protest campaigners, environmentalists and those choosing 'alternative' lifestyles. She has written several journal articles and book chapters on such topics. Her doctoral research examined the ways in which environmentalists in Britain use Internet technology, in the Department of Geography, University of Newcastle-upon-Tyne. She can be contacted at j.m.pickerill@newcastle.ac.uk.

Sasha Roseneil is Professorial Research Fellow in Sociology and Gender Studies and Director of the Centre for Interdisciplinary Gender Studies at the University of Leeds. She is author of *Disarming Patriarchy: Feminism and Political Action at Greenham* (1995), and *Common Women, Uncommon Practices* (2000). She has also co-edited (with Julie Seymour) *Practising Identities* (1999), and (with Jeff Hearn) *Consuming Cultures* (1999).

Alan Scott is Professor of Sociology at the University of Innsbruck, Austria. He is author of *Ideology and New Social Movements* (1990).

Peter Jay Smith is Professor of Political Science at Athabasca University. He has published on Canadian political thought, public policy and political economy. He is the co-editor (with Janet Ajzenstat) of 'Canada's origins: Liberal, Tory or Republican?'.

Elizabeth Smythe is Associate Professor of Political Science at Concordia University College of Alberta. She has published on Canadian investment policy, negotiation of trade-related investment measures at the World Trade Organisation and the multilateral agreement investment at the Organisation for Economic Co-operation and Development. Her current research interests include the role of civil society and its use of new technologies in shaping trade and investment negotiations.

Nick Stevenson is Lecturer at Sheffield University in the Department of Sociological Studies. He is the author of *Culture, Ideology and Socialism: Raymond Williams and E. P. Thompson* (1995), *Undestanding Media Cultures: Social Theory and Mass Communication* (1995), The *Transformation of the Media* (1999) and *Culture and Citizenship* (2000). He is currently working on book-length projects on David Bowie, and cultural citizenship.

John Street is Reader in Politics at the University of East Anglia. He is author of *Politics and Popular Culture* (1997).

John Tomlinson is Professor of Cultural Sociology and Director of the Centre for Research in International Communication and Culture, Nottingham Trent University. His latest book is *Globalization and Culture* (1999).

Howard Tumber is Professor of Sociology and Dean of the School of Social and Human Sciences at City University. His work has concentrated mainly on the sociology of news and journalism. He is the editor of *Media Power, Professionals and Policies* (2001); and *News: A Reader* (1999). He is the author of *Television and* *the Riots* (1982) and co-author of *Reporting Crime* (1994); and *Journalists at War* (1988). He is the co-founder and co-editor of the new journal *Journalism – Theory, Practice, Criticism*.

Neil Washbourne is presently Lecturer in Media Studies at Leeds Metropolitan University.

Frank Webster is currently Professor of Sociology at the University of Birmingham in the Department of Cultural Studies and Sociology. He has also been Docent in the Department of Journalism and Mass Communication, University of Tampere, Finland (since 1997). He is the author of many articles and books, including: *The New Photography: Responsibility in Visual Communication* (1980); *Information Technology: A Luddite Analysis* (1986) and *The Technical Fix: Computers, Industry and Education*, both with Kevin Robins, (1989); *Theories of the Information Society* (1995); *The Postmodern University?*, edited with Anthony Smith (1997); *Times of the Technoculture: From the Information Society to the Virtual Life*, with Kevin Robins (1999) and *Understanding Contemporary Society: Theories of the Present*, edited with Gary Browning and Abigail Halcli (2000). He is currently working, with Kevin Robins, on *The Virtual University?*

Abbreviations

CMC	Computer-Mediated Communication
ESRC	Economic and Social Research Council
FoE	Friends of the Earth
GiS	Geographical Information System
GM	Genetically Modified
IMF	International Monetary Fund
IT	Information Technology
LGDO	Local Government Development Officer
LGNP	Local Government Networking Project
MAI	Multilateral Agreement on Investment
NGO	Non-Governmental Organisation
NIMBY	'not in my back yard'
OECD	Organisation for Economic Co-operation and Development
SMO	Social Movement Organisation
UKCOD	UK Citizens On-Line Democracy
WTO	World Trade Organisation
WWF	World Wide Fund for Nature

1   A new politics?

Frank Webster

Introduction

We live, it is widely accepted, at a time of unprecedented change. As historian Eric Hobsbawm (1994) observes, the years since 1975 have seen 'the greatest, most rapid and most fundamental [set of changes] in recorded history' (p. 8). In saying this there is no claim that change today is anything like so climactic or immediately imposing as, say, the fraught period of the Second World War, the terrors of the Russian Revolution, or the internecine and bloody struggles that still plague parts of the world. When it is said that the world today is experiencing unprecedented change what is being suggested is that we are living through transformations which profoundly alter our whole ways of life. Wars have come and gone, and they have been devastating for many people, but the ways in which the survivors conducted their lives have continued, by and large, as before, once the fighting ceased. People went back to the fields, and, in more recent history, to factories, if necessary to rebuild and start again. Nowadays, however, changes taking place transform our very means of existence: genetic engineering radically transforms species reproduction, robotics allow factories to do away with work-forces, occupations are decimated or disappear as activities are relocated, spare-part surgery rejuvenates ageing joints and organs . . . This is what is meant when observers comment on today's unprecedented changes: the rhythms of everyday life, our daily experiences, our routine schedules, are being transformed in ways which, by any historical comparison, are remarkable.

Not only is change today of unprecedented depth, reaching down to challenge our very conceptions of human nature, but it comes also at a speed and on a scale which, on any previous comparator, are truly astonishing. We live today through changes which are profound, yet these also happen within a time-frame of but a decade or so. The Industrial Revolution, with its steam power, the factory system, wage labour, and the railway train appeared to many contemporaries an awesome phenomenon. But it ought to be remembered that the 'Industrial Revolution' was invented as a concept in the 1880s by a historian who looked back on the previous century. It was only in retrospect that the changes then seemed to have amounted to a revolutionary upheaval. Indeed, farm labouring was by far the largest male occupation in Britain, and domestic service the overwhelmingly biggest employment for females, as late as 1870, one hundred and more years after the start of the Industrial Revolution (Harris 1993: 41; Thompson 1988: 25–7). The heartland technology of steam power took decades to permeate through the country so innovation, if real, appeared incremental to most of those who lived through it. Today, however, we need look back scarcely a decade to trace the spread of information technologies through office, home and education. In space of a very few years digitalisation has become a routine part of life, whether it be through the television set, the PC, or the mobile telephone. At the same time, nowadays change occurs on a much grander scale than ever before. No longer is something pioneered in Lancashire then introduced, years after, into Nottingham. Now a decision or technology may come out of San Jose and its impact can be felt in Swindon only weeks later; and currency deals on the London stock exchange can affect Singapore or Indonesia days or just hours afterwards. . . .

Not only this. Change is now so much a part of the routine of life that no-one expects things to remain the same for even a decade. On the contrary, we live with the expectation that our ways of life are unstable, that the only surety is that things will continue to change. And added to this is the widespread acknowledgement that this pace of change is accelerating, so much so that for many people, perhaps even for most, a sense of uncertainty – exhilarating for some, frightening for others – comes with the territory in the twenty-first century.

In sum, we may characterise life today as something undergoing unprecedented change which yet continues to accelerate, which is of a profundity so deep that it is reshaping just about all aspects of our everyday lives, from our intimate behaviour to the supply of household goods, and which yet possesses a geographical reach which, against all previous comparisons, is enormous.

Themes of change

Since social scientists, like other observers, are struck more by the new than the familiar, it is not surprising that many have paid close attention to these more recent changes, and that most have concluded that they signal most momentous change. Let me review some themes which recur in this sort of writing.

1. *Technology* is usually a privileged element in accounts of recent change. The sheer scale, scope and speed of technological innovations, from home entertainment systems to the latest missile defence, from new medical treatments to *in vitro* fertilisation techniques, draws the attention of commentators. Information and communications technologies (ICTs) especially, followed closely by biotechnology and genetics, are presented as the main motors of change, as innovations which are bringing about radical social transition. We are all familiar with this sort of account, and it is indeed hard to resist its lure: new technologies are transforming all ways of acting, whether it is robotics in the workplace, interactive television at home, pacemakers on our bodies, or – currently a focus of attention – the Internet pervasively. There is a well-established genre of writing on the 'high-tech' society dedicated to assessing technology's impact – and this is adjudged to be massive and ongoing.

2. *Globalisation* identifies a tendential process of increasing interpenetration and interdependence of activities on a world scale which take place in real time. One of the dominant refrains in business, media and academic circles, globalisation emphasises a shift towards relationships being organised on '7/24' bases from anywhere around the world. In the language of the social scientist 'time–space compression' means that life today is subject to a more frenetic pace than hitherto, and that developments originating from just about anywhere in the world can have rapid consequences for people living thousands of miles distant. Examples are legion: currency dealings on stock markets exceeding a trillion dollars per day which can rock economies and dismay national governments, the relocation of production from Birmingham or Sunderland to another part of Europe, fresh-cut flowers arriving daily in London from Central America. . . .

3. A corollary of globalisation has been a relative *decline in national sovereignty*. It is often suggested that the period, dating from the Treaty of Westphalia in the mid-seventeenth century, during which the nation-state was the central organising feature of life, is now in on the wane. It is not often suggested that the nation-state is set to disappear in the foreseeable future, but there is thought to have been a decisive reduction in its room to manoeuvre. No longer capable of effectively controlling affairs inside its territorial boundaries, for example because financial relationships transcend frontiers and take place instantaneously or because decisions taken by super states such as the European Union or United Nations may take precedence over national desires, the days of the sovereign nation-state seem to have passed.

4. The collapse of the USSR's satellites in 1989 and of the USSR itself two years later were events of prodigious significance, both in their practical consequences and the effects on the imagination. They announced the *end of the collectivist experiment* and of the ideological struggle between communism and capitalism which had dominated most of the twentieth century and a good part of the nineteenth. And that struggle ended with the out-and-out victory of capitalism which had demonstrably trumped communism as a system capable of offering both economic prosperity and democratic order. Margaret Thatcher announced well before 1989 that 'there is no alternative' to the market system, and to many commentators it appears now that she was correct. Since 1989 TINA has been the order of the day across the world. No longer having to look over its shoulder at the spectre of communism, capitalism is now unassailably triumphant almost everywhere. Even social democratic systems which favoured limited nationalisation, robust public services and a welfare state have found themselves on the defensive against the expansionist, confident and dynamic free market. Privatisation and deregulation today represent a consensus around the world, with few redoubts still holding on to even the social democratic keep. Capitalism is today the uncontested organising way of life, and with it comes an emphasis on continuous upheaval driven by competition and the unrelenting search for growth.

5. In part a question of technological innovation, but much more than this, we have witnessed in recent years a *pervasive spread of media* both around the world and ever deeper into the private realms of life. Today we have round-the-clock

television services combined with networks of institutions which combine satellite and cable delivery systems that ensure coverage can be made available virtually instantaneously from pretty well anywhere. The Internet consolidates this trend and allows twenty-four-hour-per-day communications. To say this is not to deny that there are important differences regarding access to new media within advanced societies and, still more dramatic, between metropolitan centres and the poverty-stricken parts of the world. However, what must be conceded is that, most emphatically in western Europe, Japan and North America, the television monitor (increasingly enhanced for interactivity) is central to everyday life and is a crucial window on the world for most people. It is exceedingly hard to make definitive statements about television's effects, but what is beyond dispute is that its location inside the home and its contents that are continuously available are important elements of human experience in much of the world today.

6. Advanced as long ago as the 1960s, but today considerably more palpable, there has been a *recomposition of stratification* and a consequent decline in the salience of the working class in political (and other) life. Industrial restructuring, relocation, automation and, above all, a marked shift towards white-collar employment have meant that the organised working class is diminishing both in size and influence. Coal mines, steel works and large manufacturing plants are in terminal decline, and with these are going the characteristically male manual occupations which predominated in those industries. Accompanying this decline has come a weakening of the local communities and associated patterns of interaction and value systems which were disposed towards codes of togetherness, loyalty and mutual support among 'us' against 'them'.

7. Consonant with this decline of the 'solidaristic' working class has been an expansion of individualism and an increase in the self-consciousness which is its accompaniment. This is in part associated with the growth of white-collar occupations, but it is also shaped by a long-term trend towards what Anthony Giddens has called *heightened reflexivity*. There are many dimensions to this, but combined they mark a move towards greater scepticism about received ways of behaving and an increased self-consciousness about how to conduct affairs. In turn, this has stimulated an ethos of choice in life which endorses positions not because one has been reared to adopt them, but because it is a personal decision not to eat meat, to lend support to a political proposition, or even to wear one's hair in a certain way.

8. Together these developments have stimulated the continuing *decline of community* and its replacement with associative relationships based more and more on active choice. Indicative of this is that there is now considerable suspicion cast on notions of community since these evoke compulsion, conformity, intolerance and even forms of fundamentalism. Commentators readily point to expressions of community such as ethnic cleansing and militant Islam which demand uncritical support from adherents and threaten the lives and liberties of outsiders. In place of community can be identified a postmodern relativism in which values and conduct are regarded as highly differentiated 'lifestyle choices' which are incommensurable.

New times, new politics

With all such concentration on the new, it is not at all surprising that there is also a good deal of interest in the implications for, and responses of, politics and politicians. After all, if class structures are transforming, then it is evident that political parties must reassess their established appeals to voters. And if globalisation is subverting the nation-state, then politicians must come to terms with these changed circumstances which, potentially at least, throw awry nation-centred policies. Again, if there is evidence in contemporary society of an increasing diversity of lifestyles that are perceived to be incommensurate, then there are inevitably dilemmas for practising politicians.

This is the context in which this book makes its appearance. So much seems to be changing that many announce the arrival of a radically new politics. At one level this is the situation from which comes talk of a 'Third Way' and of the creation of New Labour. But there are many other issues to be addressed: changes in campaigns, in the adoption of computerised technologies, in new kinds of activists, in new agendas for politics, in innovative forms of protest. . . . Brought together for an Economic and Social Research Council (ESRC)-sponsored conference at the University of Birmingham, the contributors addressed a series of questions that arose from the suggestion that we do indeed inhabit new times.

As I have said, the themes which recur in suggestions that we are amid a new era find expression in a diversity of social analyses. However, many of these themes are conveniently drawn together in the recent writing of Manuel Castells, whose trilogy *The Information Age* (1996–8) has had an enormous effect on contemporary thought within and beyond the academy. Castells is a thinker with whom all contemporary social analysts must come to terms, whatever might be their specialist interest, since he presents in *The Information Age* an extraordinarily encyclopedic, empirically rich and synthetic vision of the world today. In *The Information Age* the themes outlined above are each afforded lengthy discussion and yet are integrated into a remarkably coherent account of the character of the world today. In view of this it will surprise no-one that several of the contributors to this book feel compelled to engage with Castells's account.

For purposes of this book I need only highlight Castells's arguments which pertain to the 'new politics' proposition. They run along the following lines.

We now inhabit a 'network society', one in which the *flows of information*, and the handling, assessments and decisions made on the basis of information, decisively alter previous ways of life. In the 'network society' the global is a key point of reference, not least because, courtesy of a world-wide infrastructure of ICTs, place is no longer the inhibitor to action that it once was. And neither is time: in the 'information age' activities may take place in real time on a planetary scale. The instantaneity of information flows means, in Castells's view, that we must come to terms with the 'systemic volatility' that is its accompaniment, since the unceasing movement of information results in change being both routine and unpredictable. This is one reason why the 'network society' undermines the nation-state and so many of its once-entrenched institutions (e.g. state-run utilities, trade unions, domestic oligopolies) prove incapable of containing the protean forces of globalisation.

Castells goes on to identify as central to the 'network society' those who are the creators, designers and disseminators of information flows. Together these constitute 'informational labour', being those who think, plan and conceive in situations of great uncertainty. Informational labour exacerbates uncertainty by constantly seeking to make change happen while simultaneously being especially well suited to coping with change itself. This is because informational labour is, perhaps above all else, highly educated and thereby capable of 'self-programming', a capacity bestowed on those who have 'learned how to learn' and which allows for the maximum flexibility that is the requisite of survival in the volatile information age. In contrast, 'generic labour' is that which is characteristically rigid and inflexible, the sort of work once typical of manual employees who had received a training in set tasks with the expectation that they would continue to do the same job for the rest of their lives. To Castells such labour is in constant jeopardy from informational labour of one sort or another which may use its skills perhaps to automate generic labour out of a job, or to relocate it abroad where labour is cheaper or more diligent, or even to invent a new product or process that leaves it far behind. Either way, informational labour is the class of the future while generic labour is doomed.

In terms of politics these changes, while rooted in economic organisation, have important consequences. First off, with the decline of older forms of stratification, the class bases of politics are denuded, and with them are undermined the nationally based institutions which helped legitimate them (e.g. the welfare state, the labour movement). In their place come 'identity politics' which are simultaneously global and local, irreducible to straightforward class affiliations, and, in key respects, capable of capturing and expressing cultural shifts in sensibility. This is not to ignore the continued salience of material issues in politics (nor is it to suggest that classes were once concerned solely with economic matters), but rather to acknowledge a heightened role in the realm of 'identity politics' for cultural matters, broadly defined to encompass 'feelings', 'differences', 'lifestyles' and 'affectivity'. The remarkable response to the death of Princess Diana and the conduct of her funeral in 1997 testifies to this new quality of public life (and beyond) in the UK, when many people appeared to be deeply moved by emotion, and when many found themselves able to speak about matters that hitherto had been hard to voice (sexualities, inadequate families, self-esteem). Sasha Roseneil (Chapter 7) deals precisely with this moment in British life, when the borders of politics, public discourse and the personal were breached in several ways.

Second, Castells emphasises the primary importance of new social movements which offer promise of gaining collective identities to participants (he is not so persuaded as some of the full development of individualism) and herald novel forms of political agitation. Here he instances especially environmental and feminist social movements which, while diverse, manifest the global outlooks and transnational connections his 'network society' theory announces.

Third, politics in the 'information age' is, in Castells's view, either on the informational networks or it is irrelevant. That is, contemporary politics is necessarily media-centric since 'outside the media sphere there is only political marginality' (Castells 1996: 312). The days of the hustings, when politicians got on the stump to meet the electorate and where public oratory was a requisite of political efficacy, are now in the past. Today's core skills for the politician include an easy manner, a persuasive voice, a well-prepared brief, and a willingness to address the voters through the television console. And, of course, the politician today must be supported by those competent with computerised technologies, able to design an attractive website and to update it regularly, capable of maintaining and sorting electronic lists of voters' dispositions, and supported by the findings of carefully selected focus groups. Effective campaigners in the new political movements, as well as in the political realm proper, must possess abilities common to all informational labour, namely excellent communication, analytical and information-processing skills. Activists now must be, in Castells's terms, 'symbol mobilisers', able to adopt a 'networking, decentred form of organisation and intervention' (1996: 361, 362). For instances of this new phenomenon think of Amnesty International, Oxfam or Greenpeace. These are campaigning organisations which promote particular agendas (human rights, world poverty, environmental spoilation) through appeals to people across the world who are not readily persuaded by the language of class solidarity and party loyalty, but who may be more open to notions of global citizenship, freedom of speech, and saving the planet from environmental damage. Note too that these organisations target not only 'their' government – or at least not only their own national government – but also a global constituency, attacking issues in particular locations while marshalling support from across the world. Moreover, their campaigns are handled with considerable expertise by adroit and experienced media activists, able to present their 'symbolic politics' persuasively in a 'soundbite' culture, at ease with technical issues of law or science yet capable of moving smoothly into the language of everyday people, and supported by the latest in communications and computer technologies.

Fourth, Castells observes that established politicians and parties endeavour to manage 'informational politics'. We are familiar enough with spin doctors, the packaging of policies and photo-opportunities to recognise this easily enough. However, it is Castells's view that today's information networks make it impossible for politicians to maintain effective control, try as they might. The networks are simply too fluid, too leaky, too undisciplined and too rampant to allow the politicians to maintain an effective hold.

This is related to a fifth feature of the new politics, one in which negative campaigning predominates, especially that which foregrounds scandal and sleaze. Castells dismisses the thought that politics today are significantly more corrupt and politicians more venal than previously, hence he is drawn to account for the current stress on scandal and sleaze as an outcome of the rise of networks which facilitate 'leaks' and 'exposures'. In this respect it may help to think in terms of what Thomas Mathiesen (1997) conceives of as the 'synoptic' character of life today, i.e. of a world in which celebrities and stars (and even politicians) are obsessively scrutinised by a pervasive and intrusive media. In addition, one needs also to reflect on the ease with which information may now be put on to websites to appreciate the era of new politics being one in which information control is beyond the reach of even the most talented politician, however hard he or she may strive to attain it.

Sixth, Castells believes that these features, when combined, announce a 'crisis of democracy in the information age' (1996: 302), with traditional nationally located parties being undercut by global trends, identity politics that bring together cultural aspirations and material concerns rising in importance, and electorates becoming increasingly sceptical of established politicians who seem corrupt and ineffectual when it comes to addressing issues such as animal welfare, child abuse and human rights. Finally, Castells wonders whether this scepticism might be overcome by the further development of 'informational politics' which might revitalise locations such as towns and cities by adopting electronic technologies which can enhance participation. He notes that there are countervailing tendencies here, yet is open-minded about the prospects of a 'yet to be discovered, informational democracy' (1996: 353).

An agenda for research

Awareness of themes announcing the novelty of the present era, and sensitivity especially towards Manuel Castells's analysis of the 'network society', provides a ready agenda for this book. It is this which explains the organisation of the text. In Part I we concentrate on matters of *representation*, concerning ourselves especially with the ways in which media, including new media, represent politics and politicians, the present and the possibilities of politics. Howard Tumber (Chapter 2), for instance, notes a 'crisis of journalism' induced by the coming of cyberspace and a plethora of immediate and round-the-clock media coverage. He observes that the risk of delegitimation of politicians seems to be increasing through a surfeit of scandal and rumour which can be all-enveloping. Thirty years or so ago people queued to buy hard copies of Lord Denning's report on the Profumo affair (when a Minister of State, John Profumo shared the sexual favours of a prostitute with a Russian diplomat, one Captain Ivanov) from Her Majesty's Stationery Office in Holborn. But in 1998 CNN broadcast live the Starr report on the Monika Lewinski affair as it was released line by line on the Internet. More and more, new media seem to allow for unfiltered assertion and abuse, concentration on personal foibles, and a dumbed-down concern for trivia and ill-informed opinion. Asking what might be the consequences for democratic processes, Tumber casts a clear eye on the dangers of these trends and he assesses the promise of a renaissance through 'public journalism' seizing on the Internet in hopes of establishing a more reliable media coverage than that offered by a concentrated and commercialised corporate media industry.

John Tomlinson (Chapter 4) extends this concern for how politics may be shifting in a media-centric era in an imaginative way. His major concern is with the cultural consequences of globalisation, something which encourages feelings of 'proximity' to other people and events though these may be many miles apart. Tomlinson lays emphasis on the ambiguous aspects of this process, but sees in it at least possibilities of extending political options and agendas, notably perhaps as regards 'cosmopolitan' outlooks that may be encouraged in a world of 'proximity politics'.

As is evident from this comment, representation necessarily involves examining the marked 'cultural turn' in politics, a turn in which politicians seek to appear on chat shows to show off their 'ordinariness' and in which lifestyle displays, even carnivalesque displays, intrude into the polity. Alan Scott and John Street (Chapter 3) centre on just this development, offering an appreciative if quizzical analysis of the rise of 'cultural politics'. To be sure, they concede, there has been some aestheticisation of politics, as there has been a significant politicisation of the aesthetic, yet Scott and Street remain doubtful that we are entering radically new times. Nick Stevenson (Chapter 5) shifts the discussion towards questions of morality and ethics in his contribution. His interest is in ways in which new media may allow different forms of conversations to enter political life, while closing off others. Prominent among these are questions of human rights, issues intimately connected to transnational media and processes of globalisation. Kate Nash (Chapter 6) unabashedly centres on the 'cultural turn', arguing for nothing less than a rethinking of politics, and of traditional political analysis, in terms of *cultural* politics. The final chapter in Part I takes us to perhaps the most remarkable cultural moment of recent times – the death and funeral of Princess Diana. Here Sasha Roseneil (Chapter 7) delves deep into that imbrication of culture and politics which, if centred in London, brought in millions of others around the world (cf. McGuigan 2000). Drawn together at this event was a politics of affectivity, an intoxicating mix of the personal and the public, the embrace of the marginal (gays, ethnic minorities), a combination of the sombre and the joyful, the high and the low (Verdi and Elton John), and soap-operatic drama (*that* speech from Diana's brother) confronting pomp and circumstance (Westminster Abbey and the Guards).

In Part II of the book we shift emphasis towards questions of *mobilisation*. Here our authors centre on new social movements, notably environmental campaigns, to look at the character of their activities, their adoption of new technologies, and whether they portend a new politics. These chapters illuminate much about political activism in recent years. They range from the theoretically focused and clarificatory such as Mario Diani (Chapter 8), to a case study of Friends of the Earth's use of ICTs to test Michels's iron law of oligarchy from Neil Washbourne (Chapter 9), to detailed empirical accounts of different protest movements such as is offered by Jenny Pickerill (Chapter 10), to a close analysis of resistance to the Multilateral Agreement on Investment (MAI) in which alternative and imaginative uses of the Internet were effectively used by opponents (Peter Jay Smith and Elizabeth Smythe, Chapter 12).

As would be expected, several of the chapters here engage directly with the work of Manuel Castells, and in all of the contributions his concern with the new politics of today is present. Yet a refrain running through much of the writing in this book is that it is *premature* to announce the arrival of a new politics. To be sure, there are interesting new expressions of politics in the current era. Attention is readily and rightly drawn to issues like the 'Battle in Seattle' late in 1999 when some 40,000 protesters, from some 1,000 organisations, gathered to oppose the World Trade Organisation (WTO) and proposals to further marketise agriculture. Any social scientist worth his or her salt will have an eye to movements that bring together old-style trade unionists with environmentalists, as they will be intrigued by the 'electro-hippies' who attempted – with some effect – to shut down the WTO's web-server through swamping it with messages. Contemporary use of the Internet to mobilise protesters – as happened at Seattle, and later on at Washington, as well as, on a smaller scale, in London – is sociologically interesting. More recent still, the 'guerrilla gardening' in Parliament Square on 1 May 2000 when turf was dug up and replanted with 'alternative' crops, and when the statue of Sir Winston Churchill was defaced, evokes the interest of the social analyst. All these stimulate the curiosity of the social scientist, but evidence that they are indicative of profound transformations in politics is rather slight, and certainly failed to convince most contributors to this volume. On the evidence of research gathered here, while we can see innovation and imagination at work, the weight of established practices and political parties presses hard.

As I have said, several of the authors here engage with Castells, but many do so in critical ways. His concern to identify the demise of old political cleavages, to announce the import of new political movements and the centrality of information networks gets due attention, but several authors here take issue with Castells's conclusions. For instance, Mary Mellor and Alan Dordoy (Chapter 11) criticise Castells from the position of an 'ecofeminist political economy' which reminds us of the continued importance of class divisions amid environmental disputes. Elsewhere, and from a somewhat different perspective, Nick Stevenson (Chapter 5) charges Castells with over-instrumentalising new forms of campaigning and of lacking a normative position. Relatedly, Kate Nash (Chapter 6) provides a post-structuralist critique of Castells, tracing a cultural politics to Michel Foucault.

The weight of the past

Though by no means all of the criticisms of Castells in this book revolve on doubts about his embrace of the new, there are enough of them to ask serious questions of an approach which is so insistent that we live in 'new times'. At this point we may alert ourselves to the dangers of what has been called *presentism*. This warns us of a common conceit among the living, that which presupposes theirs is a time of singular significance. Of course, all history is particular, to some degree different from that which went before, but it is too easy to overlook important, perhaps decisive, elements of continuity – even of consolidation – which tell often on contemporary political phenomena.

For instance, the globalised world we inhabit today is undeniably different in many ways from what it was even fifty years ago, yet it remains capitalist in ways not so dissimilar to those pertaining in the nineteenth century. Furthermore, capitalism's globalising tendencies were present and acutely observed by none other than Karl Marx and Friedrich Engels in much-quoted sections of *The Communist Manifesto*, a pamphlet published as long ago as 1848. Before we rush to insist that today is so different from yesteryear, we might recall that these *enfants terribles* declared of capitalism in the mid-nineteenth century that 'constant revolutionizing of production, uninterrupted disturbance of all social relations, everlasting uncertainty and agitation . . . All fixed, fast-frozen relations . . . are swept away, all new-formed ones become antiquated before they can ossify. All that is solid melts into air.' Contrary to the expectations of Marx and Engels, capitalism has triumphed over all of its challengers to date, and it rules without sign of any serious usurper. Moreover, capitalism has succeeded in extending its hold both across the globe and deeper into the everyday lives of people in ways which Marx and Engels could scarcely have imagined. Nonetheless, this world remains capitalist, displaying the following distinguishing characteristics for any impartial analyst to see:

- ability to pay is the major criteria determining provision of goods and services
- provision is made on the basis of private rather than public supply
- market criteria – i.e. whether something makes a profit or loss – are the primary factors in deciding what, if anything, is made available
- competition – as opposed to regulation – is regarded as the most appropriate mechanism for organising economic affairs
- commodification of activities (i.e. relationships are regarded as being amenable to price valuations) is the norm
- private ownership of property is favoured over state holdings
- wage labour is the chief mechanism for organising work activities.

These are old features of capitalist enterprise, as recognisable in 1850 as they are now (Webster 2000). This being so, why ought commentators go to such lengths to seek out novelty in a world founded on such recognisable foundations?

On grounds of similar logic, it does not seem obvious to me to look to the spread of information networks to account for an apparent excess of sleaze and scandal in politics today. Of course, there are now more opportunities to expose the misdemeanours of politicians and other public figures, but it could well be a signal of the absence of politics in face of today's neo-liberal orthodoxy. Capitalism has established itself over the last twenty years as a worldwide hegemon and communism have been thoroughly disgraced even in the eyes of those disposed towards anti-capitalism. Given this, what surprise can there be at the 'death of politics' when all major political players accede to market strictures, setting the laissez-faire economy apart as something beyond politics? What then remains for politics except for negative campaigning about the credentials, capabilities and character of opponents? And how may the independent and critical journalist, employed nowadays almost invariably in commercialised media conglomerates, demonstrate his or her campaigning commitment other than by exposing personal failings? The days of the journalist, even of the politician, with an alternative vision seem almost to have gone. What then is left but to indulge in stories of sleaze, scandal and spin?

To underscore the point that continuity is a manifest feature of capitalism in the twenty-first century one might look somewhat more quizzically than is usual at pronouncements of the 'death of class'. While it is undeniable that occupations have changed over the years, still there is a remarkable persistence of class inequalities and privilege over time (Halcli and Webster 2000). While there have been general rises in living standards, there remain patterns of distribution of wealth and income that are not so different from at least fifty years ago (Scott 1994). And one may still identify a capitalist class at the helm of society, if not ruling then certainly playing a massively disproportionate role in political, economic and cultural affairs. Though it has been transformed in important ways – not least in becoming technically equipped to be involved in corporate affairs – and while it is undergirded by a much expanded and fragmented middle class of managers, a capitalist class may still be distinguished by its concentration at the top of society, by its ownership of property, and by its capacity to transmit its wealth and other advantages to its descendants. This capitalist class is not of course hermetically sealed from entry to outsiders, yet still it seems remarkably able to retain its property and influence by interlocking involvement in the upper reaches of business and finance (Scott 1997; Zeitlin 1989).

One might add too that the most remarkable recent protest movement in Britain (and, indeed, across large parts of western Europe) was the road hauliers' and farmers' blockage which prevented the distribution of fuel and almost brought the country to a standstill in September 2000. While aspects of this were novel (notably the adept use of mobile phones to co-ordinate a widely dispersed set of activities), it was decidedly familiar in its emphasis on material interests and in its emanation from a particular segment of the class structure. The unequivocal demand of the protesters was for a reduction in the price of petrol so they might directly improve their circumstances. The style of the protest undoubtedly owed something to the direct action and flamboyance characteristic of alternative social movements (and, in media interviews, numerous farmers and truck drivers acknowledged just this), but its substance was pressure for material resources and its driving force a particular social group, the self-employed petit-bourgeoise. It was surely for this reason that the most popular explanatory concept used by commentators was 'Poujadism', a term conceived in the 1950s to identify and account for small business protests in France against taxation and 'big government' which was perceived to be damaging these business interests. There is little sign here of a 'new politics'.

Finally, though there has been a good deal of attention placed on the carnivalesque and lifestyle aspects of much contemporary political protest, it is noticeable that so much of the ire at Seattle and London has been determinedly anti-capitalist and anti-corporate. Targets of protesters are not very likely to be their own national governments, but they are recurrently the major logo-bearing likes of McDonald's and Sony plus key institutions of global capitalism such as the World Bank and the International Monetary Fund. I would not wish to suggest that this indicated the positing of an alternative or even a serious challenge to contemporary corporate capitalism, but would argue that the targets of protest indicate that capitalism remains entrenched in our world today.

Conclusion

This chapter opened with the commonplace statement that we live in a world of accelerating and unprecedented change. It went on to highlight themes prominent among commentators who are drawn to promote and examine the new. It continued to review features of the argument which claims that 'new politics' is part of the tumultuous change that envelops us. From this point of view, new social movements, novel forms of campaigning, high-tech, media-sensitive and lifestyle politics appear to be taking over the political ground.

That was certainly the agenda for the conference at which most of the papers collected here appeared. It is odd then that much of their content casts doubt on the accuracy of such claims. Odd perhaps, yet it may be heartening for the way in which the value of intellectual analysis and evidence is reasserted. Of course, the contributors acknowledge the particular circumstances and characteristics of the present era – one cannot be blind to the presence of the Internet, the heightened importance of culture in contemporary politics, and the prominence of environmental concerns among protesters. It is just that, time and again, reasons and evidence are found to reassert the importance of rather well-established relationships. This is not to say that the chapters uniformly insist on arguing that nothing much has changed. Not at all. It is rather that most remind us that, amid change, other features persist.

I invite readers to examine the chapters which follow. Some are empirical, others more theoretical in orientation, some are drawn to underline change, though most cast doubt, in one way or another, on claims that we live in an age of 'new politics'. All are meticulously researched and carefully composed. Anyone interested in politics today, and its nexus of media, high technology and globalisation, will find stimulation here.

Part I

New media, politics and culture

2 Democracy in the Information Age

The role of the Fourth Estate in cyberspace

Howard Tumber

Introduction

Recent work in journalism studies and mass communication has concerned itself with debates about the relative openness or closure of the communication system. In particular, interest has centred on the character of the public sphere and the various positive and negative influences on democratic communication.

Journalism is in a period of change and transition. Change in the production, distribution and consumption of news is raising debate about the nature and role of journalism in the public sphere. Recent newspaper stories, for example, 'Press in Peril' (*Guardian*, 4 Jan. 1999: 20), 'Putting Freedom to the Torch' (*Financial Times*, 13/14 Mar. 1999: i), 'The Journalism That Doesn't Bother to Check its Facts' (*Herald-Tribune*, 3 Mar. 1999: 8), suggest that journalism is in some form of crisis. The media, or journalism in particular, are cited as failing to provide or uphold their supposed traditional duty of holding power to account.

Two main factors are contributing to journalism's changing role within the public sphere. First, the globalisation of the media industries and, second, the development of new electronic communications technologies. The breadth of the changes taking place has serious implications for the public's access to information and requires a reassessment of journalism's role in the new media environment.

This chapter questions whether journalism can perform its traditional and normative Fourth Estate functions in the Information Age.

Globalisation, the Internet and the changing nature of news

The deregulatory environment prevalent since the 1970s has hastened concentration within the media industry leading to intense competition. Media companies are now huge conglomerates with the trend towards corporate marriages set to continue. The growth of the entertainment economy is forcing the mergers of broadcasting, music, publishing and telecommunication companies into mega corporations in a struggle to maintain dominance in the market. In that horrible phrase that media executives and consultants often use, 'the battle for eyeballs' is now upon us.

In the United States a redefinition of news, that has been financially driven, has taken place in network television. The separation between the business of news organisations and the product side is now joined (McManus 1994; Kimball 1994). The growth in monopoly and the changes in ownership within the communications industries are leading to serious problems for news workers who have to comply with corporate interests. There is now a serious curtailment of newsgathering by the television networks. There is a decline in importance of political coverage, particularly of the State Department, and a reduction in the number of correspondents covering the different world regions. In addition, news and television coverage of Congress is truncated with the result that the public is starved politically of the workings of the democratic system. Correspondents are demoralised by the changes as they witness the end of an era in broadcast history as the cable subsidiaries can provide cheap news programmes at a profit, a feat not possible by the traditional network news organisations (Kimball 1994: 165).

In Britain and the United States over the last fifteen years the gap between the quality broadsheet papers and the popular tabloid papers has narrowed. As competition intensifies, the quality broadsheets co-opt a more sensationalist veneer to the news product. The broadsheets compete for the same market as the tabloids, an interchange of editors between the tabloids and the quality broadsheets takes place and a downmarket product is established. The crisis is due to the competition for advertising, and more expensive newsprint, leading to a lack of interest in both foreign news and investigative journalism. The decline in the amount of foreign news is the most serious charge against the broadsheet papers and television. The subsequent lack of serious analysis, while increasing a human interest for it, is providing a retreat from the world. Despite the increase in television outlets the news is now a processed product and another branch of entertainment (Samson 1996; Franklin 1997). In Britain the moving of the main evening commercial terrestrial television news programme 'News at Ten' to an 11 p.m. slot is a potent symbol of the movement of news away from prime time to the periphery of terrestrial television.

Scandal news

A further manifestation of the new commercial environment is the journalism of scandal, smut and intrusion. As Harold Evans (former editor of the *Sunday Times*) remarked, 'Watergate gave American journalists a halo, people would trust journalists and honour them, now the coverage makes them angry. There was a culture of investigation but now it's without purpose. In its stead there is a culture of inquisitiveness' (quoted in Lloyd 1999: i). The initial point in the process is the allegation, followed by the speculation, and ending with the counterallegation. The public is left vulnerable to manipulation, as a journalism of unfiltered assertion makes separating fact from spin and argument from innuendo more difficult. The demands of twenty-four-hour cable news channels inhibits verification of stories – 'journalism is becoming less a product than a process, witnessed in real time and in public' (Rosenstiel and Kovach 1999: 8).

The resignation of Nixon is often cited as a culmination or high point of investigative journalism. By exposing corruption in government or other institutions, the news media may alter the direction of public policy and can cause people to be removed from office (Altschull 1995: 33). In this way the press acts in its role as the Fourth Estate checking on government and rectifying abuses of power. Indeed for scandals to arise the presence of a free press is a necessity (Ginsberg and Shefter 1990; Markovits and Silverstein 1988).

Some believe that Monicagate brought out journalism in its most aggressive forms and part of the current crisis of journalism is directed at the developments in the electronic media. It is what Rosenstiel and Kovach call 'the new mixed media culture' and argue that this is a sign of developments to come which bodes ill for the nature of public discourse. They argue that America is moving towards a journalism of assertion rather than that of verification, with obvious costs to society. The main culprit or the main catalyst for this journalism of assertion comes from on-line gossip/reporters such as Matt Drudge. A journalist's job is to sift out facts from allegations and to provide citizens with accurate, reliable information upon which they can self-govern and that process is now at risk. However, the information revolution is more about speculation and argument than about gathering information. The continuous news cycle makes verification more of a problem. Initially comes the allegation, then follows the speculation until the counter-allegation is issued.

> The demand to keep up with this to and fro leaves journalists with less time to sort out what is true and significant. The public gets the grist, the raw elements. There is more news on the air but it's delivered piecemeal with little context. A journalism of unfiltered assertion makes separating fact from spin, argument from innuendo, more difficult and leaves society more susceptible to manipulation.
>
> (Rosenstiel and Kovach 1999: 8)

The proliferation of media scandals across the global landscape has prompted an interest in whether there are common characteristics that account for this rise. Many commentators try to locate the increase in media scandals in a much larger picture of the 'crisis of democracy'. Castells sees media scandals as phenomena of many liberal democratic countries, particularly those where the political parties that have been in power for many years have collapsed. If one contends it is unlikely that corruption generally is at a historical high point, why is it coming to the fore now and in addition why is it affecting political parties, politicians and institutions so much in the 1990s? (Castells 1997: 333–5).

A number of structural factors and macropolitical trends have weakened political systems, making them more vulnerable to turmoil created in public opinion. The move to the centre and the breakdown of ideology in political parties have left a blurring of political positions, leaving the public more attuned to the reliability of parties and personalities of candidates than to their professed positions on issues. The breakdown of the post-war order destroyed the certainties characteristic of the Cold War. Geographical and ideological reference points of political actors were lost.

> Political corruption can be viewed as a further manifestation of the contemporary crisis of western democratic states. The revelation of widespread political corruption helped undermine one of the support structures – the claim to operate on the basis of public accountability – which had underpinned western democracies in the post-war world, and distinguished them from communist regimes.
>
> (Heywood 1997: 417–35)

One of the principal features of recent change in the personalisation of politics is the move from a reactive mode of behaviour to a proactive one involving the increasing use of long-term promotional strategies by governments, political parties, institutions and corporate interests to promote their image and influence policy-making (Tumber 1993: 345–61). A culture of promotionalism has been taking over many areas of public life. For government the breakdown of party identification and partisanship is leading politicians to turn increasingly to political consultants and public relations advisers to get themselves elected and, once in office, to continue to employ these spin doctors and professional communicators to promote themselves and maintain public approval for their policies. Information management is thus pervading all aspects of government behaviour whether it is directed towards domestic or foreign policy (Wernick 1991; Berkman and Kitch 1986).

The promotional culture and the mass media are providing politicians with the main way of publicising themselves. At the same time it makes them vulnerable. Governments and institutions of the state 'are constantly faced with the risk of loss of legitimacy' and 'can have their institutional personal authority deconstructed by the media' (Ericson 1991: 233). Scandal has become big business for the tabloid newspapers. The potential now exists for politicians and other elite personalities to lose control over the definitions of events and the subsequent interpretation by the public.

The rise of the global criminal economy is a further factor. State institutions in many countries are affected by crime, giving ammunition for scandal-making and enabling politicians to be blackmailed (Castells 1997: 336). Financial corruption stems from the fact that the political actors are chronically underfinanced, so that in order to make up the deficit they have to rely on underhand contributions from business and interest groups in exchange for government decisions in favour of these interests. Once corruption then becomes widespread, everybody in politics and the media realises that if you examine more closely and for long enough, damaging information can be found on almost anyone. In that way the hunt begins and advisers prepare ammunition to attack or defend and journalists attempt to fill their roles as investigative reporters finding stories to increase both audience and sales. Once the market of damaging political information is created, then further allegations and insinuations (and possibly fabrications) enter. Indeed the strategy in scandal politics does not necessarily aim at an instant blow on the basis of one scandal. It is the relentless flow of various scandals of different kinds and with different levels of likelihood, from solid information on a minor incident to shaky allegations on a major issue . . . What counts is the final impact on public opinion by the accumulation of many touches.

(Castells 1997: 338)

The superior stage of scandal politics is the judicial or parliamentary investigation leading to indictments and often imprisonment of political leaders. A symbiotic relationship is formed between judges, prosecutors and investigative committee members and the media. The media are protected and nourished with leaks and in return the investigators become media heroes. In essence Castells contends that 'Scandal politics is the weapon of choice for struggle and competition in informational politics' (Castells 1997: 338).

This argument echoes that of the 'crisis of publication communication' that politics is now 'enclosed in the space of the media' (Blumler and Gurevitch 1995):

The media have become more powerful than ever technologically, financially and politically and their global reach allows them to escape from strict political controls. Their capacity for investigative reporting and their relative autonomy vis-à-vis political power makes them the main source of information and opinion for society at large. Parties and candidates must act in and through the media to reach society.

Rather than acting as a Fourth Estate, though, the media instead are the ground for power struggles (Castells 1997: 337; Waisbord 1994: 19–33).

Waisbord has argued that in the case of Argentina, news media have gained increasing importance both as an arena for battling out political confrontations and as a locus for pushing government accountability.

Scandals are unthinkable without the intervention of the mass media; the latter not merely covers but, more importantly, often originates political investigations . . . press organisations are essential for publicising political sins that have remained concealed. Thus scandals need to be treated, above all, as news events, as stories unmasking formerly secret political peccadilloes. The press is not the only institution responsible for media exposés, yet a scandal-hunting press is indispensable for turning abuses of political power into public events . . . The combination of institutional political dynamics and a few news media espousing a muck-raking ethos is essential for understanding the recent series of scandals in Argentina . . . Scandals are not inherent but sporadic phenomena, breaking the surface in specific historical and political environments. Some violations of trust never cross the threshold into public awareness, others remain potential affairs stifled by diverse interests or missed or ignored by the media and others become fully-fledged political exposés.

(Waisbord 1994: 21)

In looking at the study of scandals it is important to focus on the reasons why some secret official wrongdoing turns into a public event rather than on the factors giving rise to this behaviour. The recent wave of press disclosures of political corruption in Argentina should be considered mainly as a signal of the spread of scandal politics rather than an increase in corrupt practices. Now, while Waisbord argues that the confusion of these two, the causes for corruption and the causes for scandals, is not uncommon in analyses of the Argentine case, in its most simple version the upsurge of scandals is attributed to rising levels of government corruption. He suggests that interpreting scandals by alluding to official corruption does not seem productive – the reason for this is that the evidence is hard to gather and both the processes and institutions transforming corruption into scandals are often ignored. Similarly, arguments claiming that corruption is a consistent feature of the country's politics present difficulties in accounting for the release of a scandal (Waisbord 1994: 22).

The development of the Internet has provoked further debate about whether the World Wide Web enhances the public sphere or disperses public discourse. Some argue that the new electronic technologies are empowering citizens to participate in new democratic forums not only between government and the governed but also among citizens themselves. This communitarian view argues that the Internet is creating new 'virtual', as opposed to physical, social formations, thereby providing a basis for a new politics and greater political participation by citizens.

New citizenship linkages and virtual communities are emerging in which participation, whether around political affiliation, social issues or local community interests, suggests a move away from a unified public sphere to a series of separate public spheres. A single public sphere becomes obsolete as groups maintain their own deliberative democratic forums. The problem with this view, as Gitlin articulates, is whether the proliferation of separate public 'sphericules' damages the formation of a unitary public sphere.

> The diffusion of interactive technology surely enriches the possibilities for a polarity of publics – for the development of distinct groups organised around affinity and interest. What is not clear is that the proliferation and lubrication of publics contributes to the creation of a public, an active democratic encounter of citizens who reach across their social and ideological differences to establish a common agenda of concern and to debate rival approaches. If it is to be argued that a single public sphere is unnecessary as long as segments constitute their own deliberative assemblies, such an arrangement presumes a rough equivalence of resources for the purpose of ensuring overall justice. It also presupposes that society is not riven by deep fissures which are subject to being deepened and exacerbated in the absence of ongoing negotiation among members of different groups.
>
> (Gitlin 1998: 168–74)

Communicating with the public

To counteract the increasing tabloidisation of news and fragmentation of news outlets political leaders constantly attack the media for their negative coverage and have sought to bypass the traditional media by appealing directly to the public. Techniques to assess public opinion, such as opinion polls, focus groups, electronic town meetings once used only during election campaigns, are now a vital feature of governance. Attempts by governments, politicians and political parties to communicate directly with their publics are not new. Town hall meetings go back to the seventeenth century. Recent elections in the United States witnessed candidates appearing on talk shows thereby attempting to bypass hostile questions from journalists. The interesting phase now taking place is the conduct of campaigns and the electronic delivery of political communication. Through their own websites political parties, candidates and elected representatives can all now communicate directly and constantly with voters.

Tony Blair, the British Prime Minister, recently attempted to appeal directly to the public via regular Internet broadcasts. Blair began weekly 'webcasts' in early 2000 to spread the message about his government's achievements. However, early monitoring of the response found that fewer than 4,000 people a week visit Blair's section of the website (www.number-10.gov.uk). In contrast 30,000 people look at the part where the briefings of Alastair Campbell, the Prime Minister's press secretary, are available. How many of these are journalists is unknown.

In response to the new forms of political and government communication with the public websites that promote participation rather than spectating are developing. For example, the UK Citizens On-line Democracy (UKCOD) group established in 1996, runs a permanent site, and set its objective as bringing politicians together with the public around a virtual table. It facilitated the first UK on-line discussion between politicians in the run-up to the 1997 general election, including statements from each of the three main political leaders. Its most significant activity was acting as on-line consultation on the British Government's Freedom of Information White Paper. The role of UKCOD was specifically referred to in the White Paper and this was the first time the Government had used an external agency to consult the public via the Internet on its legislative proposals.[1]

A further important phase is the delivery of government information messages and services via new electronic delivery systems. In Britain successive governments have promoted the development of services that will enable the public to access information and electronic form filling via home computers or interactive television and in kiosks placed in public arenas such as libraries, post offices and shopping centres (Tumber and Bromley 1998: 159–67). Dutton *et al.* highlighted one of the barriers to innovation in the provision of public services. A potential risk is the 'negative reactions from citizens who do not want to be treated purely as "customers" or "clients" and who might see ESD as a wedge for the introduction of inappropriate business methods into the public services' (Dutton *et al.* 1996: 270).

To envisage what might be in store for the citizen it is useful to examine the strategies of the commercial world in attracting the public to use the Web. Here the change from the industrial age to the information age is viewed as enabling the key sources of competitive edge to change from internal production efficiency to communications, transactions and the customer interface or 'go-to-market efficiency'. The rather sinister potential nowadays is seen in marketing innovation rather than product innovation. An article in *New Media Age* set out the future:

> The industrial age offered up huge leaps forward in our ability to process matter, 'things' more efficiently. The information age offers us up huge leaps forward in our ability to process information more efficiently. Result: the key sources of competitive edge are changing . . . Marketing innovation is becoming more important than product innovation. This is true of banks, bookshops and even cars. After decades of factory automation, nowadays one-third of the final price of the average car is accounted for by the costs of sales, marketing and distribution. . . . Lean marketing follows after lean production. So far, few companies have digested the full implications of this shift. One such implication is that traditional thinking in terms of categories such as consumer or audiences is now a positive brake on progress because it blinds us from the richer source of improved go-to-market efficiency, customers themselves. Internet banking transactions aren't only cheap, because they obviate the need for bank branches, they also obviate the need for bank tellers too. In Internet banking, the customer does the bank teller's job for free. Enclosed loop marketing companies learn how to better mould and develop their services and products from their interactions and trans-actions with their customers. Their customers become their best market researchers, the source of their most valuable ideas and insights for free. One of the reasons why Amazon.com, Yahoo, etc. got to where they are today is because of word of mouth recommendation where customers do the brand's marketing and advertising for it for free. Now with the Associates' Programme, Amazon is recruiting customers to become its paid distribution agents too. Terms like 'consumer' and 'audience' assumes that people are mere passive receptacles of a one-way process called marketing. This is an obsolete, industrial-age notion. The alternative is to see the customer as an active agent, as a prosumer, as the visionary Alvin Toffler called it, co-producer or simply as a commercial partner in one of the most valu-able of all marketing and distribution resources. That's the irony and the challenge. Breakthrough, go-to-market efficiency is now a key source of competitive edge and what creates this edge is the customer itself. The customer as self-service agent, the customer as source of information ideas, the customer as brand ambassador spreading the word to friends and family. That completely transforms marketing. Getting customers to part with their hard-earned cash is just the half of it, recruiting them to volunteer their labour, their ideas and their enthusiasm for your brand as opposed to your

rival's brand is the much harder half. Increasingly this is what cutting-edge Internet strategies are about.

(Mitchell 1999: 8)

This cynical business-oriented scenario is still some way short of fulfilment, but the dissemination of government information electronically has the ability to bypass traditional forms of mediation. Direct interactive communication between government and the public has the potential to replace the government–media–public system (Tumber and Bromley 1998: 165). Other agencies and institutions also have the ability to communicate directly with the public and bypass the news organisation filters. For example, the first court case to be broadcast live and unedited over the Internet took place in Florida in August 1999. Bypassing media organisations that in the past were allowed to televise court cases and broadcast them over the Internet, the Orange County Courthouse in Florida provided its own on-line service using existing security cameras, a basic audio system and an Internet server able to transmit the images. The technology is much less cumbersome and cheaper than the mobile editing suites and satellite dishes used by television companies. The public are able to see the law courts at work without relying on the established media. The court case naturally was not a boring fraud trial that the public would not understand but the trial of a woman accused of trying to murder her daughter to avoid being put in a nursing home (*The Times*, 14 Aug. 1999).

The role of journalism

Thirty years ago members of the public queued outside Her Majesty's Stationery Office in Holborn, London, to buy the report of the investigation by Lord Denning into the Profumo affair. In the television coverage of the release of the report, pictures showed members of the public queuing outside the office to purchase their copies of the report. For details of the content, viewers relied on summary and comment by reporters. The public were presented with a mediatised version of the report. In stark contrast in 1998 the report of the investigation into the various Clinton scandals by the special prosecutor Ken Starr was delivered live on the Internet. CNN decided to televise the report as it appeared with a correspondent reading the text straight from the computer. It was a symbolic moment. As Mike McCurry, Clinton's former White House press secretary, remarked,

> All the filters that are present in the world of journalism evaporated. Raw information was available in mainstream. The US public had to serve the role of editor, deciding what to show. It was instantaneous information without any of the editorial standards and filters that define what we think of the modern business of journalism.

(McCurry 1998)

The public's involvement in government and legal proceedings is being trans-formed and the problem for news organisations and journalists is how to respond to this new political and communications environment. For journalism the 'crisis' has two main components. The first is the increasing trend of concentration and its consequent increased commercial pressures and the second is the development of new electronic communications. One response to what is seen as the increasing void between citizens and government and the failure of journalism to foster public debate and participation is the development of the public journalism movement in the United States. The movement started in the late 1980s and early 1990s, spreading from working papers and workshops to proposals and projects. The 1988 presidential election was a key event in the movement's development. The campaign was depicted as a horse race with most of the coverage concentrating on the strategies of the candidates rather than on the substance of the issues. Citizens did not have access to a supposed democratic process, rather the process was 'so specialised and limited that only its own professionals – politicians, policy experts, journalists, pollsters, pundits – could be reasonably described as its participants' (Glasser and Craft 1998: 205).

Within a framework of an analysis suggesting that trust in all institutions, and particularly journalism, is in decline, Jay Rosen, Dave Merritt and other key figures recently produced a body of work setting out their ideas about how the growing gap between the citizen and the government may be bridged by a new or different kind of journalism. The state of disillusionment existing not only among the general public, but also within the journalistic profession stems in part from the crisis in the economic structures that support journalism. Merritt, for example, sees no coincidence in the decline in journalism mapping the decline in public life (Merritt 1995: 1–11). Participants in the public journalism move-ment argue that journalism is a major contributor to the malaise in public life. The failure of the profession is leading to calls for new forms of reporting requiring a change in the profession necessary for journalism once again to be a primary force in the revitalisation of public life. The public journalism movement believes that journalism is suffering a fundamental loss of authority and regaining that authority must be journalism's first step towards revitalising itself. Explicit in the attacks on conventional journalism by the public journalism movement is the professional idea of objectivity. The principle of balance removes any obligation and indeed risk that people with different views would be offended. In addition the idea of objectivity and balance provides an element of conflict, whether real or contrived into the story (Merritt 1995: 1–11). It is the framing of stories in this way that Merrit claims creates a deficiency of accuracy by polarising stories to the extremes. It leaves most people out of discussion of particular stories.

In its rejection of objectivity, the public journalism movement does not advocate a partisan approach. Champions of democratic means, not democratic ends, is the slogan.

> Public journalism's concern for the quality of public discourse widens and to some extent clarifies journalism's view of politics by recognising citizens as a source of political wisdom. This optimistic view of the electorate invites the press to expand the scope of political coverage beyond politicians and the

issues that they regard as salient. More than that, it encourages journalists to appreciate the press as an agency not only of but also for communication, a medium through which citizens can inform themselves and through which they can discover their common values and shared interests.

(Glasser and Craft 1998: 205)

Public journalism therefore invites the community at large, reporters and readers alike, to consider that our ideas of the meaning of democracy are dependent on the kinds of communication by which politics is conducted (Carey 1995, quoted in Glasser and Craft 1998: 207).

Glasser and Craft see the idea that good public journalism will enhance a newspaper's standing in the market place by attracting more and better readers as one of public journalism's most controversial claims. The controversy rests with the belief of Jay Rosen's proposition that it is in newspaper interests to have a healthy public sphere. Appealing to editors caught in the web of market-driven journalism, Rosen attempted to show the connection between a newspaper's vitality and the vitality of public life (Glasser and Craft 1998: 207). Public journalism, by aiding readers to be involved in continuing debate, provides added value to newspapers and makes good 'economic sense' (Charity 1995: 155, quoted in Glasser and Craft 1998: 207).

Criticism of public journalism has come from journalists and academics. Some view its lack of objectivity as inherent (Gartner 1995: 86). Others fear the new movement will eliminate journalism's watchdog role and its tradition as the fourth branch of government, warning journalists not to stray into the world of social engineering and away from libertarian ideals (Merrill 1996). Critics such as Hanno Hardt pose a more radical objection, seeing the public journalism movement as failing to examine the nature of news work and the ownership of the means of production, prerequisites of journalistic practice. Hardt sees the advocates of public or civic journalism appealing to the civic conscience of individual journalists or, more damningly, with management support asking for compliance with their new rules of civic engagement. Like Merrill, he views the arguments replacing those of previous discussions around the development of a Fourth Estate model of the press which tended to focus on the institutional representation of such a state while at the same time the position of the journalists as members of the Estate and their relations with the owners of the means of communication were not problematised. In essence, he sees that what is lost in these new 'grand schemes to improve journalism for the benefit of society is an opportunity to broaden the spectrum of public communication by empowering journalists as intellectual workers and privileging the concerns of the underprivileged' (Hardt 2000: 216).

The debates about public and civic journalism revolve around questions of the public sphere. In Britain debate on the public sphere has tended to focus on the desirability of public service broadcasting as a space within which a wide range of views may be articulated. James Curran has recently called for a revision of the official objectives of public service broadcasting 'in order to foster a shift in its style of journalism' (Curran 1998: 205). It is difficult to believe Curran envisages a public journalism for the BBC and other broadcasters but what he wants to see is a kind of added-value pluralism alongside the old traditional obligation of due objectivity. This pluralism requirement arises from what Curran sees as a powerful reform movement within broadcasting 'intent on extending social access and expanding the range of voices and views on air' (Curran 1998: 196). Phone-in programmes, audience-participation formats and access slots are seen as the manifestation of the movement and according to Curran should be given 'public recognition and legitimacy' (Curran 1998: 196).

Curran's democratising view of entertainment news programmes stems from the belief that these media platforms provide forums for discussing social issues. Critics, though, view them 'as lowering the standard of debate to conform to entertainment politics' (Davis and Owen 1998: 103). In the USA these kinds of programmes are enveloped by controversy and their contribution to the public sphere is hotly contested. Talk radio, for example, while taking a major role in engaging dialogue between citizens and politicians is viewed by some as the arena for citizen participation and by others who label it hate radio (Davis and Owen 1998: 10). This latter pessimistic view has certain credence if one accepts that entertainment values are dominating news organisations and that profit motives are winning out against public service responsibilities. In this new media world 'public discourse is compromised' as sensational stories replace political news and debates 'about issues and leaders are reduced to gossip' (Davis and Owen 1998: 104).

This new range of voices seen in broadcasting access also requires addressing in relation to the Internet and this is the second component in the 'crisis of journalism'.

There is a singular lack of theorising and empirical studies about the relationship to journalism and the new technologies and the future of news in relation to the information society. The development of news via the Internet from direct sources is making the old-style correspondent redundant and affecting the traditional task of journalism. How will the public itself view this new form of news? If the new interactive services provide an increase in communications between citizens and their leaders what will be the role of journalists in this unmediated landscape? Bardoel sees the position of journalism as a unified profession as no longer tenable. The new media formats will lead to two types of journalism. First, orientating journalism where background commentary and explanation are given to the general public and, second, instrumental journalism that provides functional and specialised information to interested customers. The new information services require mostly these new kinds of journalists or 'information brokers' while the classical media would seek all journalists. Within this media-sector segmentation the call for a new type of journalist will expand whereas the need for the old type of classical journalism may die out (Bardoel 1996: 283–302).

At a recent conference Steve Yelvington, editor of Startribune.com, pronounced that the era of the journalist as gatekeeper was over: 'There are no gates to be kept, the city walls are down.' Instead the new role of the journalist is that of 'trusted guide' (Yelvington 1999). He criticised some of the news websites for looking inward and not connecting users with other useful Web resources. They are charged with abdicating this role to Yahoo and other new players. He calls for journalists to broaden their definition of public service to include other areas alongside investigative journalism and the coverage of breaking news: being a servant on the World Wide Web means engaging in what we're beginning to call 'service journalism'. A restaurant guide, a website index and an on-line employment centre are not the sort of things a journalist might first imagine when thinking about public service – but they are. In a very optimistic view of the future, Yelvington talks of the revolution in journalism in which the public are telling their own stories on the Internet. This 'People's Journalism', as he coins it, communicates through e-mail, Usenet discussion forums and personal Web pages. He cites the example of Slashdot where all the contents come from participants who discuss and criticise references to news elsewhere on the Web. Most newspapers, he claims, do not understand people's journalism but there are some that have adapted to the new electronic environment. The *Sun Herald*, a weekly in the popular retirement community of Port Charlotte in Florida, became an Internet service provider instead of just putting the news on the Web. It taught Internet skills and built Sunline on the Web as a community resource with almost three-quarters of the customers having their own Web pages. 'They became participants, not just consumers' (Yelvington 1999). Does 'people's journalism' mean the demise of institutional journalism? Yelvington thinks not. 'Individual empowerment doesn't mean the end of the organisation of the state' (Yelvington 1998).

Others, though, see the culture of virtual communities shaped by the marketeers. Aufderheide states that

> it is easy to imagine the role of on-line journalism in fomenting this existing trend, it is much harder to imagine how journalism in an electronic age can cultivate a sense of community, of respect for, and curiosity about, difference. ... The larger question is the fostering and reproduction of democratic culture in the age of marketing. ... Journalists ought to need to act as empathetic but not sycophantic ethnographers of cultural pluralism and daily democracy. The values and lifestyle controversies of today are not frivolous. They are genuine manifestations of majestic pressures on individuals in highly fluid cultures. Feature writing and lifestyle issues have become front-page material for legitimate reasons as well as because of consumer centred marketing strategies.
>
> (Aufderheide 1998: 53–4)

Aufderheide believes journalists need to see themselves as the facilitators of responsible public discussion not the guardians of public knowledge. Similar to Yelvington's journalist as guide, Aufderheide sees journalists as 'the people who help us make the connections between pieces of information that we are too busy or harried or ignorant to make for ourselves. Whether they do that by hyperlink or snail mail doesn't change the basic task. It does not get any easier with new technologies, it just might be done creatively and well with them' (Aufderheide 1998: 54).

In the new communications environment what can the journalist actually do for democracy? Herbert Gans suggests that part of journalists' failings can be located in the shortcomings of what he calls 'the journalistic theory of democracy' (Gans 1998: 6–12). The theory has three parts: (1) the journalist's democratic role was to inform citizens; (2) the more informed these citizens are, the more likely they are to participate politically; (3) the more they participate, the more democratic the country is apt to be. Gans's main argument is that the theory gives journalists a central role in maximising democracy by stressing the informed citizen. But the theory does not suggest how citizens are to be informed or indeed the kind of news that may be offered. 'When journalists do their regular job, the theory assumes, citizens will be informed or will inform themselves' (Gans 1998: 6). Gans points out that the question of whether supplying the news informs citizens enough to enable them to perform their democratic responsibilities is still unknown. He also points out that many audience studies show that better-informed people are more politically active but the cause is not necessarily their being informed, but due to their socio-economic position and level of education. However, citizens who are uninformed often become politically active and lack of information has not been an obstacle to participation in protest or in political activity. In the third part, Gans suggests that citizen activity doesn't necessarily mean that it will produce democracy. What he is saying, in effect, is that journalists need a better or stronger theory of democracy and one that reflects the government and political system on which they report: 'That theory should correct the current inaccuracies about the informed citizenry but it must also say something about how and why citizens participate or do not and what citizens need to participate – that is, what makes for an informed and participating citizen' (Gans 1998: 9).

Conclusion

Journalism faces assault from two dangerous areas. From one direction it has to cope with its new owners, the media conglomerates that have exacerbated the traditional problems of professional news. From another direction, the Internet is displacing the traditional journalistic role of providing information and interpretation for the citizen. It is customary to look for notes of optimism within this bleak scenario. There are of course oases of resistance to the corporate control of news – public service broadcasting still survives in limited form, and some independently owned news organisations still exist. The future of the Internet provides more fertile grounds for optimism, albeit limited. Citizens on-line will still require interpretation and meaning of events. The political struggle over control of cyberspace is at an early stage and the role played by journalism will be crucial in determining how the balance finally evolves.

Note

1 UKCOD has recently been granted charitable status. Sponsors to date include the Joseph Rowntree Trust, Sun Microsystems, GX Networks, Rowe and Maw Solicitors, AOL, Internet Vision, European Telework Development and Digitrade. Among its other activities it has acted for public consultations of council tax levels for the London Borough of Brent, the first such consultation by a local authority in the UK; a civic discussion among prominent individuals on the European Monetary Union on behalf of the UK Office of the European Parliament; a closed on-line discussion on the data protection legislation run on behalf of the Parliamentary Office of Science and Technology, the first such consultation run by Parliament.

3 From media politics to e-protest?

The use of popular culture and new media in parties and social movements

Alan Scott and John Street

Introduction

The growing use of cultural symbols and mass media by political actors, whether in the mainstream of politics or in social movements, has been taken as evidence of a 'new politics', one marked by new forms of political communication and political action. Such claims form part of more all-encompassing arguments for a 'cultural turn' (Chaney 1994) in 'late' or 'reflexive' modernity (Beck 1998b), and for the emergence of a 'new political culture' (Clarke and Hoffman-Martinot 1998). This chapter argues that claims about the 'cultural turn' in the 'new politics' can easily be exaggerated, and that the 'newness' of new politics needs to be analysed more carefully. In particular we suggest that, while the new politics does draw heavily upon popular culture and the media techniques associated with it (Hart 1994), these new methods in politics can simply represent a refined instrumentalism, in which culture is as much a manipulative device as an expressive one. To this extent, the 'newness' refers to the details of political practice, rather than marking any more fundamental change. Two examples are taken to develop this case: New Labour's highly self-conscious adoption of a cultural *modus vivendi* and recent social movement campaigns (in particular, the Carnival Against Capital of 18 June 1999).

While both institutionalised and marginal actors have learned (have, in the context of an information society, had to learn) techniques for the manipulation of cultural material, these lessons can still be explained by the kind of 'political' language used by theories of resource mobilisation (in the case of movements) or interest intermediation (in the case of 'normal' politics). The cultural turn argument presupposes a greater historical and theoretical shift in the place of culture than is in fact the case. Earlier generations of political sociologists (notably the elite theorists) were aware of the interdependence of the political and the cultural, but were not tempted to take this as evidence of a qualitative shift through which stages of modernisation could be periodised. We argue that the kind of politics-versus-culture view implicit both in much political science and among its sociological critics is an unnecessary hindrance to understanding the continuities and differences between the 'old' and 'new' politics. Just because cultural forms and practices feature in contemporary political practice, it does not follow that this change needs to be explained in culturalist terms. The cultural dimension may be a consequence of old-fashioned instrumentalism.

Old politics in new practices: popular culture and political parties

> By means of the spectacle the ruling order discourses endlessly upon itself in an uninterrupted monologue of self praise.
>
> (Debord 1992: Thesis 24)

One development that is claimed to mark the emergence of a 'new politics' has been the increasing use of popular culture to promote the interests of political parties. During the 1992 UK general election, the Liberal Democrat Party distributed a leaflet in London. It read 'Vote Liberal Democrat. We are hard core.' This appeal was not directed, we may assume, at those voters with a taste for pornography. Instead, it was aimed at young clubbers with a taste for a particular genre of music; or at least (given that the party promised no special policy for fans of hard core), it was meant to indicate that the Liberal Democrats were hipper than the rest. The party was using popular culture to evoke an image and to attract political support. However laughable such examples may seem, they are symptomatic of a now familiar and increasingly discussed phenomenon: the use of popular culture to promote politicians and their parties.

For the 1999 European elections, a Labour Party election broadcast ended, not with a politician, but with Alex Ferguson, manager of Manchester United Football Club, cajoling his audience to 'Vote Labour' for continued success in Europe. Meanwhile, the Conservatives' European broadcasts borrowed the conventions of soap opera and the Gold Blend coffee advertisements to chart the domestic discussion of a young couple ('your friend Tony Blair said he was going to . . .'). For the 1997 UK general election, Labour made a video, aimed at young voters, which took its title ('Do it') from a Nike advertising campaign and its soundtrack from the pop group D:Ream ('Things can only get better'). In another broadcast, Labour took the storyline from the Hollywood film *It's a Wonderful Life* and had an angel (played by Peter Postlethwaite) foretell of the effects of a Conservative victory. In yet another party election broadcast, there was an 'intimate portrayal' of Tony Blair at home which used jump cuts and shots of no more than ten seconds, a deliberate imitation of fly-on-the-wall documentary techniques (Butler and Kavanagh 1997: 152–3). After the election, Tony Blair was one of the guests – together with Elton John – on the *Des O'Connor Show*, where he recounted anecdotes about family pets and his mother-in-law.

These pieces of propaganda did not just borrow their styles and icons from popular culture, they also used its practitioners. The Blair profile was made by Molly Dineen, who later directed a portrait of Geri Halliwell, the ex-Spice Girl. The parody of *It's a Wonderful Life* was directed by Stephen Frears (maker of *My Beautiful Launderette*). The Conservative Party's European broadcasts were produced by an ex-creative director at Channel 4, the man responsible for pairing Johnny Vaughan and Denise Van Outen on *The Big Breakfast* TV programme.

This practice of promoting parties through the use of the genre conventions, idols and creators of popular culture has been seen to mark a 'new politics'. It is taken as evidence for the emergence of 'the new political culture' (Clark and Hoffman-Martinot 1998), of the integration of 'celebrity and power' (Marshall 1997), of the 'packaging of politics' (Franklin 1994) and of a 'designer politics' (Scammell 1995). For some of these observers, this new politics is to be welcomed as a democratic opening up of the political process; for others, it marks a dumbing down of political discourse. 'Television', writes Hart (1999: 10), 'makes us feel good about feeling bad about politics.' In contrast, Liesbet van Zoonen (1998: 196–7) writes: 'Popular political communication should be seen as an attempt to restore the relation between politicians and voters, between the people and their representatives, to regain the necessary sense of community between public officials and their publics.' What all are apparently agreed upon is the novelty of the alliance with popular culture and its significance for political discourse. The use of popular culture is seen as creating a new means of claiming popular legitimacy (pop icons as symbols of popularity), of communicating political ideas (the subtexts of adverts and soaps) and of laying claim to forms of representation (the images and performances of politicians on chat shows, etc). In other words, it is establishing a new form of political discourse in which politics acquires a new language and new criteria of judgement.

It is worth pointing out here that the term 'popular culture' is being used to encompass a number of different phenomena. It is referring to the stars of mass entertainment, to the styles of address associated with that entertainment, and to the industrial infrastructure that produces these stars and genres. 'Popular culture' is made to stand for a form of culture which is consumed by a large audience via a highly mediated process, legitimated by claims to populism and ease of access. But as will be obvious, any such definition is itself partial and political, entailing arbitrary distinctions and loaded judgements. Our argument does not, however, depend upon any settled definition of popular culture. It is merely concerned with the general observation that parties have chosen to draw upon the conventions and practitioners of mass entertainment and leisure to advance their political cause, and that these are different from those traditionally used.

In the next two sections of this chapter, we ask whether this use of popular entertainment does indeed signal a significant shift in the character of contemporary electoral politics. The idea that using popular culture represents some kind of 'new politics' is premised upon two ideas. The first is that it is, in some way, unprecedented. The second is that the explanation for this development lies in recent fundamental changes in the political order. There is a third idea, which is not addressed here, that using popular culture allows politics to be discussed in a new political language ('Cool Britannia'). Put another way, the changes may be real, but superficial – and hence not 'new' in any significant way; equally, they may have precedents, but the causes for their appearance now may lie in major shifts in the political terrain – they may not appear to be new, but may actually be the product of radical change.

Is the link between politics and popular culture new?

In one sense, the relationship between politics and popular culture has an immensely long history. In *The Republic*, Plato discusses at length the moral and political consequences of musical pleasure. He distinguishes between the beneficial and detrimental consequences of particular harmonic and rhythmic forms. Such an argument creates the basis for censorship, for the idea that the state needs to censor popular culture for fear of its effects on the dominant order. We need only observe the strictures of the Taliban regime in Afghanistan, or revelations about the CIA's propagandist promotion of culture, or remember the treatment of pamphlets and broadsides during the English Civil War.

Paralleling the long history of the state's politicisation of popular culture has been another history, that of oppressed groups for whom popular culture provides some means of expressing defiance and resistance, a means of creating solidarity and communicating grievances. James Scott (1990) writes of the 'hidden transcripts' that are embedded in the popular cultures of subservient peoples, and Eugene Genovese (1976) has documented the way slaves used song to challenge the order constructed by their masters. And popular culture continues to act as a political weapon, whether in the polemical subtext of films by Spike Lee, Oliver Stone or John Sayles, or in the subcultural practices with pop styles from rock'n'roll to punk to dance culture.

These two general trends tend to preserve, formally at least, the separateness of politics and popular culture. On the one hand, there is the state imposing its interests and values on popular culture; on the other, there are artists and audiences who invest popular culture with political meaning and significance in defiance of the state. But there is a third, less confrontational tradition in which popular culture is tied into politics. Here popular culture presents itself as a kind of 'trophy' to be used in the enhancement of personal and political reputation. Its modern incarnation is the way in which political leaders attend high-profile events in the popular culture calendar (football cup finals, awards ceremonies) or when they invite pop and film stars to receptions at the White House or 10 Downing Street. This is the contemporary variant of a long-standing practice, one illustration of which can be found in 1930s Britain when society hostesses courted sporting heroes and popular performers (like Noel Coward) as illustration of social standing (McKibbin 1998a: 30–1). These figures became adornments to their social life, and markers of their reputation. The same is now true in the political realm; cultural success is appropriated for political gain (albeit at some potential cost, as when Noel Gallagher and other British pop stars, who had been used to embody Labour's version of 'Cool Britannia', expressed disillusionment with the Blair project).

There is, therefore, nothing novel in the linking of politics to popular culture, at least as far as these three traditions are concerned. However, there may be a case for seeing some element of novelty insofar as the three traditions have become more intimately entwined. Politicians have become part of the popular culture that they also seek to control, and popular artists take on the guise of politicians.[1] The case of the former is represented by the appearance of politicians in cultural formats that previously they chose to avoid or which chose to exclude them. In the UK in the 1980s, examples of this included Mrs Thatcher's appearance on a chat show hosted by Michael Aspel or on a daytime pop radio station (the *Jimmy Young Show* on BBC Radio 2). Meanwhile, her opposition rival, Neil Kinnock, reviewed pop videos on a Saturday morning children's TV show and also actually appeared in one such video (with Tracey Ullman). Not to be outdone, the UK's third party, the Liberals, produced their own rap song, 'I feel Liberal all right'. This political symbiosis with popular culture, as we have seen, has been administered increasingly by people whose background is not that of the traditional party apparatchik, but rather of media and popular culture.[2]

The divide between politics and popular culture has not just been breached from the political side. In popular culture, the last decades have witnessed ever more direct cultural intervention into politics. This is most dramatically illustrated by popular music. From Rock Against Racism in the late 1970s, through to Red Wedge and Live Aid in the 1980s, pop musicians have become engaged directly in a variety of political causes and campaigns (Frith and Street 1992). Of course, there were earlier examples of this, most notably folk musicians' involvement in the peace movement or soul musicians' involvement in the civil rights movement, but what was distinctive about the 1980s was the ways in which the musicians took on political responsibility and became engaged with mainstream political parties (to the extent that now stars and executives of the record industry sit on government advisory committees, and government ministers actively promote British pop).

What we want to suggest, then, is that there are precedents for the so-called 'new' politics, but what may be different is the degree of intimacy of politics with popular culture. This brings us to the second question about the 'new' politics – can these linkages be seen as the product of fundamental changes in the conditions under which politics operates?

New political conditions for a 'new' politics?

Are there major shifts in the conditions of party political practice that might lead to the conclusion that party politics, in adopting popular culture, has entered a new phase?

Imitation

British political use of popular culture can be seen, as can much else, as an imitative response to the American example. It is widely reported that both the British Conservative and Labour parties spent time observing their US equivalents and drawing upon the experience and expertise developed across the

Atlantic (Butler and Kavanagh 1997: 56–7; Kavanagh 1997: 29–30; Norris *et al.* 1999: 58). The use of the icons and techniques of popular culture, long employed in the USA, may be one such borrowed technique. But in noting the possibility of imitation, we do not get much closer to the question of whether the trend represents a radical innovation. It only moves the explanatory task back one stage, to the question of why the originator of the technique came to this solution (and why it is this example being imitated and not some other). The answer to this lies in the particular political structure of parties in the USA and UK, and in the political context in which they operate. Paolo Mancini and David Swanson (1996: 17–20) argue that the adoption of the 'modern model of campaigning' is linked to, among other things, the structure of party competition, the electoral and media system, campaign regulations and political culture.

Rational choice

An alternative explanation for the adoption of popular culture lies in the rationality of electioneering. Antony Downs (1957), and the many who have followed him, have pointed to the disincentives for voters to acquire detailed information about any given set of political alternatives. The costs of acquiring information outweigh the calculable benefits of allocating an individual vote to any given party. This same logic, since it applies to all voters, does also suggest that if all others abstain, it pays to vote, since that vote will be decisive. The point is that these competing logics create a state of affairs which encourages the parties to provide information in an easily accessible form, to reduce the cost of information acquisition. Hence, there is a drive towards 'branding' rather than detailed policy detail. Pippa Norris and her colleagues (1999) observed exactly this move during the 1997 election. They write (Norris *et al.* 1999: 59) of how Labour realised the need to devote as much attention to symbols as debates, that the party had come to the belief 'that style was as important as substance' and that the chosen style 'was a deliberately "non-political" style'. This alternative 'style' was provided by popular culture. The need for this derives – in part, at least – from the pressure created by rational action in a world where information is costly and imperfect. But what is clear is that if this was the reasoning behind Labour's strategy, it constituted a continuation of traditional practices, and popular culture was no more than another instrument. It did not signal a 'new' politics. For this to be the case, there has to be an answer to the question *Why now?* Why does the logic take hold at a particular juncture? If the adoption of popular culture is simply a response to the problems caused to parties by rational voters, then this move merely represents one amongst many solutions. It would only be 'new' if there were some significant alteration in the character of voters' relationship to party and the application of rationality.

Dealignment

One way in which the voters have been claimed to have changed, in ways that make popular culture more salient, emerges through accounts of political dealignment. This can be represented as the erosion of traditional (non-rational?) forms of political allegiance (and the rise of rational forms). If traditional ties of party and class loyalty have been eroded, then, the argument runs, political issues become more salient in determining party preference (Crewe and Sarlvik 1983). Prior to this, party loyalty was a product of a process of socialisation, and the position adopted by citizens on any given issue was predetermined by their party loyalty. Now it is suggested that the relationship works in reverse – policy preference determines party choice. If this is the case, perceptions of parties and of the policies they advocate become crucial to party political strategy. Parties cannot rely on traditional ties, they have to sell themselves. The mass media represent a key forum, and advertising a key language, for this sales technique.[3] Within this account of voting behaviour, media representations become central elements in the formation of allegiance. However, not all theories of voting behaviour place the same emphasis on the media, and some are sceptical not only of the degree of dealignment but of the impact of the media on political behaviour (Curtice and Semetko 1994). In a sense, though, this is not the issue, since what is important is not whether, in fact, the media affects behaviour, but the *belief* about the media's influence. The party elite believed in the importance of creating particular images, and acted on this basis in reforming the party structure. Labour created, for example, the Shadow Communications Agency, and elevated people like Peter Mandelson to positions of power (Kavanagh 1995). But while the belief may be as important as the reality in accounting for the internal logic of political actors, the question of whether there has been a funda-mental shift in the conditions of voter behaviour, and whether this provides an incentive for the use of popular culture, is a matter for the psephologists to resolve. What we can say, though, is that the new, culturally sensitive approach to the voters may owe as much to the fact that parties have invested heavily in people (and agencies) who think in these marketing/media terms as to any more fundamental shift.

Technological mediation of politics

An alternative strategy for establishing the claim that we are witnessing a new politics is to focus on the technology which delivers both popular culture and political discourse. The massive penetration of television into domestic life, and the widely held view that television is now the main source of political infor-mation, is seen to create the drive towards parties' strategic focus on the medium (Negrine 1994). More than this, though, it is argued that the formats and nature of television, its particular character as a medium, have shaped the mode of address adopted by the parties. Joshua Meyrowitz (1985), for example, argues that television by its nature – its use of close-ups, its intimate tone – works against a declamatory oratory and leaderly aloofness. Instead, as he suggests, leaders are brought down to our (the viewers') level. Political communication is forced to take on the style of television's naturalism, and to adopt the codes and conventions that television demands. It is a view echoed by Hart (1999: 2) who argues that television 'has changed how politics is conducted and how it is received'. Politics becomes 'more private'. The modern politician is required to seek popularity according to prevailing norms, and the current norm, according to David Marshall (1997), is that of 'celebrity', itself a direct product of the popular culture of film, television and pop music. It is this pressure which lies behind the adoption by politicians of the formats and icons of popular culture. Politics takes on the generic conventions of the medium – politics becomes melodrama through the recounting of personal anecdotes; interviews become therapeutic encounters (Hart 1999: 25–9). In other words, the medium of modern politics invests it with a particular language and style, both of which derive from popular culture. The claim for a 'new' politics rests here upon three arguments: the first is that a new technology now mediates political discourse; the second is that this technology imposes its own logic on the conduct of politics; and the third is that television representations of politics diminish the discourse. Put crudely, if technology is seen merely as an instrument of political will, then the use of popular culture will be viewed as just another device of the powerful to maintain their power, and in no sense a break with previous practice.[4] Equally, it is has to be *shown* that the current media representations of politics are, in some way, qualitatively (democratically) diminished – that we learn less about Tony Blair from seeing him interviewed by the crooner-comedian Des O'Connor than by the journalist Jeremy Paxman. This cannot be assumed; it has to be demonstrated by a critical reading of the relevant examples. Is it actually the case that an appearance on O'Connor's show is less revealing of Tony Blair's politics than one on *Newsnight*?

The commodification of politics

If technology does not in itself cause the reshaping of political practice, then the focus shifts to the interests that organise those technologies. For this we need to focus attention on the political economic context. Here claims about the commodification of politics suggest a distinct reason for the adoption of popular culture and for a new politics. Nicholas Garnham (1986), drawing upon Jürgen Habermas's account of the commercialisation of the public sphere, argues that mass communications are now organised around advertising. The 'public' is now the 'market', and media now address and constitute citizens as *consumers*. In a similar vein, Marshall (1997: 205) argues:

> The product advertising campaign provides the underlying model for the political election campaign. Both instantiated the prominence of irrational appeal within a general legitimating discourse of rationality. Both are attempts to establish resonance with a massive number of people so that connections are drawn between the campaign's message and the interests of consumers/citizens.

By this account, the use of advertising and of celebrity endorsements is less about a pragmatic adoption of communicative conventions, and more about the enforced denial of full political participation and debate. The suggestion is that the political economy of communications introduces a powerful logic which links popular culture to political practice, but that the use of popular culture is continuous with a pre-existing commercial logic.

The politicisation of popular culture

While the previous arguments go some way to accounting for the political adoption of certain formats and stylistic conventions, they omit one crucial dimension: the contribution made by popular culture (as a supplier of icons, endorsements, styles and creators). Although parties have drawn upon expertise within advertising for some time, there has been a reluctance on the part of the youth/popular culture to associate itself publicly with political parties and explicitly political causes. It may have joined ad hoc campaigns, but typically these fell outside the formal political arena or commanded almost universal support. But from the late 1970s there has been an increasing involvement of stars in politics, not just as benefactors but as endorsees and as political actors in their own right. The explanation for this cannot rest simply with a changing political consciousness of these performers, but has also to take account of the changing popular economy of popular culture (Frith and Street 1992). This is perhaps best illustrated by the movement of rock music into the mainstream, and its increasing function as a form of corporate leisure (Rolling Stones tours sponsored by prestige companies) and advertising (Rolling Stones songs advertise Microsoft operating systems and i-Mac computers). The political role played by rock performers (like Bob Geldof) is a product of their new status as popular entertainers, not as dissident radicals in exclusive subcultures. Whatever interpretation is put upon such developments, the point is that any talk of a 'new' politics must incorporate an account of the changes in the political economy of popular culture.

Once again the answer to the question as to whether we are witnessing the emergence of a 'new' politics receives an equivocal answer. Much depends on how the use of popular culture is explained, whether it is assigned to accounts which stress recent or fundamental breaks with previous practice, or whether it is assigned to long-established patterns of politics. There is not space here to explore further this issue; it is sufficient to say that the claims for a 'new' electoral politics need to be built upon firmer foundations than are supplied by those who either celebrate or decry the development. There is a need for closer examination of the conditions affecting the relationship between popular culture and politics, and a closer reading of the texts which are held to represent this relationship. Only then will it be possible to establish whether we are witnessing old politics conducted through (new) practices or a new politics, at least insofar as it is conducted through the iconography of popular culture.

So far we have considered the suggestion for a new politics in relationship to the electoral politics of established parties. We want to move now to look at the same question in relation to social movement politics, and in particular, the Carnival

Against Capital. Do interventions like this represent something newer than the new social movements?

New(ish) politics in new(ish) practices

All that was once directly lived has become mere representation.
(Debord 1992: Thesis 1)

As anyone who has caught the internet virus can attest, virtual activism may serve as a substitute – and not as a spur – to activism in the real world.
(Tarrow 1998: 193)

On 18 June 1999, depending on whose figures one believes, between 3,000 and 10,000 people marched through the City of London; unremarkable, except for: (i) the estimated £2 million damage done (*Financial Times*, 21 June 1999: 1) in what was widely characterised as the worst violence in London since the poll tax demonstration – 'by 6 p.m., the streets around the London International Financial and Futures Exchange looked like a riot zone' (*Financial Times*, 19/20 June 1999: 9); (ii) the fact that the usual arrangements and planning agreements between organisers and the police authorities had not been made; (iii) that the march was co-ordinated with similar events throughout the world timed to coincide with the G8 summit in Cologne; (iv) that the organisation was conducted almost exclusively via the Internet. So this section of the chapter starts from an observation and a puzzle. The observation is that recent campaigns in Britain such as anti-roads campaigns (e.g. Tyford Down, Newbury Bypass), protest against GM foods and the Carnival Against Capital in London on 18 June appear to have a stronger than usual family resemblance. Likewise, the groups typically involved in these campaigns – Earth First!, Reclaim the Streets, London Greenpeace, June 18th Network – appear to adopt a similar *modus vivendi* and share a common organisational form. But beyond the national context, the Carnival Against Capital was both an imitation of the highly successful use of the Internet by the Zapatista movement in Mexico and foreshadowed (or was in turn the model for) the protest events surrounding the World Trade Organisation conference in Seattle in December 1999. The family of resemblances may be characterised as follows:

- In terms of strategy and style of protest there is an emphasis on spectacle, gesture, ridicule, carnival and/or on what Brian Doherty has called 'manufactured vulnerability' (Doherty 1999b).
- In terms of organisation they have decentralised 'light' styles of organisation, but nevertheless these afford a high level of co-ordinated action; what we might call 'organised spontaneity'. It is tempting to characterise these campaigns with their network-like and often overlapping organisations and their focus on culture and lifestyle as typical 'new social movements' (NSM). But on the

tion that our initial observation is correct, the catch-all new social
nent label appears too broad to capture the specificity of this family of
campaigns. In other words, they may in some respects be 'newer' than
is. Although there is clear continuity with NSM repertoire, we want to
est that these innovations possess a new 'action repertoire', or at the very
least a distinctive synthesis of older themes. Perhaps this point can be best
pursued by considering the nature and origins of that action repertoire.

Doherty (1999c) points to other campaigns – especially Greenham Common
– as the key source of this new(ish) repertoire. This seems plausible, but we want
to suggest that there are other inspirations from outside the social movement
sector which campaigns have drawn upon and reference to which offers a fuller
explanation of their distinct common characteristics. To generalise the point,
social movement analysis has paid considerable attention to the ways in which
action repertoires are copied across social movements, but perhaps has not yet
paid sufficient attention to the way in which movements adopt repertoires from
beyond the social movement sector. Of these broader influences the following
are central: carnival, avant-garde artistic practices and popular culture.

Carnival – the 'aestheticisation of politics'

Carnival, originally pre-Lenten festival in Catholic countries, has long been open
to adaptation and innovation, for example as gay marches and 'love parades'.
Carnival now appears to have been taken as a paradigmatic model for many
recent social movement campaigns. Abner Cohen in his splendid ethnography
of the Notting Hill Carnival offers an account of carnival as an event in which
political (intended and rational) and cultural (unintentional and non-rational)
elements are mixed in a 'continual interplay between cultural forms and political
relations' (1993: 7):

> As a blueprint, carnival is a season of festive popular events that are charac-
> terized by revelry, playfulness and overindulgence in eating, drinking and
> sex, culminating in two or three days of massive street processions by
> masqued individuals and groups, ecstatically playing loud and cheerful music
> or as ecstatically dancing to its accompaniment.
>
> (Cohen 1993: 3)

This carnival blueprint was precisely that adopted and adapted by the
organisers of the 18 June Carnival Against Capital whose website appeared more
like a call to party than to arms. Thus the London march included the 'Associations of Autonomous Astronauts' protest against the militarisation of space;
the one in Boston was to start 'with a conga line, music, puppets, street theatre
and leaflets. There's a rumour that Zapatistas may ride in on horseback to show
their solidarity' (Second J18 Bulletin, //bak.spc.j18/bulletin2.html). Participants
protesting against the G8 summit in Cologne (which occasioned the events) were

invited to form a human chain 'with as much noise as possible – bring drums, whistles and rattles along!' and after that they were invited to a concert on the Deutzer Werft and advised to take in a little sightseeing (Come to Cologne, //www.oneworld.org/jubilee2000/action/cologne.html). While much protest has a carnivalesque quality, carnival seems now to have been elevated to the defining characteristic of the event, transplanting the language of the mid-1980s hippie convoys and free festivals into an urban context: 'By lunchtime, more than 3,000 people had gathered in Liverpool Street Station, where, led by a samba band, they entertained City workers by crawling over the marble façades of the insurance houses, dancing in the sunshine and waving flags' (*Guardian*, 19 June 1999: 5).[5]

Along with this urban transfer we also seem to have here the reverse of the process of reclaiming 'liminoid space' described by Kevin Hetherington in his account of New Age travellers and of the contention of space around ancient sites such as Stonehenge. In such cases 'the margin becomes socially central' (1996: 37). In contrast, the intention of Reclaim the Streets and of the J18 Carnival Against Capital was not to reclaim marginal sites for their potential 'heterotopian' function, but rather to challenge directly the meaning of spaces, such as the City of London, which are anything but marginal. Likewise, the target of such protest is no longer the state which polices such marginal sites, but rather the private commercial organisations which control these central spaces. Thus protest was typically directed against banks and companies such as McDonald's and Gap. Using similar carnivalesque forms of action, these recent campaigns attempt something like a symbolic (and spasmodically also a physical) assault on central social space rather than the kinds of defensive transgressions at the margins described by Hetherington. Although, as Cohen also shows, carnival too can become a commercialised enterprise, it remains a suitable means of taking highly commercialised spaces and, at least for the duration of the event, giving them over to expressions of collective festivity or disorder.

Avant-garde artistic practices – the 'politicisation of aesthetics'

From the 1920s onwards avant-garde artistic movements, notably surrealism and Dadaism, pioneered the spectacular events to challenge or even replace the exhibition. Forms of action art have continued and developed such techniques. Sadie Plant (1992) has persuasively argued that it was Situationism in the 1950s and 1960s that provided the link between these artistic practices and political action. She demonstrates the influence of Situationist ideas both on the radical politics of the 1960s (and particularly on the events of 1968) and on postmodern social theory. Situationist critique of consumer society as a society of spectacle (reminiscent of Baudrillard's 'simulacra'), its rejection of vanguardist politics (reminiscent of Lefort and Castoriadis), its emphasis on individual acts of resistance (reminiscent of aspects of Foucault) and its absorption of anti-statism from anarchist political theory provided a synthesis which reappears as a legitimating leitmotif within recent political campaigns. So the 'newness' of these new social movements may consist in the rediscovery of a political vocabulary from the 1950s and 1960s which was carried on, for example, by so-called *Spontes* in the German environmental movement of the 1970s but which otherwise largely disappeared from the vocabulary of collective protest. But we also want to suggest that the influence of avant-garde artistic movements is not restricted to their intellectual content and to the ideas contained in their manifestos (e.g. Debord 1992 [1967]). They have also developed techniques which have been absorbed into the action repertoires of these groups. Spectacular events (such as the 18 June carnivals in London, Cologne, etc.), innovative 'shock' tactics (such as the destruction of genetically modified crops or the felling of genetically modified beech trees), and symbolic provocation and ridicule (the Cologne marchers were told to laugh at the G8 delegates) have come to form part of a shared repertoire. While modernist theorists like Habermas and Luhmann have emphasised the autonomy of spheres (the separation of the aesthetic, political, scientific, moral, etc.), we have nonetheless repeatedly seen how characteristics held to be specific to one of those spheres can spill over into any or all of the others. The mimicking of artistic techniques by political activists is merely one such case. Perhaps we can push the point further by pointing to an affinity between even more recent innovations in the aesthetic sphere and in contemporary forms of collective action. There are, for example, parallels between 'body modification' in which the artist's own body becomes the exhibit and political actions in which protesters' bodies become a chief site of resistance (see Docherty 1999b: 14).

Popular culture – as symbol, organisation and infrastructure

In developing their cognitive account of social movements, Eyerman and Jamison (1998) have drawn attention to the role of popular culture, and especially popular music, in forging collective identity. 'Through its ritualized performance and through the memories it invokes,' they write (1998: 163), 'the music of social movements transcends the boundaries of the self and binds the individual to a collective consciousness.' This is a general point about the way in which popular music operates within social movements, but the Carnival Against Capital drew on specific elements and traditions within popular culture.

At the symbolic level, the Situationist gestures are themselves a key feature of certain strands within popular culture. Indeed, in *Lipstick Traces*, the American writer Greil Marcus (1989) sketches 'a secret history of the twentieth century' which connects Situationism through punk and beyond, forging a particular identity – marked by saying 'no' to convention and commonness – that is evident in the politics of the Carnival Against Capital. The gestural politics of punk – the use of shock tactics – remain part of the practice of eco-warriors and groups such as Class War (who have promoted events similar to the Carnival Against Capital).

But popular culture was evident in more than the symbolic repertoire it supplied. It also formed part of the organisation and infrastructure of the movement.

The creation of networks of networks, of organised spontaneity, is itself closely linked to the techniques evolved by the organisers of the illegal warehouse parties and raves of contemporary dance culture (Collin 1997). These parties were the product of a system which operated with little centralised authority or easily identifiable leaderships. A loosely linked system of answerphone messages, and now website addresses, provides a mechanism for assembling large numbers of people in one place without warning or publicity. Rave culture has also provided the basis for more permanent social movement activity, most notably around such entities as the Exodus collective in Luton (Malyon 1998).

These elements drawn from popular culture help to mark as 'different' the Carnival Against Capital and the anti-GM movement (which also practises organised spontaneity). But in underlining the difference from other forms of social movement, their reliance on popular culture does not necessarily establish their novelty. As George McKay (1996) has pointed out, though there are clear continuities between rave culture and certain social movement forms, there are also precedents for them in the fayres and politics of the 1960s. A similar sense of history emerges from Christian Lahusen's (1996) authoritative survey of the place of popular culture in political mobilisation. But these precedents are not, in themselves, proof of endless repetition, but rather a flourishing of a submerged current in the history of cultural politics.

One could make much of this shift in action repertoire, i.e. assert that it is not merely a new variation on old themes plus a couple of minor innovations, but constitutes a final break from the old bureaucratic/military action repertoire classically characterised by Michels. Above all, the days of the ordered (and usually orderly) mass demonstration appear to have given way to a wider variety of smaller-scale but spectacular 'events', combined with longer-lasting protest.

But is this cultural story enough? So far our interpretation of a highly selective set of recent political campaigns appears to have taken the 'cultural turn'. We have accepted two of Melucci's central contentions: first, that collective action has increasingly adopted a cultural form and, second, that political institutions and actors are of declining significance as addressees of these actions (Melucci 1996). But does a cultural *interpretation* of a movement's *modus vivendi* imply the need for a culturalist *explanation* of why such a *modus vivendi* was adopted in the first place? We want to argue that it does not. More precisely, we shall argue that however innovative the action repertoires of these campaigns are, their adoption can be quite adequately explained by rather more conventional – and more political – styles of analysis of the kind to be found within theories of resource mobilisation and within 'new institutionalism' in sociology and political science. We also want to suggest that the motives for collective protest movement in adopting these kinds of repertoire are not so different from those of the political parties discussed in the first part of the paper.

To support this argument our general claim is that the concept of 'opportunity structures' should be extended beyond the sphere of political institutions to include media and new media. But we also want to argue that conventional (i.e. press and TV) and new media present social movements with quite distinct opportunity structures. This can be best illustrated by comparing the kinds of opportunities and consequences of the use of traditional media and the use of the Internet. Conventional media will tend to induce 'source professionalization' (Schlesinger, quoted in Neveu 1999: 52), that is, the 'professional management of media' and 'intellectualization of protests' (Neveu: 51–2), the narrowing of the gap between social movement and commercial campaigns (Baringhorst 1998), or the emergence of a mail-order 'protest business' (Jordan and Maloney 1997). Examples often referred to here include FoE and Greenpeace. But it is exactly against these professionalised movements that groupings like Earth First!, Reclaim the Streets and London Greenpeace react (see Doherty 1999c). The Internet on the other hand opens up a quite different set of opportunities. The Net is attractive for social movements for four broad reasons. First, it facilitates what Gerhards and Rucht (1992) call *'mesomobilization'* namely, it allows a high degree of co-ordination between movement networks across a broad geographical range without creating a fixed hierarchical organisational forms (a *network of networks*). Second, this in turn affords an enormous reduction of costs: high impact on little resource. In other words, the Net provides social movements with the same kinds of opportunities as it does a commercial enterprise: namely, the opportunity to create an effect disproportional to the size of the enterprise – a characteristic nicely captured by the *Observer*'s headline 'How virtual chaos beat City Police' (20 June 1999: 9). Third, unlike conventional media, the Net provides activists with 'editorial control' over the image they convey, for example enabling them to counter newspaper and TV reports with their own alternative news media (it is attractive to political parties for the same reason). Finally, the relative lack of regulation of the Internet at present offers the option of secrecy and of bypassing the state.

With respect to all four points the argument of della Porta and Diani (following Tarrow 1998b) holds:

> The expansion of both printed and electronic means of communication permitted an 'externalization' of certain costs . . . If highly structured organizations were previously required to get a message across, today a lightweight one which can gain media attention is sufficient. The diffusion of cheap global means of communication (such as faxes and electronic mail, for example) reduces the costs of co-ordination, though the level of professionalization required for mobilization increases.

> (della Porta and Diani 1999: 152)

We would differ from this analysis only on the final point because, as suggested above, new media do not lock social movements into this level of professionalism. In part this is because of the increasing simplicity of website design and publication, but it is also because of the newly won level of editorial control which means that they are no longer caught in a 'symbolic weaponry race' (Neveu 1999: 52) with the press and media in which a high degree of professionalisation of the presentation of self is a prerequisite for success ('the days of Swampy appearing on TV shows and Jonathon Porritt sounding measured are gone', *Observer*, 20 June 1999: 9). Professionalisation can be confined to the technical proficiency required to produce high-quality Web pages and links (and here the J18 sites are indeed highly professional). The Net can in this respect be seen as the (post?)modern equivalent of the backroom duplicator, but with infinitely greater potential.

Its greatest potential lies in the sphere of organisational flexibility, particularly in regard to mesomobilisation by which Gerhards and Rucht mean not the mobilisation of individuals but of groups: 'first they provide a structural integration by organizationally connecting groups with each other . . . Second, they aim at *cultural integration*[6] of the various groups and networks in developing a common frame of meaning' (Gerhards and Rucht 1992: 558). The Net enabled the organisers of the 18 June events to plan and to co-ordinate simultaneous events across the globe – or, more accurately, to sequence events according to local time zones. It also enabled them to stage the event as spectacle by bypassing the normal co-ordination of marches with the police authorities. As newspaper reports noted, this element of surprise made the size and form of the event difficult to assess and to police, one side-effect of which was the difficulty in controlling incidents of violence. At the same time the Internet enabled the organisers to remain all but hidden, affording them the strategic advantages of a cellular secret society (cf. Simmel 1950): 'We do not know who is behind this. But they got what they were looking for. Our resources were overstretched. Tactical decisions were made as we went along' (a senior police officer quoted in the *Observer*, 20 June 1999: 9). For social movements and political parties alike one further major advantage of the Internet is the possibility it opens up for bypassing existing institutions. Political parties, and indeed governments, can bypass political conventions and the press by appealing directly to voters. Social movements can bypass nation-state institutions by appealing directly to potential protesters and targeting international companies simultaneously in a variety of global locations.[7]

But in addition to these organisational and resource advantages, access to Internet technology also facilitated the process of creating a 'common frame of meaning'. The frame turns out to be much more conventionally political than that associated with the protests of New Age travellers in the 1980s.[8] Critiques of economic globalisation and of neoliberalism have revived a generalised critique of capitalism very similar to the 'master frame' characterised by Gerhards and Rucht in their analysis of an anti-IMF and anti-Reagan demonstration in Germany in the late 1980s (see 1992: 576). The major difference is that 'neo-liberalism' now stands where 'imperialism' once stood as the core characteristic of the system against or around which the master frame defines itself. In other words, those movements which we are keen to describe as 'new' in their *modus vivendi* appear to be a revival of older campaigns with respect to their frames of meaning – or, if you prefer, ideology. There is, for example, the same association between anti-capitalist activism in metropolitan centres in the West with the struggles of, say, the landless in Latin America or the new jobless in the ex-Soviet Union, or for that matter striking dockers in Liverpool (Reclaim the Streets). So, for example, J18 websites contain links to sophisticated critiques of neoliberal capitalism (e.g. Michel Chossudovsky, 'Financial warfare', //www.corpwatch.org/trac/globalisation/financial/warfare.html). Thus the claim made by analysts like Doherty (1999c) and Barry (1999) that recent campaigns lacked a single ideological frame may largely describe a familiar point in a social movement circle, namely, that, shortly before movement, intellectuals develop such a frame. What the critique of neoliberalism and economic globalisation appears to have done is to strengthen the belief that the nation-state and its political institutions are irrelevant and that the targets of actions should be global financial and retailing concerns: 'demonstrators trashed a McDonald's, wrecked part of the Futures Exchange, set fire to a bank, and destroyed cars and empty flats in the City of London' (*Guardian*, 19 June 1999: 5). Such an analysis also fits neatly with the Situationist diagnosis, which likewise marginalised the state and focused upon commercialisation as the key defining quality of the society of spectacle.

The Internet is thus both organisationally and ideologically perfectly suited. Organisationally it offers flexibility, speed of response and the possibility of a cellular and secret organisational form. However, we wish to emphasise that although IT in general and the Internet in particular can facilitate these forms of action and has an affinity with what one might dub 'techno-anarchism', there is no simple one-to-one or determinist relationship. The current opposition to the inclusion of the right-populist FPÖ in the Austrian Government illustrates this vividly. While the use of IT by opposition groups such as SOS-Mitmensch and Demokratische Offensive has been no less sophisticated, these have generally taken the form of bulletin boards announcing demonstrations or disseminating information (for example, while writing this sentence one of the authors received an e-mail analysis of effects of political pressure on the news content of the previous evening's ORF news bulletin). In general the repertoire of these opposition movements has remained broadly conventional (e.g. small 'spontaneous' marches or large well-organised protest co-ordinated with the public authorities).

The level and efficiency of organisation afforded by the Internet and the ease of framing meanings in the absence of will formation among participants not only raise familiar questions of the democratic accountability of movements to their 'members' and supporters, but also a more basic question: beyond the point at which IT is merely an information and co-ordination service does the virtual organisation exist for the sake of the protest event or does the protest event exist for the sake of the virtual organisation, as advertisement and as demonstration of its potency?[29] To ask this question of conventional political parties might seem entirely uncontroversial – of course, parties act to create issues and agendas with the sole purpose of promoting their own organisational interests. To ask it of new social movements is more contentious, but it does need to be asked if the claims for a 'new politics' are to be sustained.

Conclusion

The above arguments can be summed up as follows: both conventional political parties and unconventional political actors have increasingly adopted cultural modes of action but their motives for doing so have remained largely familiar, conventional and instrumental. They are responding rationally to technology- and media-driven changes in their environments by learning new techniques for managing their presentation and mobilising actors as either voters or protesters. They have, in this sense, simply exploited the opportunities offered by particular technologies and modes of communication. They have added to the repertoire of political gestures and devices, and to this extent we are witnessing new kinds of political practice (although there are, as we noted, precedents and pre-existing trends). It is not clear, however, that we are seeing the emergence of a new politics in the sense that parties and movements now relate to voters and supporters in entirely novel ways. Parties and movements operate in instrumental ways to promote their interests as organisations. Just as e-commerce has opened up new markets for firms, so it has opened up new techniques of mobilisation and lowered the costs for social movement organisations. But to say this is not to deny the cultural dimension to their activities, it is just to strike a note of caution to those who see the cultural as an alternative to the instrumental. Our suggestion is that they are linked, and the confusion over the idea of a new politics stems from the failure to recognise their connectedness. Notions such as 'political opportunity structures' and 'social movement sectors' (where the analogy is with the business sector) need to be extended and not abandoned to culturalist modes of explanation in the light of these IT-dependent developments.

While culture and politics are frequently seen as alternatives within academic discourses, within social practices themselves they are always mixed. The point has been well made by the anthropologist Abner Cohen, to whose work we have already referred:

> Culture and politics were dynamically related in the development and structure of the carnival, but the event, like all other symbolic forms, is not reducible to either. It is a multivocal form, an ambiguous unity of political and cultural significance, combining the rational and the non-rational, the conscious and the non-conscious.
>
> (Cohen 1993: 120)

Cohen's characterisation of carnival as a *multivocal form* applies no less, as he here hints, to any other form of symbolic collective action. Thus, while we can speak of a shift of weight between the cultural and political we need to recognise that these multivocal forms are also unstable forms; so unstable that efforts at periodisation using the politics/culture divide as a *differentia specifica* are doomed to failure. At the same time, this is no argument for celebrating the use of carnival as necessarily a form of expressive politics. The Carnival Against Capital acted highly instrumentally in its manipulation of people and signs (and it is an irony of the Situationist-inspired use of the spectacle for political ends that the Situationist movement itself was intended as a *critique* of spectacle (Plant 1992)). The implications of this extend beyond our understanding of social movement activity. To the extent that both parties and new social movements act instrumentally, they may both be contributing to the degeneration of public sphere, to what Zolo (2000) calls an 'antipolis'. Despite the appearance of public engagement in politics through populist use of popular culture and spectacle, this engagement may offer no more than the experience of managed spectatorship.

The changes we have described in the modes of action of political parties and social movements, although important, are not unique. They mirror changes elsewhere – in the business sector, for example. The comparison between the party or social movement sector and the business sector holds up remarkably well (see Zald and McCarthy 1987). However, recent developments may suggest a degree of reversal in the direction of influence. Shifts in the character of parties and social movements echo, and are echoed in, changes in the nature of contemporary business organisations. For example, Stewart Clegg and his colleagues in their analysis of 'embryonic industries' describe the way in which the search for a successful model of organisation shifts from the more innovative American multinationals to new companies on the 'periphery' and emphasise that cultural pluralism is now a key source of new ideas and personalities within firms. Not only do such developments chime with multicultural and difference discourses, but also specific political movements – notably Greenpeace – become models of the contemporary company. The business and the 'social movement sector' merge and aspects of the social movement repertoire are taken over wholesale.

This possible reversal of the direction of influence is also supported by the arguments of new institutionalists like DiMaggio and Powell (1991). They propose the thesis of '*institutional isomorphism*' by which they mean the tendency for institutions to mimic successful models within or outside their field of operation thereby reproducing and decimating dominant institutional forms. Given (a) that firms, parties and movements face similar organisational and resource problems and (b) that media and information technologies present them with new and similar opportunity structures – and particularly the possibility of lighter, less hierarchical, but nonetheless co-ordinated forms – we should not be too surprised to find a convergence between them around some new model. Novel developments do not necessarily demand novel explanations; they do, however, require the adaptation of these models of explanation to the opportunities and conditions now emerging.

Notes

This chapter is based on a paper given at a workshop on new politics and new technology at the University of Birmingham in September 1999. We would like to thank the organiser of the conference (also the editor of this volume), Frank Webster, and the other participants for stimulating discussions.

1   The political ambitions of Jerry Springer and Warren Beatty are just recent examples.
2   Peter Mandelson's career is emblematic of this. Mandelson was recruited to the

Labour elite at a meeting, hosted by one of his colleagues in television (where he worked as a producer), at which he was introduced to Philip Gould, who at the time worked in advertising. Years later, as the minister responsible for the UK's Millennium Dome, Mandelson visited Disneyland in the search for 'best practice'.

3 This logic does not hold just for the 'dealignment thesis' of voting behaviour. It also applies to structuralist accounts in which voting allegiances are seen as the product of the management of ideology, where people are organised into particular political preferences (Dunleavy and Husbands 1985)

4 This is the implication of the quotation from Debord that begins this section.

5 The carnival atmosphere seems to have been infectious if the following report is to be believed: Lord Levene (Lord Major of London) forsook his official Bentley for a motorcycle taxi and 'dressed in a T-shirt, tracksuit trousers and a baseball cap, he saw protestors fake cases of police brutality using "stage blood", according to the Corporation's spokesman' (*Financial Times*, 21 June 1999: 1).

6 Interestingly, in the first version of the paper (published as Discussion Paper FS III 91–101, Wissenschaftszentrun Berlin für Sozialforschuung, 1991) Gerhards and Rucht characterise this as 'ideological' rather than 'cultural' integration.

7 The political possibilities created by the Internet need also to be contrasted with those linked to television, and referred to in the first case study. There communications technology is viewed negatively as a conservative force. The risk with both arguments is that posed by 'technological determinism'.

8 Greg Martin (1998) has argued that a culturalist interpretation of the aims of New Age travellers was really only ever applicable to the first generation who had the kind of 'choice' Hetherington describes. Martin notes a politicisation of New Age traveller ideology as a second generation, more exposed to a decline in the welfare state and to post-Fordism, emerges. For this generation, travelling represents an economically rational choice rather than an elective lifestyle.

9 The recent announcement of a Web-organised campaign against poverty, starring figures from showbiz (George Michael, the Corrs, etc.), and the suggestion that the Conservative Party make more use of the Web, both indicate that the Internet lends itself to very different political purposes (*Guardian*, 12/13 Aug. 1999).

4   Proximity politics

John Tomlinson

'Proximity politics' as I employ the term here refers to a certain set of new political problems and issues that the globalisation process confronts us with. I encountered these problems while trying to understand the *cultural* implications of globalisation (Tomlinson 1999) and no doubt this primary interest in culture inflects my approach to the political. Nonetheless it is some *general* political principles – rather than what might be thought of as specifically 'cultural politics' – that I want to address here. Very often in cultural debates about globalisation I have found myself persuaded by quite different – seemingly opposing – political principles. What follows is an attempt to make some sense of these ambiguities.

The term 'proximity politics' is used rather than 'globalisation politics' partly in order to register an important limitation in the discussion. What I am interested in is the sort of new political issue the process of globalisation forces upon us as it draws us all closer together both 'structurally' via the complex institutional inter-connections of globalisation, and 'phenomenologically' via the sort of *experienced* proximity that is provided in time–space bridging technologies – particularly communications and media technologies. It seems to me that this relational close-ness – in a complex set of interactive modalities – presents its own distinct order of political problems.

These problems seem to me to be (at least partly) distinguishable from the political debates about the globalisation process itself: debates about the sources of globalising forces – particularly about the progress of global capitalism – about the relationship of this to class politics, the magnification of global inequality and forms and strategies of opposition, resistance and so forth. Now there is certainly a strong body of opinion that *this* is the main underlying political agenda, and, indeed, there is a politics involved in one's critical attitude to this agenda. What I mean by this is that to show a concern for the politics of proximity as I have defined it might be taken to indicate a sort of capitulation before the advance of capitalist-driven globalisation: treating it, in Armand Mattelart's phrase, as 'global inevitability'. There is a rather crude form of this position pretty widely distributed within the political-economy tradition which simply insists that globalisation be treated as the globalisation of capital, and thus reduces acceptable critical response to a ritual condemnation of the power of transnational corporations. But there is also a more nuanced version which argues that the interests of capitalist expansion are well served by the representation of globalisation as in some way an abstract condition of late modernity – a simple 'fact of life'.

This argument, which plausibly recalls Marxian arguments about strategies of ideological concealment, is nicely captured in the Mexican cultural theorist Carlos Monsivais's quip: 'Globalization means never having to say you are sorry' (quoted in Mattelart 1999: 3). It has been recently put in a sophisticated form by Slavoj Zizek who expresses a deep scepticism about the political force of contemporary critical theory and cultural studies, arguing that these are 'doing the ultimate service to the unrestrained development of capitalism by actively participating in the ideological effort to render its massive presence invisible' (Zizek 1997:46). For Zizek, more or less everything I shall be discussing will probably rank as distraction from engagement with the one great 'universal' of the capitalist world system.

I am, however, unrepentant. For I hope to show that the *immediate* political issues which global proximity forces upon us are real, significant in their own right, and not in fact solvable by appeal to some 'higher politics' of capital. This is not, of course, to deny that the capitalist market is thoroughly implicated in the structuring of global interdependencies; but it is to suggest that, once established, such proximities pose their own independent and irreducible political problems.

Let me begin then with an implication of proximity that is currently receiving a good deal of attention: the idea of cosmopolitanism, conceived simply as 'world citizenship'. Roughly the idea here is that the increased interconnectedness, the enforced proximity of the globalisation process, is both making the old eighteenth-century utopian dream of a single world political community possible and, perhaps more importantly, making this sort of world polity a necessity. Typically a cosmopolitan political arena is seen as necessary to the political agendas of environmentalism, of international peacekeeping, the control of international crime and the drugs trade, and the regulation of various global 'flows': of capital, of knowledge and information, of cultural commodities and influences, of people (say, as labour migrants or as political refugees) and so forth.

A good example of this cosmopolitan position is the stance of Charter 99: 'A Charter for Global Democracy'. Charter 99, launched on 24 October 1999, had the aim of placing an agenda for democratic global governance before the September 2000 United Nations Millennium Assembly and Summit. The Charter lays out a number of areas for urgent action, for instance, to 'open all international institutions to democratic scrutiny and participation', to 'monitor and regulate international corporations and financial institutions', to 'make the UN Security Council fair effective and democratic', to 'create an international Environmental Court' and to 'create equal world citizenship based on the Human Rights Declarations and Covenants'. It challenges the representatives at the UN Millennium Assembly to adopt these and other aspects of democratic global governance as an alternative to what it describes as the de facto 'world government' that already exists:

It is not to be found at the United Nations. Rather, the UN has been sidelined, while the real business of world government is done elsewhere. Global policies are discussed and decided behind closed doors by exclusive groups, such as the G8, OECD, the Bank of International Settlements, the World Bank, the International Monetary Fund, the World Trade Organisation and others. These agencies are reinforced by informal networks of high officials and powerful alliances such as NATO and the European Union. Together they have created what can be seen as dominant and exclusive institutions of world government. All too often they are influenced by transnational corporations which pursue their own world strategies. These agencies of *actual* world government must be made accountable. If there are to be global policies, let them be answerable to the peoples of the world.[1]

The democratic character of Charter 99 seems unimpeachable. The main problem might thus appear to be the practical one of its implementation; of how far these radical institutional changes are realisable within the fragile and uncertain set of accords that describes the context of current world politics. One way of putting this is to ask how far the proposals constitute, in one prominent signatory's formulation (Anthony Giddens), a project of 'utopian realism' rather than mere utopianism. And to interrogate this properly one would have to go beyond issues of institutional reform and ask more searching questions about the possibilities of profound *cultural* change within local constituencies of interest that would be necessary to sustain such institutional reform. Charter 99 draws some of its inspiration from the 1995 Commission on Global Governance, and as the report of this body stressed in its central metaphor of a 'Global Neighbourhood', institutional change ultimately depends on a shift in cultural identification and accompanying forms of solidarity, from narrowly local to global contexts. But once we start to examine the project of global governance – and the cosmo-politanism that inspires it – from this cultural perspective, new sets of difficulties emerge: not merely ones of practicality, but of principle. It is these problems of conflicting political principle thrown up by the structural changes of enforced proximity – principles of universalism versus the demands of cultural difference; ethical interventionism versus the principle of sovereignty – that I want to explore. To try to make some sense of this extremely complex set of issues, I am going to simplify matters by squeezing them into a good, old-fashioned, four-domain matrix (see opposite).

To explain, briefly, the dimensions of the matrix : 'inclusivity' and 'exclusivity' refer to political–cultural principles and attitudes that order ideologies, insti-tutional politics and political action in relation to the increasing proximity that globalisation is producing. 'Exclusivity' is for the maintenance and institution-alisation of strong divisions between cultures mapping on to strong political divisions (to use the Commission on Global Governance's metaphor, keeping high fences between neighbours). Inclusivity, by contrast, is the principle which stresses commonality, intercultural commerce and flow, mutual involvement

	CONTEXT OF REGULATION	CONTEXT OF DEREGULATION
Politics of Exclusion	-1- Nation-state system Nationalism Sovereignty Cultural Protectionism Cultural Imperialism Policing of Borders	-2- Breakdown of nation-state 'Identity Politics' 'New Wars' Vicious Particularism Romantic or Fundamentalist Localism 'Multi-Communitarianism'
Politics of Inclusion	-3- Universalising cosmopolitanism Maximise Global Responsibility Human Rights Global Governance INGOs 'Global Commons' Eco-Politics Ethical Interventionism	-4- Pluralising cosmopolitanism Maximise Local Autonomy Cultural Rights 'Cultural Polyvalence' Hybridity Politics Localist Environmentalism Pragmatism

Figure 4.1 Vanishing and emergent positions in proximity politics

and shared responsibility, mixing and hybridisation, and respect for cultural differences.

'Regulation' and 'deregulation' are broader and less precise categories, but regulation is meant to convey the idea of concerted political control, invoking enlightenment ideals of order and the regulation of life by rational institutional means: rules, conventions, governance and so on. Deregulation in this broad context implies either the simple absence (or withdrawal) of such regulatory frameworks, or the idea that certain forms of social life – for example, cultural processes – are not amenable to such regulation, or ought not in principle to be regulated. Or, perhaps more frequently, deregulation implies that forms of regulation need to be 'softer', less institutionalised, more fluid, open-ended, dialogic or pragmatic.

The combination of a politics of exclusion and a context of regulation in *Domain 1* more or less describes the nation-state system at the zenith of high modernity. Here strong state structures contain internal cultures within one dominant (if regularly internally contested) version – a national culture – which is institutionally sponsored, maintained and protected. The state is assumed to be capable of regulating cultural practices within its sovereign territory. The typical themes of cultural politics here are: the policing of political–cultural borders, the exclusion – or at least strict nomination, surveillance and control – of aliens, inter-state rivalry and fears of cultural invasion by more powerful national cultures (an obvious example of this last being the perceived threat of 'Americanisation' in Europe). Typical cultural policies are those of what Michael Billig (1995) calls 'flagging the homeland' – the mundane deixis of national belonging in politics, the media, education and so forth – along with strong immigration laws, and combined cultural and economic protectionist measures. This is the world of strong nation-states containing strong 'unified national cultures' which many argue is fast disappearing under the pressure of globalising forces. Though there are arguments about how quickly, or how totally, this is likely to occur, and indeed claims for the ultimate resilience of nation-state cultures (Smith 1995), it is clear that the accelerating process of deterritorialisation – the severing of the ties of mundane cultural experience from geographical localities (Garcia Canclini 1995; Tomlinson 1999) – means that no-one actually lives in such an ideally regulated discrete territorially defined cultural space any more. Though many would probably wish to, most notably the inhabitants of Domain 2.

Domain 2 indicates what can occur where exclusivist politics are in the ascendant in a context of the collapse of a strong nation-state: in fact as a result of the failure of the regulatory politics of Domain 1. This is what, according to people like Mary Kaldor, has occurred in what she calls the 'new wars' of the era of globalisation like those in Bosnia-Herzogovina, Kosovo and Rwanda. Kaldor argues that 'new wars' are wars fought around a vicious form of 'identity politics' rather than over the ideological and geopolitical goals of nation-state 'old wars'. Identity politics, as Kaldor (narrowly) defines them, refers to 'movements which mobilize around ethnic, racial or religious identity for the purpose of claiming state power' (Kaldor 1999: 76). They are not generally a straightforward expression of the emancipatory struggle of repressed cultural groups; rather these wars frequently arise from the violent struggle for dominance of particularistic interests within a locality which generally involves both the suppression of other cultural identities and deliberate terror against civilian populations. They are, Kaldor says, 'a mixture of war, crime and human rights violations' (1999: 11). Kaldor sees these wars as emerging in the uneven, culturally fragmenting wake of globalisation, but not as an inevitable consequence of the process. They result rather from a destructive response to globalisation – a vicious particularism of (racial, religious or ethnic) identity positions constructed in crude and spurious labels: politics centred purely on division and exclusivity. Hardly anyone in fact wants to live in this sort of world. Certainly not the ordinary citizens who suffer the violence and the loss of civil society. But not even the factional armies, whose ultimate aim is really to return to some form of the regulation of Domain 1. The aim of identity politics as Kaldor says is ultimately state power. The only people who may wish to inhabit this grim landscape of deregulation/exclusivity are, in its reality, the opportunistic warlords who live off the violence itself, or, in imagined versions, romantic or fundamentalist communitarians – one thinks of the 'survivalist' fringe cultures now emerging in North America.

The implications of Kaldor's analysis of new wars is that the only rational, progressive cultural–political response to the fragmentary impulses of globalisation is in a new form of regulation based in cosmopolitan global governance. This is the space defined in *Domain 3*, the intersection of regulation and a politics of inclusion. Kaldor's unabashed universalism is evident here. She is on the side of 'those who support cosmopolitan civic values, who favour openness, toleration and participation' as against 'those who are tied to particularist, exclusivist, often collectivist political positions' (1999: 147). What this comes down to in direct policy terms is the advocacy of international intervention – 'cosmopolitan peace-keeping' – in wars like those fought in the Balkans. Kaldor sees such intervention, directed specifically towards, and legitimated by, the protection of universal human rights, as the responsibility of a global community – perhaps organised along the sort of federal lines envisaged in Kant's famous cosmopolitan politics (Kant 1991).

This sort of regulatory position is typical of what might be called 'universalising cosmopolitanism' as distinguished from 'pluralising cosmopolitanism'. However, I have tried to indicate with the broken line in Fig. 4.1 that differences between the co-ordinates of Domains 3 and 4 are not nearly so sharp as those between any of the other positions. There is a great deal of definitional slippage here and so the main point is not to contrast these two types of cosmopolitanism starkly so much as to explore their possible common ground. To see, in a context where reversion to either forms of a politics of exclusion is off the agenda, what emergent political themes and possible tensions stretch across the field of cosmopolitanism. For reasons of space I shall discuss just one key issue here: that of how different political agendas relate to the key idea of universalism.

Kaldor's advocacy of a global peacekeeping force exemplifies the humanist, ethical interventionism of universalising cosmopolitanism. Here the ethical motive and justification is the preservation of universal human rights. But equally strong within this way of thinking is the idea of concerted intervention to protect a common global environment from the threats of unregulated pollution. The politics of inclusion in both these examples is focused on shared involvement, care and responsibility, summed up in Ulrich Beck's (1992) claim that we inhabit a world 'in which there are no others'. This sort of inclusiveness – which transcends the conventional politics of sovereignty in the name of a higher unity – sets the political agenda for a wide range of INGOs – Greenpeace, Amnesty, Médecins sans Frontières, Human Rights Watch and so forth. And it can also be seen in recent shifts in inter-state politics – from the sort of international regulatory conventions and protocols that have been agreed on environmental issues (Yearley 1996), through the much promised but rather elusive 'ethical foreign policy' of the New Labour administration in the United Kingdom, to NATO's military intervention in Kosovo.

But, as the Kosovo case illustrates, there are obvious dangers in this sort of inclusivism. Ulrich Beck's recent 'Cosmopolitan Manifesto' (1998a) points out the risks that 'a "cosmopolitan façade" arises which legitimises western military intervention . . . Subordination of weak states to the institutions of "global governance" opens up space for power strategies disguised as humanitarian intervention' (Beck 1998a: 29). The point is clearly well made.

Notice, however, that this is a danger of a power play disguising itself as a good ethical–political principle. It is not that universalism or humanism – as somehow intrinsically 'western-enlightenment' principles – inevitably promote the interests of the West – as, for example, the neo-conservative critic John Gray (1997) has argued. It is rather a case of the familiar ideological tactic – noticed by Marx in relation to the interests of the bourgeoisie – of the particular disguising itself as the universal: universalism as 'masquerade'. Now there is undoubtedly a good deal of this around today in certain sectors of the popular political consciousness of powerful countries like the United States. To give just one egregious example we can consider the claims of Ben Wattenberg's (1991) book The *First Universal Nation*:

> We are the first universal nation. 'First' as in the first one, 'first' as in 'number one'. And 'universal' within our borders and globally. . . . We don't much read, watch or listen to their [Europe's and the Third World's] stuff. Is it that Americans are provincial, insular, parochial boors? More likely it is that we have a taste for just what the rest of the world now enjoys. . . . Only Americans have the sense of mission – and gall – to engage in benign but energetic global advocacy. Hence the doctrine of 'neo-manifest destinarianism', to help form a world that is user-friendly to American values.
>
> (Wattenberg, quoted Brennan 1997: 60)

As Tim Brennan suggests, the fact that such gross ethnocentrism is easy meat for academic critique is besides the point. It is the immediate popular emotional appeal of such rhetoric (Wattenberg's book was adapted and screened as a television documentary with support from right-wing bodies like the Heritage Foundation) that makes it significant.

But where do sentiments like Wattenberg's belong in the matrix? Not in Domain 3 but actually back in Domain 1. It can be read more plausibly as a form of nostalgic wishful thinking – a tugging back to the certainties of state-ordered regulation and the politics of exclusion – than as a part of the politics of universalising cosmopolitanism.

Regulators like Kaldor and Beck can claim, plausibly, then that their position is quite distinct from familiar ethnocentric universalist projections, and thus not inherently prone to slip back to the politics of strong state regulation and, moreover, is not incompatible with the agenda of pluralising cosmopolitanism in Domain 4.

In *Domain 4* the focus on the maximisation of local autonomy implies the protection, for instance, of differential cultural rights as distinct from overarching human rights. But this, importantly, does not imply the sort of exclusivist cultural protectionism typical of Domains 1 and 2. Rather, cultural rights are seen here as part and parcel of the open-textured cultural mix that Zygmunt Bauman refers to as 'cultural polyvalence' – a category, stressing the inherent hybridity of post-modern cultures, that Bauman refines out of Alain Touraine's distinction between an inclusivist 'multi-culturalism' and an exclusivist 'multi-communitarianism'.

The degree of potential agreement on such issues across Domains 3 and 4 is evident in Kaldor's position. She not only accepts as legitimate the defence of cultural rights, but goes on to define cosmopolitanism as involving 'a celebration of the diversity of global identities, acceptance and indeed enthusiasm for multiple overlapping identities' (Kaldor 1999: 88). And this degree of rapprochement is further reinforced by what we might call the 'new universalism' in cultural analysis evident among some postmodernists. Bauman, for example, concludes his recent book with a section called 'Recalling universalism from exile' in which he argues that:

> Universality is not the enemy of difference.... The pursuit of universality does not involve the smothering of cultural polyvalence or the pressure to reach cultural consensus. Universality means no more and no less either, than the across-the-species ability to communicate and reach mutual under-standing – in the sense ... of 'knowing how to go on' ... In the face of others who may go on – have a right to go on – differently.
>
> (Bauman 1999: 202)

Could it be said then that there are no very great tensions between pluralising and universalising cosmopolitanism? It is not, I fear, quite so easy. I shall now try, briefly, to draw out some of the issues that continue to separate Domains 3 and 4.

In the first place there are different, politically less flexible, definitions of universality than Bauman's in currency which, while speaking in the name of global rather than of particular interests – not, then, examples of universalism as mas-querade – are nonetheless far less tolerant of cultural differences. I think here, for example, of Nicholas Garnham's advocacy, following Habermas, of a strong regulated 'global public sphere'. Garnham's hostility to the pluralising bent of postmodernism – which he describes as 'a utopian and romantic pursuit of difference for its own sake' – leads him to approach global problems in an uncom-promising universalist way, looking for the 'one rationally determined course of interventionist action' which 'has to be agreed consensually or has to be imposed, whether by a majority or a minority' (1992: 371–2). The problems with this particular hard line scarcely need adumbrating.

At the other end of the philosophical and political spectrum we find a more complex set of positions: varieties of postmodernists, postcolonial theorists, cultural anthropologists, pragmatist philosophers, 'green localists' and neo-conservative political theorists all find common cause in objecting to the totalising rationalism of Enlightenment humanism and universalism. John Gray, for example, whom I have already mentioned, objects to universalism in the most unequivocal terms, describing it as: 'one of the least useful and indeed most dangerous aspects of the western intellectual tradition ... the metaphysical faith that local western values are authoritative for all cultures and peoples' (1997: 158). This is to object to universalism as masquerade; but Gray's objections go deeper, extending indeed to a more general antipathy towards cosmopolitanism itself – 'the Enlightenment project of progress towards a universal human civilization' (ibid.) or 'the left project of universal emancipation in a cosmopolitan civilization' (1997: 160). All such ideas (presumably including the principles informing Charter 99) are, for Gray, along with the global capitalist free market, and the ideals of Enlightenment humanism, equally the follies of a universalising cultural imagination. One of Gray's reasons for objecting to universalism is an apparent belief in the intrinsic value of cultural difference:

> The disposition to constitute for itself different cultures or ways of life appears to be universal and primordial in the human animal. Yet the idea of a human universal civilization, as we find it in Condorcet, J. S. Mill, Marx and Rorty, is compelled to treat cultural difference as transitory or epiphenomenal, a passing stage in the history of the species. Modern thinkers have been led accordingly to misconceive the telos of political life. The end of politics is not the construction of institutions that are universally rationally authoritative. It is the pursuit of a modus vivendi among cultures and communities.
>
> (Gray 1997: 177)

Gray cannot on this evidence be counted in the cosmopolitan camp, and his assumption that culture is founded 'universally' in difference is in many ways problematic (Tomlinson 1999: 67ff.). However, his point about 'the pursuit of a modus vivendi among cultures and communities' as a political goal contrasts starkly with Garnham's position and chimes with others whom we might more readily describe as pluralising cosmopolitans. And here again the fluidity of positions along the cosmopolitan axis is striking. To underline this, in conclusion we can consider Richard Rorty's recent interventions.

Rorty's pragmatist philosophy – often interpreted as allied with postmodernism – might be taken as equally antithetical to Garnham's universalism as Gray's. While he subscribes to the idea of a culture of human rights (Rorty 1998), he sees no basis for this in abstract transcultural universals – particularly not in the idea of a universal human nature (Geras 1995). However, in his recent writing we find an interesting version of pluralising cosmopolitanism emerging which, while not daring to speak its philosophical name, is not all that distant in its practical implications from what I have called the 'new universalism' emerging in thinkers like Bauman. In his 1999 article 'Pragmatism, Pluralism and Postmodernism', Rorty takes his distance from 'a mindless and stupid cultural relativism' that some postmodernists feel drawn to by a combination of the rejection of 'grand narratives' and a partisan attitude towards any non-hegemonic culture. He does this by arguing that his pluralist position, while continuing to reject an ahistorical abstract notion of Enlightenment 'reason', can nonetheless find rational means to distinguish between better and worse cultural–historical–political developments:

We have learned quite a lot, in the course of the past two centuries, about how races and religions can live in comity with one another. If we forget these lessons we can reasonably be called irrational. It makes good pragmatic and pluralist sense to say that the nations of the world are being irrational in not creating a world government to which they should surrender their sovereignty and their nuclear warheads . . . and that Serbian peasants were being irrational in accepting Milosevic's suggestion that they loot and rape neighbours with whom they had been living peacefully for 50 years.

(Rorty 1999: 275)

There is no reason, then, why a respect for, and toleration of, cultural difference has to harden up into a disabling stance of ethical–political abstention, on 'theoretical' grounds, in the face of manifest follies, injustices and violences. Of course this does not make Rorty a 'regulator' in any robust sense. He probably remains a fair way from endorsing the ethical interventionism of people like Kaldor (let alone Garnham) and his rather vapid faith in the cultivation of 'moral sympathy' of 'the sort that whites in the United States had more of [towards blacks] after reading *Uncle Tom's Cabin*' (Rorty 1998: 180) will seem to some (e.g. Eagleton 1996: 27) the epitome of liberal quietism. With Rorty, it sometimes seems that the best we can hope for in terms of tackling human rights abuses is that the offenders might be brought to see the world in the same way that their victims, and 'we cosmopolitan pragmatists', do. And yet there is some utilitarian sense in this too: 'The reason to try persuasion rather than force, to do our best to come to terms with people whose convictions are archaic and ingenerate, is simply that using force, or mockery, or insult, is likely to decrease human happiness' (Rorty 1999: 276).

Rorty's pluralist cosmopolitanism obviously leaves many difficulties unaddressed, but the virtue of it to my mind is that, while being philosophically acute, it allocates a reasonably modest role to matters of philosophical/theoretical principle in the task of imagining a viable democratic proximity politics. This brings me to my final point. Clearly political as well as philosophical differences will continue to exist across the field of cosmopolitan politics both in terms of agendas and in terms of potentially incompatible real interests. Local interests seem likely to clash with global ones, for example in the area of environmental regulation, and a facile one-worldism is not going to solve these difficulties. They will always require detailed 'local' negotiation and, probably, compromise. To this extent, the line between Domains 3 and 4 cannot be entirely removed. But what I have tried to show is that some of the bigger fears of incompatibility of principle are probably exaggerated: there is in fact a good deal of room for manoeuvre on this cosmopolitan terrain.

Critics from Domain 3 can accommodate localist cultural claims without fear of either the theoretical abyss of cultural relativism, or the more immediate threat of these assertions of difference necessarily slipping towards a vicious identity politics. Equally, critics in Domain 4 can lose their general suspicion of universalism by recognising that there are benign versions, friendly to cultural difference, which do not inevitably slip back to nation-state hegemonies or fetch up in a dirigiste leftist global rationalism. It is within the sort of 'conversation' possible between these positions that the genuine differences of interest which proximity throws up have to be negotiated.

Note

1   Charter 99, *Observer*, 24 Oct. 1999: 19. Also at: www. Charter99.org.

5 The future of public media cultures

Morality, ethics and ambivalence

Nick Stevenson

Introduction

A series of ambivalences and oppositions make themselves apparent if we consider the nature of globalised media cultures.[1] The first, and perhaps most obvious, is the capacity of electronic media to transport images, text and voice through time and space opening us to the interrogation or indifference of 'others' who live in contexts far removed from our own. The modern media then in certain respects remind us of the ways we live on a shared planet. However, we only have to consider for a moment the contexts and social settings within which we gather information and this picture is complicated further. Most of us engage with the media chiefly in privatised contexts where we are rendered largely passive. The media of mass communications is permanently caught between dialogue and fragmentation and engagement and boredom. The global media's capacity to make us aware of common concerns then is mitigated by the comparatively isolated contexts within which we make our interpretations. Alternatively we might view this contradiction as falling between the circulation of the knowledge necessary for us to decide upon common norms, rights and obligations and the rise of the home as an entertainment centre. Add to this the further complication that media audiences continue to be fragmented along the lines of taste, class, gender, race, age and nationality in terms of the media they consume and the picture that emerges is far removed from McLuhan's idea of the global village. The modern media therefore continues to be constituted through the dual processes of unification and fragmentation. I shall call this the dialogic problem.

Second, the rapid development of media technologies has increased the volume of information available, imploded established distinctions between public and private, and speeded up the delivery of information more generally. The rapidly emerging information highways, the multiplication of television channels, the increasing power of communications conglomerates and the development of media technology are all driven by the instrumental logics of science and profit. The question as to whether more channels will enhance our ability to communicate with ourselves about issues worthy of public attention is rarely asked. The ambivalence here is again that, while we can point to instrumental logics within communication that are contributing to processes of commodification, feelings of meaninglessness and a wider culture of superficiality, we can also connect these processes to the problematisation of previously repressed areas of social experience. These would include questions of gender and sexual identity, ecological questions and relations between different world regions. I shall call this the problem of instrumental reason.

As Charles Taylor (1991) has made clear the problem of public recognition versus the subjective turn inwards, and the problem of instrumental reason as opposed to more hermeneutic concerns can be reconfigured as questions to do with the individual and community, and strategic goal-oriented thinking as opposed to more open-ended forms of conversation. My argument then is not to press the originality of these dilemmas but to open out their inevitably ambivalent natures, and to look at the ways in which they have become transformed in heavily mediated cultures like our own.

To these questions I want to add a third related issue which is the problem of identity. It seems to me at least that the development of media cultures not only poses questions concerning dialogic involvement and instrumental reason but also opens issues connected with identity. This can be understood optimistically, as opening out a form of cultural cosmopolitanism where humanity in general experiences new forms of cultural openness and engagement with previously excluded others. However, such processes can also be understood to stumble on some of the more enduring features of modernity from the powerful centres of global capitalism to the relative endurance of the national ideal. Again it seems to me that in seeking to understand the new communications environment or the development of modernity more generally we need to resist the idea that it is necessary to bet on one side against the other. Here I am questioning the impulse that makes us want to definitely decide questions rather than hold them in tension. For example, the development of a multichannel universe may well lead to audience fragmentation, the undermining of public service ethics and a relative decline in shared television experiences. Yet it might also herald new possibilities for local television companies, autonomy with the use of hand-held cameras and videos, more choice for the viewer, and make it increasingly difficult for the state to censor debate. We might then equally look forward to a world which increases the power of large-scale multinationals and where new possibilities for interrupting the discourses of the powerful are utilised by citizens and new social movements alike.

Here, however, I want to press the argument that these questions cannot be decided theoretically but will inevitably be the outcome of social and political processes. In order to explore these issues further I want to investigate a number of reactions within the literature to the ambivalences that might be associated with contemporary media cultures. Put simply they are the arguments that the global recognition of rights to communication (as part of a human rights initiative) would empower ordinary people against states and large-scale media conglomerates, and the claim that the technological development of Internet cultures will lead to an energised and more participatory civil society. Both of these positions raise questions in connection with dialogics, instrumental reason and identity. They differ in that the first is primarily a political initiative whereas the second is largely the result of technological change. Yet both imagine a future that has more successfully resolved our three problems than the time we currently inhabit. I want to offer a judgement of the feasibility of these and similar perspectives by considering more pessimistic counter-claims. This is done not to dismiss the imagination of the two viewpoints out of hand, but to conceive of the fate of media cultures through over-optimistic scenarios inevitably invites criticism of a more pessimistic nature.

Human rights, social movements and global media

One of the most significant moral and political achievements of humanity remains the 1948 Universal Declaration of Human Rights. The principles laid down in this document recognise that everyone irrespective of national boundaries is entitled to the rights and freedoms held out in the Charter. The Charter has provided the basis for international law setting out common standards that might reasonably be expected by all peoples (Falk 1995a). The Charter, in Article 19, contains a defence of the freedom of information and rights of expression, that includes the right to impart and receive information irrespective of frontiers. Article 19 has provided the inspiration behind attempts by Third World nations in the 1970s to challenge Western media dominance, and a series of commissions and reports that issued declarations on the rights of peoples and the responsibilities of the global media. One such report, by the MacBride Commission, sought to safeguard the rights of journalists to 'exercise their profession'. That such rights are no closer to fruition than they were at the time the report was drawn up has been made evident in conflicts from the Gulf War to the genocide in the former Yugoslavia. More recently Cees Hamelink (1994, 1995) has argued that the globalisation of mass communication has led to a disempowering of ordinary people when it comes to exerting power and control over their communicative environments. Globalisation processes have increased the power of large-scale media conglomerates and flooded the world with cheap standardised media products. These processes can only be reversed through a human rights initiative that enables participation within cultural and political life by providing peoples with access to information so that they might make autonomous decisions. Thus whereas global media empires are disempowering in that they infringe upon local cultural space and privatise access to information, human rights approaches treat knowledge as a collectively owned common good to be shared, debated and contributed to by equal citizens. The reduction in cultural space enables the West to control the flow of information and disempower 'other' peoples from developing their own sense of identity.

Starting from local networks, the world's peoples are encouraged to search for alternative sources of information exchange that emerge underneath the disciplinary power of the state and the commercial imperatives which govern global media empires. The development of a genuine people's media through community radio and newspapers and the burgeoning of a people's community network over the Internet could form the beginning of local and global sources of information that provide alternative sources of communication. Politically we can afford to be optimistic about such movements due to the 'revolt of civil society'. By this Hamelink means that alternative networks of communication will arise along with social movements like ecology and feminism. The emergence of a 'double citizenship' or what Albrow (1996) has termed 'performative citizenship' means that such movements point to a new form of politics that seeks to link the struggles internal to nations to more global levels of interconnection. As a first step in building upon these civic initiatives, Hamelink proposes the worldwide adoption of what he calls a 'People's Communication Charter'. The main aim of the charter is to raise the awareness of individuals and social movements as to the shared importance of securing both human and cultural rights. The charter then builds upon Article 19 of the 1948 declaration by granting people rights to form an opinion freely, gain information, enter into public discussion, distribute knowledge, protect their cultural identity and participate in a shared public culture among others. The idea then is to make this both a movement of non-governmental forces (groups such as Amnesty, CND, Greenpeace, etc.) and to have the charter adopted by the United Nations.

The most obvious and immediate objections to such arguments are that the declaration of human rights is not legally enforceable and without the reform of the United Nations itself such charters have historically had little impact. The 'People's Communication Charter' on this cynical view ends up adding to the meaningless pieces of paper that are produced by the United Nations' bureaucracy. These proposals could be further criticised in that they are unlikely to have any lasting impact on the dominant rationale and structures of the global media. Such arguments, however, are as insightful as they are mistaken about the politics of human rights and their connection to questions of cultural citizenship and the media of mass communication.

The first point to make is that the widespread acceptance of a 'People's Communication Charter' is not solely dependent upon its ability to produce legal effects. Like other human rights that are widely accepted among non-governmental organisations its 'cultural' existence gives groups something to appeal to and build a social struggle around. It is undeniable that in terms of its perceived moral legitimacy such a process would be greatly enhanced if the charter was accepted by the United Nations. This would then give new social movements a platform to perform a form of immanent critique whereby signatories could be embarrassed by their refusal to uphold the principles they had formally agreed. Human rights documents in this respect are important in that they help create a set of general political and cultural expectations which when violated potentially attract the attention of the media and political movements alike.

There are of course no guarantees in this respect, but if movements for social change are able to point to international treaties or other collectively agreed documents it will aid them in making interventions into the global televisual arena. The argument being proposed here is that the economic (wealth and resources), political (influence over state policy) and cultural (modelling stocks of discourses and concepts) power of the new media order is such that an inter-national recognition of people's rights in respect of information exchange could indeed have an empowering effect upon the interrelation between local, national and more global public spheres.

The other argument is that without the reform of the United Nations and the eventual evolution of a world state such resolutions are unlikely to have much impact. Indeed it is significant that while media, economics and security systems have become globalised the institutional organisation of democracy remains very much on the level of the nation-state. In this view, the United Nations, if drastically reformed, could be the forerunner of a global parliament. This could be an integrated structure dependent upon local, national and regional bodies finally leading to the global level. If such a demand seems somewhat utopian in the present climate, we could begin this process by reforming the UN. Such reforms might include the empowerment of poorer nations in the Security Council, the alteration of the veto system, the creation of a new human rights court that did not proceed on an ad hoc basis, etc.

The argument here would be that each age has had to rework democracy to fit specific cultural contexts. Direct democracy worked in Athens as it was based on small homogeneous communities, national representative democracy was appropriate in that it came along with the rise of national capitalism and the nation-states, whereas a global age requires a global state and democracy. Further, we might continue, that direct democracy implies a mostly oral public sphere of face-to-face relations, national democracy evolved along with print securing national 'imagined' communities, and what McLuhan would term the 'electric' age makes possible political participation less dependent upon physical space and more truly global than ever before.

Arguably such views remain somewhat utopian and overly abstract from some of the more concrete pressures and practices of the present. David Held (1995), for example, argues that so-called Westphalian models of governance (based upon national sovereignty) have been displaced by a UN Charter model which recognises that peoples have rights irrespective of their national citizenship. These universal human rights, which should be shared by everyone on the planet, offer a direct challenge to the notion that nations set the internal standards by which they are judged. Of course there is no international law requiring states to directly apply these rights; states can opt out of these treaties (a number of nations in fact refused to sign the 1948 document, including South Africa and the countries of the former Eastern Bloc) and human rights treaties contain consider-able leeway for specifically national solutions (Archibugi 1995). However, despite these restraints, we currently occupy an ill-defined zone between a world where nation-states were all powerful and more global forms of governance.

Held suggests that instead of looking upon the United Nations as the outdated relic of the post-war era we think of it anew as offering possibilities with regard to global democracy. Indeed, what he proposes is the eventual implementation of a global cosmopolitan order which is built upon local, national, regional and global levels of representation and government. The cosmopolitan order could seek to instigate a more equitable distribution of goods globally, put limits on nations' capacity to wage warfare, co-ordinate ecological initiatives and enforce internationally agreed standards for the functioning of the media. This would give charters such as the one proposed by Hamelink more active purchase on the structuration of political institutions and practice.

On the other hand, Richard Falk (1995b) argues that a global parliament would probably serve the interests of global capital, and what is actually required is a deeper more normative commitment to democratic principles, and the radicalisation of society through the acceptance of already agreed upon UN principles. In this respect, Falk treats democracy not just as a set of institutions, but as a binding ethical commitment. To be committed to democracy and cultural citizenship in general is to be committed to a set of norms which include reciprocity, listening, respect, responsibility and the recognition of difference. Of course these values do not exist outside of institutional structures, but neither are they likely to be ushered in by simply setting up new tiers of government. The rebirth of a more substantive democratic media then cannot be assumed to be the simple 'effect' of human rights treaties or programmes of institution building. Such initiatives as communitarian and socialist humanist thinkers have long since held are the products of agency and people's projects within civil society. However, the faith that we might have in the 'People's Communication Charter' then is undermined not so much by the trust it places in institutions as in people's initiatives generally. Civil society is currently made up of organisations which aim to reinstate patriarchy, ethnic nationalists, religious fundamentalists and all kinds of other causes with which Hamelink would find himself out of sympathy. This begs the question as to whether a charter that emphasises the 'right' to be heard can really solve the communicative crisis within civil society today.

This situation is exaggerated by the fact that Hamelink's manifesto fails to address what I shall call the 'cultural' question and notions of communicative obligation. The 'cultural' question remains how we go about imaginatively loosening the grip that the nation continues to have upon popularly constructed horizons. The fate of 'other' peoples is still extremely difficult to convert into a rallying point for change. People dying far away are unlikely to become a focus for change in the way running down 'our' welfare system or poisoning 'our' people could be. For most of the people most of the time notions of community remain local and national. Paradoxically it remains a 'real' political question as to how social movements might re-imagine relations of solidarity in an admittedly increasingly interconnected world. There are evidently new possibilities emerging in this respect with regard to new communications, diasporic population movements and the growth of tourism, but it remains an open question as to what kind of global civil society will come to represent such dimensions. We can perhaps take heart from the fact that, just as the sexes have only just begun to problematise how they communicate with one another, the same could be said of different world regions. The demand that we understand rather than dominate one another occupies a comparatively short period in the history of humanity. Viewed optimistically, then, we could all be on the cusp of a more globally informed cosmopolitan citizenship. However, as I have maintained throughout, there are just as many good reasons for thinking that the so-called global age could be equally marked by more insular forms of imagining. Second, the media charter's discussion of rights irrespective of obligations, given the diverse rather than harmonious nature of civil society, would not necessarily improve the quality of debate. The inclusion of more voices in an already noisy global village may have the positive benefit of getting more people heard, but actually achieve little by the way of reflexive understanding.

My argument then is that we are some way off seeing the fully fledged development of a global public sphere underpinned by widely recognised rights to communication, More likely are other developments whereby the agendas of commercial global media are interrupted by human rights groupings in a struggle for recognition, world region organisations asserting their right to intervene in the regulation of public communications and the nation continuing to dominate the collective imagination.

Technocultures, media and community

Current debates in respect of the development of new media technologies have a strong overlap with questions that are currently being asked about the nature of community. The media of mass communication are rapidly diversifying just at the point when old communal relations are increasingly open to question. Are new media technologies responsible for undermining a sense of community by robbing people of participatory public spaces or are they the sights where more diversified relations of solidarity can be made? Crudely we can divide arguments in respect of the effects and transformations brought about by new media into opposing optimistic and pessimistic schools of thought. The pessimists propose that the development of new media technologies can be coupled with the continuation of modernity and the destruction of communal forms of identification and the progressive privatisation and commodification of public life. On the other hand, more postmodern frames see the emergence of the Net, video, mobile phones and portable stereos as opening out new possibilities for voices that have been traditionally excluded from public cultures. New, more affective attachments can be formed through underground networks, fan magazines, MUD sites and phone chat lines. Unlike traditional communities in which 'individuals' are born into 'co-present' local relations, so-called postmodern communities are more likely to be the result of 'individual' choice and the product of mediation. Whereas one set of critics views the global triumph of capital as destroying the communal identifications that allow people to resist capitalism, the other views community as a more fluid site and a potential place of radical politics. To overstate the point, where one set of critics is mournful at the passing of old ties the other is celebratory in the hope that new ones might be made. Let us unpack these viewpoints.

The pessimists' camp houses a wide spectrum of political viewpoints from old-style radicals to cultural conservatives. For instance, Julian Stallabrass (1996) argues the super information highway and cyberspace will not offer a utopian domain of free communication, but the perfect market place which can operate through space and time at the flick of a switch. Those who are currently excited about the future possibilities of the Net are failing to ask who will control the information, work out to whom it is going to be made available and in whose interests it is likely to be run. The answers to these questions are all traceable to the needs of global capital. For instance, so-called virtual communities are places built upon irony and play unlike real communities which are places of obligation and responsibility. If within cyberspace we are able to disguise our identities this effectively denies the possibility of a genuinely democratic communicative exchange, where the particularity of the 'other' has to be engaged with. Instead it creates a 'kingdom of information, whose palatial halls we may wander without fear, free from chaos, dirt and obscurity' (Stallabras 1996: 67). Cyberspace becomes a zone of irresponsible consumption where the poor will never appear as subjects in their own right and only very occasionally as 'objects' for discussion. Indeed the desire to create 'virtual' communities over the Web points both to the disappearance of 'real' communal relations being trampled under the atomising effect of commodity capital, and to the fact that humans desperately need a sense of belonging and will create it with whatever tools they currently have to hand. The human need and desire for community is what is being currently manipulated by the advocates of cyber solutions. The democratic and communal potential of much of the new media turns out to be an old con-trick performed by capital's need for ever-expanding new markets and enthusiastic consumers.

However, as I have indicated, technological pessimism is not restricted to the Marxist left. From a markedly different political perspective, John Gray (1995a, 1995b) has similarly argued that the belief that technology is going to renew our communities, solve ethical problems, and radically democratise our shared political world is the worst kind of utopian thinking. Communities are not something we change on a whim but are relatively enduring spaces of belonging and identification. The real political problem, and this is a view similar to one presented above, is that traditional communities are being destroyed by the excesses of free market liberalism. The solution to this does not lie in the reinvention of class politics, but with the renewal of social democracy that aims to preserve and rethink community in a global age. Cyberspace, on this reading, is little more than a privatised comfort zone we retreat into to avoid increasingly dangerous public places. The image being presented here is not one of technologies modelling society, but of the reverse. New media technologies are linked to instrumental reason, processes of commodification and the individualistic retreat from the public more generally. Rather than becoming actively involved in our communities we have retreated into the cosy privacy of the home.

Significantly, the development of new communications technologies have been read differently by writers who occupy less traditional frames of reference. Maffesoli (1996) questions the pessimistic projections of those who are concerned with the fragmentation and privatisation of the modern subject. He does this by articulating a notion of the subject that is continually searching for emotional connection with intersubjectively related others. Maffesoli rejects the idea of the isolated individual split away from others through the operation of mass culture, and points to what he calls the 'tribalisation' of the social. By this he means that through the creation of football teams, self-help groups, friendship networks, Internet sites and religious associations individuals are increasingly likely to belong to a number of diverse and contradictory communities. What we are currently witnessing therefore is the deindividualisation of modernity and the growth of more affective communities based less on utilitarian notions of self-interest than on sociality. The new tribes are based upon shared sentiments whether they are regular visitors of an Internet site, readers of a football fanzine or even occasional viewers of a soap opera. These new emotional communities are constructed more upon fleeting identification and periodic warmth than the stability of traditional ties. Hence the argument here is not so much to bemoan the ways in which capitalism has destroyed traditional forms of association as to investigate the creative ways in which social solidarity might be imagined in the late modern age.

Similarly, the advent of digital television, according to its most enthusiastic supporters, will rapidly expand the sheer amount of information available and provide greater interactive involvement for the viewer. Digital butlers will order and sort this information as the new smart television sets 'learn' about the preferences of their viewers. This promises no more boring nights at home slumped in front of the box, but an interactive universe where we might spend the evening e-mailing a loved one in Australia, downloading material from the *Washington Post* or creating our own camera angles at a Derby County home game (Negroponte 1994; Gilder 1992). In addition, the Internet, due to its less centralised and hierarchical nature, opens new possibilities for oppositional voices to heard. This is largely due to the fact that computer cultures, unlike the more traditional 'big media', are based upon a two-way flow of information and consequently are structured in less hierarchical ways (Kellner 1995; Rheingold 1994). The public sphere then becomes progressively unfrozen the more that technological advance allows for greater forms of participation by citizens. The Net is exciting precisely because it disrupts existing regimes of power and knowledge, whether this is within the academy or decentring the power of the previously powerful media in the public sphere.

What is immediately noticeable about this debate is that the new media technology is subversive for the optimists for the same reasons that the pessimists find it troubling. For instance, whereas Stallabrass (1996) bemoans the amount of junk and trash to be found on the World Wide Web, Sadie Plant (1996) finds the Internet liberating precisely because it bypasses the usual gatekeepers of public culture. This opposition can also be seen in the related problems of dialogics, instrumental reason and identity. The pessimists read the Internet as developing an individualistic withdrawal from the public, an acquisitive attitude towards commodities and the delights of consumptive freedom rather than deeper forms of social responsibility. For the optimists new media technology helps open new forms of critical engagement, makes public participation a real possibility (given the passing of old-style one-way flow media) and fosters new forms of belonging.

What is perhaps surprising is that critical theory with a tradition of dialectical reason and an awareness of the impoverished nature of thinking in binarisms can be so easily divided between optimists and pessimists in this way. My argument is in part that this sort of polarised thinking actually exhibits a fear of the future. The modernists cynically feel that the past will continue to grind on through the present in such a way that the future simply becomes the endless repetition of commodification, technological reason and other features which can all be associated with modernity. On the other hand, the postmodern view denies the more depressive aspects of social reality by splitting them off from the revolution about to be accomplished less through human agency than through technological modelling. To borrow the metaphors of lightness and weight from Milan Kundera (1985), the view that the future is actually the continuation of the past represents a heaviness through which history endlessly repeats itself. This closes down the prospect of human contingency. The other argument that new media cultures will liberate the future from the past appears to be light when it is actually heavy. By this I mean that the future is not so much viewed as an open possibility but as already predestined. My point is not so much that both perspectives continue to have something to offer – this much is obvious; more that each viewpoint attempts to colonise the future, deadening itself from more ambivalent possibilities. As psychoanalytic writers have pointed out, to be a mature subject is to have an awareness of the ways we have been written by wider narratives as well as maintaining a sense of the future that is open to that which is new and 'other' (Bollas 1994; Elliott 1996). The message here is that whether or not the development of new communications technologies offers new opportunities for social control or the revitalisation of democratic life will be decided by wider political and social developments. While both sides of the argument raise substantive views, it is as if each has allowed itself to be defined by the discourse of the other, and in doing so robbed us of a future defined by political agency. This brings us to the recent work of Manuel Castells.

Manuel Castells, the media and critical theory

Castells (1996,1997,1998) has come the closest of recent writers in opening some of the important political features of contemporary media cultures. Arguably, unlike the perspectives presented so far, Castells outlines a view of contemporary media cultures that both deconstructs the polarities of the earlier discussion while connecting them to processes of substantial social transformation. Castells, as we have already seen, argues that the emergent 'information society' is primarily borne of the changing relationship between global capitalism, the state and new social movements. However, he is equally clear that the development of new media, the diversification of media messages, the implosion of politics and the media, and the development of the politics of 'scandal' have all had far-reaching effects upon the public sphere. The effects of these dimensions are multifarious and move in more than one direction. Television in particular and the media in general have become central and defining institutions in modern society. Castells illustrates this by pointing to the fact that television currently frames the language and types of symbolic exchange that help define society. Unless a social movement, set of ideas, or commercial product appears on television it may as well not exist. From the advertising jingles we hum on the way to work to our opinions on the government's latest set of social policies the media frame our sets of common understandings, knowledges and languages. The media then do not so much determine political agendas, but provide the background and context to political and social struggles. The centrality of modern communications in contemporary culture therefore does not deliver a mass culture, but what Castells calls a culture of 'real virtuality'. The idea of a mass culture has now been surpassed by a media environment where messages are explicitly customised to the symbolic languages of the intended audience. The future will not so much be governed by a homogeneous mass-produced culture repressing human diversity, but by a diversified popular culture where competitive advantage comes through product differentiation and audience segmentation. For Castells (1996), 'we are not living in a global village, but in customised cottages globally produced and locally distributed'.

The newly emergent information society then is characterised by a media culture that is more individuated and less homogeneous than before. Further, the culture of 'real virtuality' opens out a world where popular moralities and perceptions opened by soap operas can have as much if not greater impact on modern sensibilities as the moral strictures of politicians. Indeed we can probably think of numerous examples where the 'popular' and the 'political' have become irreversibly intertwined. This might invoke soap operas raising political questions, the development of so-called infotainment, politicians receiving media training, protests deliberately designed to attract maximum media exposure and the development of the art of media spin-doctoring. Taken together these aspects and others speak of a new media and cultural environment that presses the case that unless you are on the media then you are not in politics. Seemingly for Castells, then, the new media politics can foster both domination and patterns of resistance. Here I shall open out two such examples from the many that appear in Castells's three-volume study: the politics of scandal and some of the avenues that social movements have explored by utilising new media technologies.

Scandal politics develops within the general context of an increasingly televisual society that has come to the fore against a backdrop where political concerns are frequently played out and reported as a cynical and strategic game. This privileges the presentation of political issues in a fast-paced and punchy style which in turn prioritises the culture of the soundbite. Further, the visualisation and corresponding trivialisation of political issues through television give an added emphasis to the 'personalities' rather than the substantive issues at stake in political debate. Television then produces a kind of binary politics where complex positions are boiled down into digestible categories. The personalisation of politics and the decline of ideological contrasts between the major political parties produce the grounds for the central forms of struggle in the age of informational politics. In an era where moral and ethical distinctions between political parties are

y being replaced by more instrumental forms of manoeuvring that
errupt themes and positions previously occupied by opposing political
e whiff of scandal can create a sense of political division and untrust-
ess. The fact that major political parties are both involved in expensive
of image-making while being simultaneously chronically underfunded
makes them increasingly likely to accept money under the table. Once this form
of corruption becomes central to the organisation of mainstream politics then
this provides ammunition for journalists and opposing political forces to expose
corruption at the highest level. Scandal politics, therefore, becomes a daily threat
if not occurrence.

Although Castells brackets off the analysis here it is not hard to imagine a
situation in the future where parties might seek to attract support by constructing
agendas and political teams that are 'above' scandal. Yet, if Castells is correct,
such attempts are likely to prove fruitless. We might even further extend this
argument by pointing to the future possible development of a kind of 'scandal
fatigue' among the electorate. Just as the reporting of distant wars, famines and
human rights abuses has arguably fostered compassion fatigue, so scandal fatigue
could equally lead to an unshockable form of cynical indifference among the
vast majority of the population. Scandal fatigue then would open out a situation
whereby the public sphere became drained of meaning and politics detached from
wider questions of value. At this point Castells's concerns come close to those of
Williams and Habermas in respect of the closing down of public space and discourse. These are all evident dangers in contemporary media-saturated societies.
However, if Castells retreads familiar themes within critical theory, demonstrating
how media politics has become detached from ideological positions, these agendas
are in turn seemingly interrupted by a variety of social movements from below.
Castells (1997) characterises a variety of social movements as developing highly
skilful media techniques in creating largely reactive and defensive responses to
economic globalisation. By this he means that the movements under review do not
so much articulate a vision of a future emancipated society, but a more conservative attempt to preserve current social identities. For example, the Zapatistas
in Mexico (who Castells describes as the first informational guerrilla movement) made skilful use of image manipulation (videos, Internet, etc.) to convert a
small local struggle for dignity, democracy and land into a movement that has
caught the attention of international public opinion. Indeed the Zapatistas' media
connections made it impossible for the Mexican Government to use the state
apparatus to repress their movement forcibly. This brings out one of the distinctive features of the network society: that is, while the concentration of power and
wealth is increasingly distinct from local contexts, our collective forms of meaning
are more readily to hand. The task then of any oppositional movement must
be to connect local experiences to a more global agenda, and absolutely crucial
in this process is the medium of mass communication given its capacity to shift
information through time and space.

Castells argues that new media technology can contribute to the building of
networks among new social movements that might serve to reinforce relations

of dominance or alternatively call them into question. This picture is further complicated elsewhere in discussing who actually uses the Net. Here Castells asserts that new media technologies reinforce existing social structures rather than transforming them. For instance, because access to the Net is dependent upon economic and educational factors it is more likely to reinforce the cosmopolitan orientation of social elites than to destroy social hierarchies in the way that some commentators have been expecting. New media technologies therefore simultaneously reinforce relations of cultural capital, hierarchy and distinction, while enabling social movements to publicise campaigns and connect with distant publics.

My argument therefore is that Castells's concern for the cultural conditions of the public sphere in the informational age offers a more substantive agenda than questions simply linked to the granting of additional rights and tracing through the 'effects' of technological change. Instead of claiming that new social movements need to be empowered by a human rights agenda he argues that they have already had a transformative effect on modern societies. Further, he breaks with the idea that we can coherently view the development of new media cultures in any straightforward way through the axis of domination or emancipation. Instead Castells's complex reading of modern informational cultures points towards a more nuanced position that views the evolution of media cultures and technologies in a structured field capable of being transformed by political agency.

By viewing Castells in terms of the tradition of critical theory we might argue that he takes a less 'pessimistic turn' than is evident in Habermas and the early Frankfurt school. What Castells most clearly provides is a social and historical understanding of the emergence of the 'information society'. Like Adorno and Horkheimer's account of the culture industry and Habermas's notion of the public sphere the 'informational society' opens out a new critical paradigm. Yet if one of the main agendas of critical theory is present, others are absent. First, missing from Castells's account is a more normative analysis that would provide us with a critical standpoint from which to evaluate social change. In answer to this charge I think Castells would make two responses: (1) that implicit in much of what he says there is an agenda that seeks to map out the possibilities for democracy and social justice; (2) that it is not for 'experts' like him to hand down blueprints for social change – the history of actually existed socialism has surely put paid to the desirability (or even feasibility) of getting social reality to conform to the wishes of the intellectual vanguard. Such reasons arguably cut critical theory off from moral and ethical questions. To put the point bluntly, if it is worth arguing that the public sphere is becoming increasingly infected by a form of cynical reason and 'show' politics it is also worth making some broad suggestions on how we might begin to construct an alternative. Further, if the media are becoming increasingly central to the self-definition of democratic societies then radical change will only come through citizens increasing their involvement and participation within wider media cultures. The question as to how democratic societies help foster public involvement as opposed to private withdrawal, communicative concerns as opposed to instrumental strategies, and publicly engaged pluralistic identities as opposed to passively construed cultures is central to the concerns of critical theory. In doing this we should indeed avoid adopting the legislative ambitions of the expert, while also sidestepping thinking that fails to open new critical possibilities. It is not that Castells believes that the world could not be otherwise, but that he misses the implications a moral and ethical agenda could have for media and culture. If Castells opens out a more complex view of the media's position in modern society than was evident in the other perspectives under review he also fails to develop a more normative response to the problems of dialogics, instrumental reason and identity.

Second, and despite his claims to the contrary, Castells offers an instrumental account of cultural processes. By this I mean that while he is concerned with agendas of social movements, state and informational capital there is little sense of a more hermeneutic agenda. That is, what are the diverse cultural meanings that might become attached to informational capitalism? This failing is most evident in his discussion of cultural processes such as the changing shape of the family.

Castells argues that the patriarchal family as the focal point of patriarchalism is being progressively challenged at the end of the century. The combined forces of the increased visibility of different sexual practices, the massive incorporation of women into *paid* work, growing control over child-rearing and the new self-definitions offered by new social movements are the social forces that are redefining gendered relations. The shaking of heterosexual norms and the disruption of the patriarchal family (primarily through the emergence of singles' lifestyles and households, divorce, the practice of 'living together' and greater autonomy in reproduction) have meant that there is an increasing diversity of family types on offer. Hence unless men are willing to enter into more equal relationships with their partners they have only two other options that can be described as workable. The first is a deeper investment in male-only gatherings which are likely, in the absence of women, to become spaces of nostalgic yearning for the more certain edifices of patriarchy. The other is gayness. Castells then views patriarchalism being torn down and ripped asunder by a multitude of social forces that can be loosely associated with changes taking place in a wider collective culture and within the economy. Informationalism then is as important to the workings of the global economy as it is to understanding the recent reported rise in oral sex and domestic violence.

Castells is correct that patriarchalism and contemporary gender relations are being reformulated at the end of the twentieth century. This will inevitably mean the emergence of a more confusing and complex terrain in terms of both gender and sexuality. As we have seen, Castells argues that there are currently stark choices facing men in this respect. My problem here is that Castells unintentionally overly instrumentalises the cultural domain. It is unlikely, for instance, that many men actually experience the choices presented to them in the stark way outlined by Castells. While he is right to emphasise the post-traditional aspects of these choices, I think it unlikely that men are likely to be as clearly grouped as Castells indicates (gay men, redundant men, men living equally with their partners). For instance, we might see the rise of a postmodern form of masculinity which is capable of combining in complex and contradictory ways different pleasures and identities. That is, in an era where identities are becoming increasingly unstable, what is to stop heterosexual men incorporating certain aspects of gay culture (this is arguably already happening in areas such as body aesthetics and the revaluing of friendship), preserving areas of male bonding and feminine exclusion (the increasing popularity of team sports and men's magazines among young men) and attempting to forge more equal relations with their partners? Rather than conceiving of culture as presenting us with stark choices (which of course it sometimes does) we might perceive the flows of culture to be like a series of overlapping circles. Of course an increasingly heterodox masculine culture is also likely to breed a counter-reaction where certain groups of men search for a less tainted and more purified identity. Our capacity to be able to tolerate 'otherness' within ourselves and a competing need for psychic certitude opens out a range of emotional and unconscious responses that Castells leaves under-theorised. For example, the turn to national-communalism in an age where some of the old levers of economic control are disappearing from nation-states depends as much upon the emotional–unconscious repertoires available to the self and community as it does upon a 'cultural' response to economic crisis. My concern in a nutshell is not that Castells reads cultural questions from the stand-point of economics, but that some of the complexities of the cultural dimension are sacrificed at the altar of informational capitalism.[2]

A short agenda for media and cultural citizenship

The importance of a moral and ethical dimension in media politics need not be seen either as turning away from the world into the comfortable certainties of the study or as pointless given the prevailing culture of cynicism and the abandonment of ideology by the main political forces. While it is true that relativistic thinking, a sense of meaninglessness, the dominance of money and power and technological reason remain determinant features of modernity, other questions and opportunities remain. New social movements, mainstream political parties, the pervasive culture of human rights, new domains of reflexivity are just some of the forces keeping moral and ethical questions alive. Indeed, unlike Castells, I think that ideological debate among mainstream political organisations is far from dead. Just as the 'end of ideology' theorists in the 1960s had to revise their proclamations due to the revival of Marxism the same can also be said of Fukuyama's more recent arguments that we have reached the 'end of history'. Fukuyama (1992) argued that ideological conflict had been brought to an end by the collapse of state socialism and the global triumph of liberal democracy. If these arguments were applied to the media then the increasing dominance of the market over the censorious state would have ensured equal rights to communication and equal forms of recognition. My argument is not only is this not the case, but that more rights, technological advance and the capitalistic expansion of the market do not necessarily lead us to understand the points of view of strangers any better than we did before. How to make a society more genuinely communicative is I think the central moral and ethical dilemma concerning the study of mass communications today. Arguably, then, we might have a really good bill of rights protecting free speech, widespread access to the most sophisticated media technology available and the greatest range of media products in human history to choose from, but still remain an uncommunicative society. Indeed one of the key questions we have to decide is the extent to which as a community we are willing to put limits on the determination of communications by economic and technical reason. Multichannel access, digitally enhanced television and a fast-moving soundbite culture might serve our interests as consumers, but as political and cultural citizens they leave much to be desired. The moral and ethical requirements for what I have termed cultural citizenship in the modern world call for concerted local, global and still overwhelmingly national strategies. Further the revitalisation of our communicative sensibilities requires a cultural politics that is more communitarian than liberal in focus. That is, if the revitalisation of our culture is not to be secured through guaranteed rights and slicker forms of technology, it will have to come through a reworking of civil society, journalistic practices and the dominant media institutions.

In this context, I use the term communitarian guardedly in wishing to distance myself from much of the illiberal and generally repressive talk that goes on under its mantle. However, I would want to point to the importance that this tradition continues to place upon ideas of overlapping communities, the critical question of obligations as opposed to rights and the key importance of civil society. In this respect, then, I would like to mark out four broad areas for critical intervention.

1. The first point is to open out an ethic of responsibility and participation in respect of contemporary media and communication within society more generally. The media in terms of the range of voices that interrogate one another should be seen as a zone of peaceful civility. One of the primary ways in which we act ethically is in the way we choose to communicate with one another. This means that when we enter the public domain we are always seeking to judge the fine line between our rights to speak and our obligations to other members of the community. While such practices are likely to remain fraught with ambivalence all mature societies will have to learn to live with the messiness of contradictory opinions and perspectives that are voiced across a diversity of channels of communication. As far as possible the mainstream media need to become channels of 'inclusion' in terms of the overlapping cultural patterns that are allowed to interrogate one another. In this sense nations cannot afford to be 'agnostic' in terms of the cultural capabilities of their citizens. The promotion of a vibrant civil society is perhaps above all dependent upon the communicative capacity of its inhabitants. However, despite attempts to promote civil exchange (that can be linked to literacy campaigns and how the education system teaches citizenship) there will undoubtedly be groups that need to be excluded. What Beck (1998b) calls 'ugly citizens' are likely to use alternative unofficial methods of information exchange to promote a sense of in-group identity and cohesion. The point here is

for public systems of communication to keep the dialogue 'open' in the hope that rogue citizens will rejoin the conversation at a future date.

2. 'Scientific' journalism needs to be held to question not only in terms of traditional notions of bias, but also in respect of the promotion of reflexivity. The media need to be opened up as far as possible in order to make sure 'alternative' voices are heard while simultaneously making clear that any picture of a society (especially when it is distant from our own) is always partial. A critical democratic public sphere then depends upon how others spatially distant from the local contexts in which we live are represented on mainstream media. Journalistic culture therefore needs to become oriented less around the search for objective factual statements (as important as this remains) and more around opening up critical questions for discussion. Media professionals therefore will need to search for new repertoires to stimulate reflection rather than adhering to well-worn stereotypes. The promotion of a culture of critical engagement and doubt requires that journalists view themselves less as purveyors of hard truths and more as interpreters of knowledges.

3. Western European societies continue to maintain a shared tradition of public service broadcasting. Despite the growth of new and alternative technologies in respect of media cultures the culture of public service is likely to remain a key site. Television remains a more powerful medium at this point in history than all of the other media combined. New pressures in terms of audience share, increasing competition and the multiplication of new channels are all placing public service broadcasting under pressure. Yet reports of its demise are much exaggerated. The culture of public service broadcasting continues to have strong supporters in elite circles and needs to be robustly maintained. This is likely to become more important rather than less given the cultural standards and guarantees that continue to regulate public service channels.

4. The move towards more transnational levels of governance (prefigured in the EU) should open the question as to the regulation of the global media. There should be increasing concern as to the quality and type of information that is regularly crossing the boundaries of nation-states. The kind of regulation required will depend upon different histories, traditions and sociological make-up of the societies in question. For instance, in the European context the threat to media and cultural diversity is posed by large media conglomerates commercialising public space and creating new exclusions on the basis of price. However, as we saw, different problems in respect of media cultures face different world regions. In the Rwandan context the crucial moral questions in terms of the public sphere could not be posed in terms of the colonisation of communication by economic and instrumental reason. Instead, the real problem was the underdevelopment of civil society allowing a so-called 'soft state' to censor and direct public debate. Again this is an issue that could be profitably taken up by different levels of governance including neighbouring African states and the United Nations.

These proposals are necessarily brief and are intended to point towards possible future debates rather than being explanatory in their own terms. What they point towards is a future public debate that takes moral and ethical problems in the context of communications seriously. Such a venture would need to link structural questions (what would a democratic and just system of communications look like?) with those of personal and group agency (how should we go about talking to one another?) in a way that recognises many of the ambivalences these issues inevitably open.

Notes

1 A different version of this paper appears in Nick Stevenson (1999) *The Transformation of the Media: Globalisation, Morality and Ethics* (London: Longman).
2 These questions are taken further in Peter Jackson, Nick Stevenson and Kate Brooks (forthcoming) *Reading Men's Lifestyle Magazines* (Cambridge: Polity Press).

6 Contested power

Political sociology in the Information Age

Kate Nash

Manuel Castells's analysis of the Information Age builds on and modifies ideas of the post-industrial and information society first developed by Alain Touraine and Daniel Bell (Touraine 1971; Bell 1973; Castells 1996). It also has much in common with theses of postmodernity and post-Fordism (Kumar 1995). In all these cases there are thought to be fundamental changes in social order that mean a historical break with the principles of modern industrial capitalism (though each theory varies in its conceptualisation and weighting of the relevant changes). Here I will focus on changes in politics, particularly those related to globalisation, the politics of 'new' social movements and the increased importance of culture and cultural codes in the contestation and consolidation of structures of domination. It will be argued that the tools of traditional political sociology are inadequate to understand new political forms, but that Castells's development of the idea of cultural politics is also limited by the theoretical framework in which he discusses it.

Traditionally political sociology has analysed politics in terms of the relation between state and society, seeing it as organised around and oriented towards the nation-state. Within this tradition there are two dominant theoretical approaches: pluralism and elite theory. It is now clear, however, that there are various aspects of politics that cannot be analysed using the theoretical tools developed within these frameworks. Although there is a good deal of controversy over whether we have actually entered a qualitatively different type of society historically, there is widespread agreement that there now exist new political forms. A model of cultural politics based on Foucault's 'analytics of power' will be proposed as better suited to their analysis than more traditional theoretical tools. This is compatible with Castells's theory of contemporary society and, indeed, it is close to his understanding in many respects. It will be argued, however, that the proposed model of cultural politics helps clarify the conceptual confusions of Castells's more empirically oriented sociological theory and encourages a more thorough and consistent examination of new forms of power and politics.

Political sociology and the displacement of the nation-state

It is impossible to do justice to the complexities of elite theory and pluralism in the confines of this chapter. Here I will simply look briefly at radical elite theory – a version of which Castells subscribes to – and the neo-pluralist challenge to it.[1] It will be argued that although they are ostensibly competitors in traditional political sociology, radical elite theory and pluralism nevertheless share similar assumptions, notably the view that politics is essentially about conflicting interests and that the nation-state is the 'power container' of modern society. These assumptions mean that they are inadequate in the face of new political forms.

Radical elite theorists are concerned with the question of how and why a minority rules over a majority. Political elite theorists are above all concerned with the decision-makers in society, those they see as holding power as a cohesive, relatively self-conscious group (Parry 1969: 13–14). Within this approach radical elite theorists argue, in opposition to liberals and classic pluralists, that the state is not a neutral arbiter of social interests and that the political process is actually dominated by the interests of the power elite (Mills 1956), or the ruling capitalist class (Miliband 1969). However, although they see the holders of power as outside democratically elected government, radical elite theorists see the state as playing a central role in the exercise of that power. In this respect, despite the broadly Marxist orientation of the approach, they follow Weber's view that the nation-state is the most powerful institution in modernity because it has the legitimate monopoly of the use of force within a given territory (Weber 1948a: 78; Hoffman 1995: 42–3).

Castells subscribes to elite theory insofar as he sees the Information Age as dominated by economic elites. He differs, however, from classical formulations of the theory in two main ways. First, he maintains that the nation-state has lost power as a result of globalisation. This is a widely held view that will be discussed more fully later in this section. For Castells it means that the economic elite attains its interests primarily through the global exchange of information, bypassing the nation-state. Second, against classic formulations of radical elite theory, Castells argues that the ruling elite forms a global network rather than a class or any kind of cohesive, conspiratorial group. Although he explicitly breaks with Miliband on this point, however, he retains an element of Marxism in his claim that the interests of the global elite dominate those of labour (Castells 1996: 473–4).

It is axiomatic for elite theorists that the objective interests of ordinary members of organisations and institutions are necessarily opposed to those of the elite. If both groups shared common interests, an elite would be nothing more than a number of individuals holding the top positions in society (Dowse and Hughes 1972: 152). In contrast, classical pluralism is opposed to elite theory in that it takes politics to be a matter of competing interest groups, none of which can dominate completely over any of the others since all have access to resources of different kinds. Neo-pluralism, however, has come closer to the understanding of radical elite theory concerning the constraints of democratic decision-making where some groups systematically have more power and resources than others (Lindblom 1977; Dahl 1985). There is, therefore, a convergence between them over the importance of corporate elites working through the institutions of the state. Neo-pluralists have accepted the Marxist point that in order to secure its own wealth in a capitalist society, the state must favour policies that facilitate the growth of private enterprise (Held 1987: 202). Nevertheless, pluralists continue to see the state itself as a set of competing and conflicting institutions, rather than as a monolithic entity which exerts its power over the rest of society (Smith 1995: 211). They therefore prefer the term 'government', even if it is generally used interchangeably with 'state' (Dahl 1991: 9–11). They further argue that that the elite is not unified, nor capable of manipulating and deceiving the citizens into accepting elite rule. For neo-pluralists, stable and enduring elites continue to exist only insofar as they are genuinely responsive to the interest groups they purport to serve (Dowse and Hughes 1972: 135–8).

Classic formulations of elite theory and neo-pluralism share an understanding of the nation-state as the principal site of politics. State power is both the stake of politics and also the principal means by which economic power is exercised. Furthermore, politics is seen as primarily concerned with conflicts of interests constituted outside the political arena. For radical elite theorists, these are the 'objective' interests of class struggle. For neo-pluralists they are the interests of social groups that try to influence the political process. Although for neo-pluralists there is a variety of such groups, both theories converge on the understanding that the interests of corporate capitalists are well placed to dominate over others.

In contemporary society these assumptions are untenable. As Castells argues in *The Information Age*, the nation-state has been displaced as *the* site of politics. Most commentators agree with Castells that politics is changing in this respect as a result of globalisation – including many who would not subscribe to his historical periodisation. Here, then, we will look only at the broadest thesis of globalisation, on which there is virtually a sociological consensus. Changing political forms may also be related to the activities of social movements. Again the claims that will be outlined here are quite uncontroversial; for the most part they differ from Castells's views in *The Information Age* only on questions of detail.

It is widely agreed that the nation-state has been displaced as a result of processes of globalisation leading to the decline of state autonomy and the development of 'pluralised sovereignty'.[2] David Held makes a useful distinction between state autonomy and state sovereignty. The autonomy of the state involves its ability to act independently to articulate and pursue domestic and international policies (Held 1995: 100). Manifestly, the state has never been fully autonomous; on the contrary, the extent to which the state is independent of industrial capitalist society is one of the chief topics of traditional political sociology, not least of radical elite theorists. However, the debate has taken on new life in that it is now argued that globalisation systematically undermines state autonomy to the point where governments are reduced to managing processes over which they have no control, even in principle, since they are not contained within national borders. Processes of globalisation mean that the capacity of the nation-state to act independently in the articulation and pursuit of domestic and international policy objectives has diminished as its control over the traffic of goods, services, technology, media products and information which cross its borders has been reduced. Furthermore, state sovereignty – the political authority to determine the rules, regulations and policies within a given territory – has also been reduced by international political institutions and law which actively enforce limits on the state's jurisdiction over its citizens. Most striking in this respect is the European Union, a 'supranational' institution in that it has the authority to make laws that can be imposed on member states. Others, like the United Nations, the World Bank, the IMF, the economic summit Group of 8 and so on, are better described as international since they are wholly dependent on the co-operation of nation-states for their operations since they have no other means of collective enforcement of their authority. However, intervention in the internal affairs of a sovereign state by international institutions has been legitimated in certain cases: the UN interventions in Bosnia, for example; and the practices of the IMF which may grant financial assistance to governments who ask for it under conditions that the government in question may have no part in negotiating (Held 1995: 109–10). In this respect, along with influential International Non-Governmental Organisations (INGOs), they provide the conditions for what is known as 'global governance': 'governance without government – of regulatory mechanisms in a sphere of activity which function effectively even though they are not endowed with formal authority' (Rosenau, quoted in McGrew 1997: 15).

Of course, this is not to say that the state is now irrelevant. On the contrary, in many respects, more powerful states have clearly gained new powers through international politics. As Held points out, however, the globalisation of political institutions means that sovereignty is now, to some extent at least, shared between national, international, and, in some cases, regional authorities; it is no longer the indivisible and illimitable power of individual nation-states (Held 1995: 135).[3] This has clear consequences for a political sociology that takes the state as the centre of political activity. Such an emphasis can no longer be justified – if it ever could be – where the state has weakened autonomy and shares sovereignty with other political institutions. The nation-state has been displaced as the centre of political activity in contemporary society in comparison with modern industrial capitalism.

Alongside globalisation, social movements have also contributed to this displacement. Social movements are currently among the most prominent political forms and they are at least as active in trying to bring about changes in civil society as they are in contesting policy and legislation enacted by the state. It is important to be clear about what this involves. New Social Movement Theory, inspired by Touraine and Melucci, has long argued that so-called 'new' social movements engage in conflicts in culture, contesting meanings and forming collective identities that may potentially transform existing social structures (Touraine 1981; Melucci 1989). For these writers, however, it is only those movements that engage in such fundamental conflicts in civil society that may be seen as such. Where there is political activity at the level of the state, this cannot be seen as 'anti-systemic' and should be understood as carried out by interest groups or political parties broadly defined. However, this seems unnecessarily limited as a definition of social movements. Although the boundaries of social movements are notoriously hard to establish, movements like feminism, the gay and lesbian movement and the environmental movement engage in activities intended to address individuals and groups in civil society as well as, on specific occasions or through specific organisations, the institutions of the state. Social movements are loose networks of organisations, groups and individuals which contest dominant interpretations of events or practices and construct collective identities to transform everyday life (Diani 2000). The politicisation of taken-for-granted power relationships in which they are engaged takes place on various levels: from the micro-politics contesting sexist and heterosexist subjectivity, for example, to challenging state definitions of citizenship rights organised around the norm of the white, heterosexual, male head of household, to subverting global corporate power in direct action against their products. The state remains important, but as one site of political activity among others.

Furthermore, social movements raise questions about an understanding of politics as organised in terms of class interests. Most obviously because the collective identities constructed in 'new' social movements are not those of class. While it might be the case, as Offe has argued, that the members of social movements tend to be drawn from the new middle classes (though I have argued elsewhere that his definition of class is over-inclusive (Nash 2000: 106)), it is certain that they do not engage in politics 'on behalf of a class' (Offe 1987: 77). Furthermore, it is not clear that we should think of social movements as organising primarily around interests at all. Craig Calhoun has argued persuasively that to think of social movements in the restricted terms of instrumental rationality is to neglect the way in which they are – and have been since the mid-nineteenth century – concerned with aesthetic and utopian dimensions of identity politics (Calhoun 2000). Contemporary social movements clearly engage in issues of identity, values and lifestyle that are not readily seen as matters of group interest (unless the term 'interest' is given such a wide meaning as to make it useless).

Finally, the politics of social movements confounds the division between public and private on which the dominant model of politics in traditional political sociology depends. 'The personal is political' is an ambiguous slogan, almost as vilified for reducing the political to the personal as celebrated for bringing the personal to political attention. Nevertheless, it is clear that it is a resonant slogan for many contemporary social movements: for the women's movement calling into question a traditional gendered division of labour, representations of women, subordinate subjectivity and so on; for the environmental movement linking personal lifestyle choices to global environmental damage; and for the anti-racist movement challenging dominant cultural norms, accepted colonialist understandings and definitions of nation. In each case these challenges cut across and confound the division between private and public. Any adequate understanding of contemporary politics must, then, allow for the way in which the very question of what is to count as political is itself an object of political struggle.

Culture and cultural politics

Alongside the emergence of new forms of politics, there have also been theoretical challenges to the principal concepts on which traditional political sociology depends. In sociology there has been a consideration of the concepts of 'power' and 'politics' that, surprisingly, has been relatively unacknowledged within the sub-field of political sociology. In fact, it is remarkable that while sociologists now take more of an interest than ever in power, political sociology itself has been rather neglected as a field of study. One reason for this may be its limitations with respect to changes in politics and the difficulty of developing it to accommodate these changes where a focus on the nation-state as the centre of politics is retained.

Famously, or infamously, sociology has recently taken a 'cultural turn'. There are actually two different cases here. First, there is the 'epistemological' case in which culture is seen as universally constitutive of social relations and identities. Those who have developed arguments to this effect have mainly been influenced by post-structuralism and postmodernism (Laclau and Mouffe 1985), but the work of 'sociologists of reflexivity' may also be seen as an example of this type of approach (Giddens 1984, 1990, 1991a; Beck 1992). Second, there is the 'historical' case in which culture is seen as playing an unprecedented role in constituting social relations and identities in contemporary society (Bauman 1992; Crook *et al.* 1992; Lash and Urry 1994). Theorists of contemporary society do not necessarily divide neatly into two camps on this question: it is possible to argue that culture is universally constitutive but that this is more evident, or more significant, in contemporary society.

Castells's analysis of the Information Age is of this third type. While he accepts the epistemological case, arguing that reality is always mediated through language, he sees culture as increasingly important in the Information Age because its 'material foundation' is information (Castells 1998: 356). Culture has shaped the development and use of information technology, but informational capitalism also shapes culture with the explosion of the mass communication system. Culture becomes, according to Castells, 'real virtuality': experience is doubly mediated insofar as people's already symbolically mediated existence is represented in a multimedia setting (Castells 1996: 373). Furthermore, this 'real virtuality' produces its own effects. Above all, according to Castells, it means there is no possible influence on society except through *cultural codes*. Culture is constitutive in the Information Age insofar as everything is framed and structured by information and communication media. For Castells, it is through cultural codes that 'people and institutions represent life and make decisions' (Castells 1998: 367). It is therefore through cultural codes that elites dominate: organising activities, consolidating structures and disorganising opposition to their dominance (Castells 1996: 415).

A principal focus of Castells's work is the analysis of new forms of politics in the Information Age. The sovereign nation-state can no longer play the role it did in modern industrial capitalism. Weakened by economic globalisation and unable to manage the crisis of legitimacy provoked by demands from within the national community which it is in no position to meet, it is now better seen as a node in a broader network of power that includes other states and global markets. Gaining control of the nation-state is only one way among others to exercise power (Castells 1997: 304–6). In this respect, then, Castells is a chief proponent of the view that traditional political sociology needs rethinking and, although he says that *The Information Age* is a book about the world, not a book about books, he actually makes some bold theoretical claims about how power and politics should now be conceptualised. It will be argued here that these formulations, impressive though they are as a way of organising the mass of information and ideas with which he works, are in some ways inadequate to his own analysis so that more conceptual work is needed to develop them.

First, Castells's understanding of the sites of power in the Information Age seems inadequate and even contradictory. Castells argues that power founded on the state, with its institutionalised monopoly of violence, is now superseded insofar as it is dependent on other sources of authority and influence (Castells 1997: 305). New power relationships, he argues, 'must be understood as the capacity to control global instrumental networks on the basis of specific identities or, seen from the perspective of global networks, to subdue any identity in the fulfillment of transnational instrumental goals' (1997: 305). Insofar as power is enacted through identities in the network society, it is, according to Castells, 'in people's minds' (1997: 359). No doubt this is a polemic turn of phrase, but it is an unfortunate one. While Castells himself makes little of the idea, it suggests that by changing consciousness it is possible to change the world. This is a voluntaristic understanding of power and it is at odds with other aspects of Castells's own theory.

What Castells wants to stress is that because the 'social morphology' of the Information Age is networks organised around information flows, there is an unprecedented fluidity and flexibility in social arrangements. He sees the relative fixity of information flows as secured by identity, which constructs interests, values and projects (Castells 1997: 360). However, it is unnecessary to see identity in terms of consciousness and Castells himself does not necessarily see it in this way. It is more useful to see it as situated in social structures, however fluid. From this point of view, identity is less a matter of consciousness than of *practices* in which social action is made meaningful in a dialectical relationship between subjectivity and structure. In this way, voluntarism is avoided. Although structure is not determining, it provides certain limits within which action is taken on the basis of decisions made in specific contexts. For example, Castells notes the proliferation of feminist identities, seeing them as 'self-constructed' (black, Mexican American, lesbian, sado-masochistic lesbian, etc.) (1997: 199). It is clear, however, that these identities are not simply invented. They are defined in ongoing social practices that make these particular self-identifications meaningful: in relation to a social movement oriented towards uncovering discrimination, where personal identity and lifestyle choices are seen as political, in the context of legal rights and so on. Such identities are not simply a matter of consciousness; they are contingent on, and realised through, ongoing social action.

The idea of power as sited in practices is actually more in keeping with Castells's own understanding of power as exercised through cultural codes. In this case power is not located in 'minds' but in the 'objective', or 'inter-subjective' structures of meaning within which events, experiences and other people are framed and understood, legitimacy is gained and what might be a possibility in an abstract sense is actually ruled out as implausible. As Castells argues, for example, elites reproduce themselves through cultural codes embedded in social structures to create lifestyles, spaces and global symbolic communities which constitute an exclusive shared identity (Castells 1996: 416–17). Other identities are not different in kind. Power must be seen, then, as embedded in the practices which, reproduced over time and space, constitute the material social structures of *The Information Age*. Even if structures are more fluid in informational than in industrial capitalism, they nevertheless constrain possibilities in various ways. I shall return to this point in the next section.

Second, Castells's definition of politics is surprisingly limited. At the end of his trilogy he uses the term 'cultural politics' to describe a future politics which will be based on information technology, enacted in the media, fought with symbols and connected with experience in the Information Age (Castells 1998: 372–3). For the most part, however, throughout the three volumes of *The Information Age* he reserves the term 'politics' for discussions of activities oriented to the state. This is curious. Although, as we have also already noted, Castells sees the nation-state in informational capitalism as a node in a global network of power, rather than as the power-container of industrial capitalism, nevertheless he tends to see the state as the dominant focus of politics, almost despite himself. For example, Castells argues that the future 'cultural politics' is prefigured in the 'symbolic politics' of Internet advocacy and the 'non-political' humanitarian causes of such organisations as Amnesty International, Greenpeace and Oxfam (Castells 1997: 352–3). He distinguishes these new political forms from traditional politics since they often involve acting outside the mainstream political process, addressing issues directly to individual citizens or to a consensus across political parties. However, it seems that what makes these activities specifically *political* for him is that 'Ultimately, their horizon is to act on the political process; that is, to influence the management of society by the representatives of society' (1997: 352).

Despite Castells's broad understanding of the sites of power, then, his understanding of politics is conceptually very limited. This is clear, for example, from the way in which, although he discusses the women's movement and the reorganisation of the patriarchal family at some length, he apparently does not see it as engaging in politics, dealing with it under the category of 'experience'. Again, while he quotes Petra Kelly to the effect that 'the primary goal of Green politics is an inner revolution' (quoted in Castells 1997: 110), he apparently does not see the creation of 'green culture' as political. For Castells, despite the claims of social movements themselves, the way he sees power as sited in 'minds' and the fact that he sees social movements as potentially the subjects of radical social change, it seems that the personal is not political.

Foucault's 'analytics of power'

At this point I want to propose a model of cultural politics that is more coherent and better captures the new forms of politics Castells is analysing in *The Information Age*. It is based on a reading of Foucault's 'analytics of power'. I will argue that it is possible to take from Foucault's work a useful theory of 'cultural politics' as a result of his innovative understanding of power in modern society.

The most significant point of Foucault's analytics of power is that power is productive. His analyses are explicitly opposed to what he calls the juridico-discursive model in which power is seen as possessed by the state, especially the law, and is used to impose order on society. This is the model political sociology has taken for granted. According to the juridico-discursive model of power, it involves legitimate prohibition modelled on the legal contract, according to liberals, or repressive legislation and policing to preserve class domination, according to radicals. It is, at any rate, essentially negative, restrictive and inhibitory (Foucault 1980). According to Foucault, to think of power in this way is to miss how it works in institutions and discourses across the social field. He is concerned to analyse power in the details of social practices, at the points at which it produces effects, as a fluid, reversible and invisible 'microphysics' of power. Power is productive in the sense that it works to produce particular types of bodily discipline and identities in practices that remain invisible from the point of view of the older model of power as sovereignty.

Foucault could not have identified the effects of power on the body and on subjectivity using a totalising theory of power. His analyses in *Discipline and Punish* and *The History of Sexuality* depend on examining the precise details of historically specific knowledges and practices as they operate differently in institutions like schools, factories, prisons, hospitals, clinics and so on to produce constraining and subordinate identities. Nevertheless, his studies have been quite extensively criticised as tending to fall back into the negative view of power to which he is opposed, portraying it as a monolithic, unmitigated force of domination (Fraser 1989; McNay 1994; Dews 1984). In his later work, Foucault's ideas about power developed in ways that meet such objections. At the same time, with the development of his ideas of resistance and domination, he also provides the elements for a model of cultural politics that is very useful for the political sociology of contemporary social life.

In 'The Subject and Power', Foucault discusses the relationship between power, domination and resistance in contemporary society. He argues that, as a matter of definition, where there is power there must be resistance. He had sketched out this idea in his earlier work, but here he develops it further, arguing that power necessarily works on what he calls 'free subjects'. It is only where there is the possibility of resistance, where subjects are not fully determined but may realise different possibilities from the range with which they are faced, that it is meaningful to think in terms of power. Slavery does not involve a relationship of power where the slave is in chains, but rather a relation of violence (Foucault 2000).

This definition of power does not immediately seem very different from Weber's: power is 'the chance of a man or a number of men to realise their own will in a communal action even against the resistance of others who are participating in the action' (Weber 1948b: 180). This is the most widely endorsed definition of power in traditional political sociology and it is the definition to which Castells also subscribes (Castells 1997: 305–6). Perhaps it would be possible to drop Weber's commitment to the juridico-discursive model of the state as a 'power container' and to use his definition of power in its widest sense. There is, however, an important difference between these formulations and Foucault's understanding of power. Weber's emphasis on 'will' as the motivation behind power is at odds with Foucault's emphasis on the construction of subjectivity through practices of power and knowledge (Foucault 2000: 97–8). Apparently in opposition to his previous assertions that 'power is everywhere' and that subjects are discursively constructed, in 'The Subject and Power' Foucault commits himself to the idea that the 'free subject' necessarily exists prior to discourse. However, he retains the view that subjects are constructed in practices of power insofar as he maintains that subjects are subjected where they are controlled by others, and also insofar as they are tied to their own identity by conscience or self-knowledge (Foucault 2000).

In fact, power takes on a relatively positive connotation in Foucault's later work, in comparison with its implied denunciation in the earlier writings. It now represents the potential fluidity of social relations. Since power only acts on those who may resist, and who may in turn act on others, there is always the possibility of reversals of power. According to Barry Hindess, in the later work Foucault increasingly uses domination as a term to analyse what is more commonly thought of as power. On Hindess's reading, Foucault used more precise terms in order to distinguish between power as a feature of all human interactions and domination as a particular structure of power in which antagonisms are consolidated in hierarchical and stable relations. Those who are dominated have such little room for manoeuvre that reversals of power become impracticable, though they are never strictly speaking impossible (Foucault 2000; Hindess 1996).

In his work on power, resistance and domination, Foucault lays out the principles of a model of cultural politics. Insofar as politics involves the contestation of relations of power, cultural politics is always possible, an inherent aspect of all social relations which are not based on violence. Insofar as power necessarily, by definition, involves resistance, power relations are fluid, always potentially reversible. This is made explicit in the definition of politics based on Foucault's analytics of power elaborated by Ernesto Laclau: politics involves opening up the possibilities repressed in the constitution of taken-for-granted and apparently 'objective' social relations and identities (Laclau 1990: 33–6). Where social relations are relatively fluid, there will be widespread and frequent contestation of all aspects of social life; where there is power, there will be politics. Where there is domination, on the other hand, there will be little political activity. This need not, however, be a consequence of state repression; Foucault's analytics of power explicitly draw our attention to instances where this is not the case. Domination also results from strong and unquestioned traditions, for example, or from a dominating 'technocratic' culture in which decisions based on scientific knowledge are not challenged. In any case, where there is domination, there will be power relations which are not contested and which therefore remain fixed. Power is in operation wherever there are relations involving human beings with real alternative choices of action. Politics is in operation wherever those relations are not consolidated into an enduring, unquestioned, 'objective' reality.

Why '*cultural* politics'? Foucault does not use the word culture and nor does Laclau. In fact, Foucault's work is somewhat inconsistent in this respect. He actually states that power is exercised in extra-discursive institutional practices (Foucault 1972: 163–5). For the most part, however, his ideas have been much more readily applied to the analysis of the rules and representations of discourse as language than to social practices and institutions (Barrett 1992). Furthermore, this is legitimate insofar as analysts take seriously his view that objects, including subjectivity, are only constituted in discourse. If this is accepted, as Laclau and Mouffe have argued, then the distinction between discursive and non-discursive is either meaningless, or is itself a differentiation which can only be made within discourse (Laclau and Mouffe 1985: 107). They therefore argue for a view of discourse as language that is always embedded in practices such that there is an indissoluble unity between language, actions and material objects. It is following Laclau and Mouffe on this point that I use the term 'cultural politics'. In my view, the word 'cultural' is preferable to 'discourse' because of the linguistic connotations of the latter – connotations which actually do not make for valid analyses of 'discourse' in these terms. Furthermore, although it is certainly true that the word 'culture' is far from unambiguous, given the proposal to address concerns in sociology after the 'cultural turn', it is surely better to use the same vocabulary where possible.

On this model of cultural politics, conventional politics at the level of the state is displaced to the periphery of vision to allow other forms of politics to come into focus. This does not mean that the state is irrelevant; on the contrary, the effects of action taken in the name of the state still provide many of the conditions of social action. It does mean, however, that politics in civil society, between civil society and the state and within the practices and institutions considered to be of the state itself must also be taken into consideration. The state itself is continually being formed and reformed according to the outcome of political struggles in social contexts where it may or may not be taken as the object of direct contestation. Putting cultural politics at the centre of political sociology involves seeing challenges to power relations as primary wherever they occur, while challenges to power relations supported or instituted by the state are a subset of the wider category of politics as such. The traditional focus of political sociology on relations between society and the state is a secondary aspect of the wider phenomena of political contestation that must be considered. Cultural politics is understood as potential in every social context in which power is at work, involving the contestation of normalised identities and social relations in which one individual or group is subordinate to another.

'Merely' cultural?

There are certain obvious objections to this model of cultural politics. Critics argue that post-structuralist theories of politics are idealist: they lack purchase where it is a matter of substantive, materialist issues and the systematic structures of inequality analysed by radical elite theorists and now accepted by neo-pluralists. In Judith Butler's words, '[It is argued that] the cultural focus of left politics . . . focuses on transient events, practices and objects rather than offering a more robust, serious and comprehensive vision of the systematic interrelatedness of social and economic conditions' (Butler 1998: 34).

I would certainly agree that the model of culture politics outlined here is limited. It is to be used in very specific ways, as a sensitising device, to deconstruct claims of 'objectivity' in which domination is concealed and to reveal the politics of particular social forms and identities. It is limited in that it cannot easily be used to construct sociological theory, to identify concrete institutions and structures that may then be deconstructed and refined. It is only by using middle-range sociological theory read through the post-structuralist model of cultural politics that an adequate political sociology may be constructed (Nash forthcoming).

This, I take it, is the strength of Castells's analysis of the Information Age. Although there may be disputes over his analysis of social and political forms, he provides a map of the contours of contemporary society, and thus opens up discussion. In fact, the principal value of the work is its attempt to synthesise information and ideas to provide a new paradigm for the study of contemporary society. However, as I have argued, the theoretical framework Castells develops to achieve this synthesis is inadequate in various ways. It is sometimes important to read books about books in order to understand the world, and the post-structuralist model of cultural politics outlined here is valuable for the more systematic and rigorous understanding of power and politics it offers.

Furthermore, in this section I want to argue that it is far from peripheral to an adequate sociological understanding of material structures and systematic domination. On the contrary, the post-structuralist commitment to the idea of politics as ontological enables an understanding of the structuring, contestation and transformation of social life which is invaluable if, as Castells and others argue, the task for sociology now is to grasp the fluidity of contemporary social life in its specificity.

In this respect Castells's assumption, shared with elite theorists and neo-pluralists, that ultimately it is interests that are at stake in politics is unnecessarily limiting for sociological analysis (Castells 1996: 415). In fact, Castells's specific commitment to the idea of 'objective' interests again seems inconsistent with the emphasis of other parts of his work on identity as organising experience and action in the Information Age (Castells 1997: 7). If, as he argues, elites work by organising society and disorganising others through cultural codes rather than through conspiracy, this can only be because their own interests, values and purposes are themselves structured through cultural codes (Castells 1996: 415). The alternative is to suppose that elites take up a God-like position from which they have access to objective reality unmediated by the perspective from which they understand how to proceed in achieving their goals. In fact, of course, Castells's view is more complicated than this. He sees the global elite, like others in informational capitalism, as relying on the knowledge generated by information technology. Furthermore, he argues against the idea that there is a capitalist class in the Information Age precisely on the grounds that the elite is fragmented: capitalists are only ever in control of specific operations of the global economy; there is no cohesive group with an overview of its systematic workings. Nevertheless, the economic elites share objective interests, he suggests, in a 'global capital network': financial flows through electronic networks whose movements structure the behaviour of individual capitalists (1996: 474).

The problem with this understanding is that elite interests in the 'global capital network' are then seen as outside politics. As I have noted, this is conceptually at odds with Castells's emphasis on identity and cultural codes as organising interests, but it is also at odds with new forms of politics. For ongoing political struggles, it is often the differences between capitalists that are most important. In the case of the campaign against GM foods, for example, what is most important is precisely that Monsanto does not have the same interests as big supermarkets (see, for example, Revolt Against Genetic Engineering's website for details: http://www.rage.org.nz/food-bytes17.html). Furthermore, the environmental movement has had some success in convincing companies like Shell, for example, of the value of environmentally friendly corporate policies despite the general reluctance of most companies to engage with such issues (Giddens 1998: 49–50). Clearly, what is important here is to understand how interests are constructed in specific ways in response to particular political contestation. It is far from obvious that even at the most abstract level capitalists share a common interest in the global capital network. While, as Castells has argued, capitalism has been restructured since the 1970s to increase flexibility, since the global financial crisis in the 1990s more consideration has been given to how flexibility might be tempered with greater stability. This raises the possibility that financial markets may once again be more closely regulated in the future and suggests that we might reasonably expect conflicting perceptions of interest among the corporate elite.

Does the multiplicity of interests in contemporary society therefore mean that the framework of neo-pluralism is preferable to that of radical elite theory? Is the model of cultural politics proposed here simply a version of neo-pluralism? A post-structuralist theory of politics does share certain common features with neo-pluralism. For both approaches, society is seen as made up of a multiplicity of self-defining groups with no natural essence, no 'objective' interests given by a position in a socio-economic structure. Furthermore, 'interest groups' may be seen from both perspectives as constructed in alliances and conflicts with others, not as based on intrinsically shared 'real' interests or characteristics. In fact, there are 'cross-cutting solidarities' between groups, as individuals belong to more than one according to how they experience their political identity in different social contexts. The lines of division, the overdetermination of political identities, and the mobilisation of power and resources across the social cannot simply be added together into one unified domain with a single sovereign centre (McClure 1992).

There are, however, differences between cultural politics and pluralism. Leaving aside the point that for neo-pluralists power is held by the nation-state – a feature of the theory that might be modified to incorporate changes in global politics z– most important is the limited definition of power with which they work. In this respect neo-pluralists are closer to Castells than to post-structuralists. For Castells, power is 'the capacity to impose a given will/interest/value, regardless of consensus' (Castells 1997: 305–6). Similarly, Dahl famously defines power as 'a realistic . . . relationship, such as A's capacity for acting in such a manner as to control B's responses' (Dahl 1956: 13). In both cases the definitions presuppose an already constituted social actor who is in possession of power such that s/he is able to control the effects produced. As critics of pluralism have pointed out, the emphasis on observable effects means they neglect the way in which the political agenda may be shaped in such a way that direct manipulation of the outcome of the political process in unnecessary (Lukes 1974). As we have seen, those influenced by Foucault would go still further to argue that the formation of the identity, capacities and concerns of social interest groups must themselves be seen as an effect of power.

In relation to the corporate elites with which both Castells and Dahl are concerned, then, an analysis in terms of cultural politics would adopt a somewhat different approach to either. The emphasis of the analysis would be less on the conflict between already formed groups, how conflict was resolved and who won. Although this is an important aspect of the politics of corporate power, it would be still more important to look at how interests came to be defined as such, how collective identities were formed in opposition to others, and how agency was constructed within perceived limits of action. It is only in this way that we do justice to the specificity of the case, revealing the political possibilities as well as the ways in which they were actually limited by existing social structures. To return again to the example of the campaign against GM foods, it would be important to analyse how Monsanto came to see its interests in expanding into the European market and the decisions made about how it should represent those interests; the construction of a consumer identity as oppositional and the possibility of action taken on that basis; the ways in which small farmers are represented or excluded; and finally the different meanings given by researchers into genetics to their work and how they influence public debates.

Cultural politics need not be idealist, interested only in what is ephemeral and epiphenomenal to material social structures. In fact, as I hope I have shown, the model proposed here takes social structures very seriously. The definition and contestation of identities and interests embedded in social structures are seen as politically fundamental in this model. Cultural politics is not confined to a particular sphere of society: as Castells – albeit somewhat ambivalently – argues, it is constitutive of social structures themselves. For this reason, I have argued here, it is more suited than radical elite theory or neo-pluralism to an understanding of contemporary political forms where the nation-state has been displaced and the very question of what is political is itself contested.

Notes

Thanks to Fran Tonkiss and Neil Washbourne for helpful comments on this chapter.

1   The other important strand of elite theory, actually dominant in mainstream political science, is 'competitive elitism'. According to this view, hierarchical political parties are the only means by which political leadership in large-scale, complex societies can be secured. Although bureaucratic institutions inevitably exercise enormous inertia in such societies, it is possible – according to Weber – for elected and administrative political elites to exercise independent leadership within the state. The competition between parties in elections is the best possible forum for the development and selection of such leaders (Held 1987: 156–9). This strand of elite theory supposes that liberal-democratic politics are the only realistic way for modern societies to be governed and that, for the most part, they are quite effective. I take it that some of the arguments employed here against radical elite theory also undermine the case of 'competitive elitists'. However, this is not the focus of this chapter.

2   Hirst and Thompson are the main exceptions (Hirst and Thompson 1996). However, their argument against an overly simplistic understanding of globalisation does not rule out the points made here. Although, as they argue, globalisation is not new, nor irreversible, this does not mean it was not qualitatively different in the late twentieth century as a result of new information technology, the growth of international institutions, transnational organisations and a global military order (Amin 1997). Furthermore, Hirst and Thompson also agree that the state must now act internationally, though they object to the simplistic idea that it has lost power entirely. The real division in the debate on globalisation is that between neo-liberals who think of it as a 'natural' consequence of market forces and those who see it as a political project instituted by neo-liberal deregulation (Scott 1997).

3   The very idea of a divided and plural sovereignty is paradoxical from the point of view of the modern nation-state. It was formed around the legitimation of sovereign rule following the problematisation of traditional authority in the religious and civil conflicts of early modernity (Held 1995: 38–9). We must, therefore, conclude that the very set of institutions named as 'the state' should be understood in quite different terms from those of traditional political sociology (Nash 2000).

7 A moment of moral remaking

The death of Diana, Princess of Wales

Sasha Roseneil

Introduction

In the early hours of the morning, on Sunday, 31 August 1997, Diana, Princess of Wales, died in a car crash in Paris. Within hours of the news breaking, people started to gather outside Kensington Palace, bringing with them flowers to lay at the gates. Images of these early mourners, visibly shocked and often in tears, and vox pop interviews instantaneously filled television screens around the world, as saturation media coverage was unleashed, and the drama of Diana's death began to unfold. The tone of the extraordinary week that followed was presaged in those first few hours, by the strikingly heterogeneous collection of individuals who chose to express their emotion in public. London-born, and not, speaking with the accents of different classes, regions and nations, black and white, European, African, South East Asian, East Asian, young, middle-aged and old, gay and straight, wearing jeans and T-shirts, sportswear, club gear, high fashion, suits and ties, twin-sets and pearls – their diversity placed its imprint on the occasion from the outset.

Between the announcement of Diana's death and the funeral a week later, hundreds of thousands of people were moved to make public gestures to mark their mourning of her death. The voices of these people, out on the streets, were relayed around the country, and beyond, and public moral discourse about Diana, her life and death, about the royal family, the institution of the monarchy and the ethics of the media, about love, loss and the meaning of life, and much more, exploded. People travelled to Kensington Palace, Buckingham Palace, St James's Palace and Althorp, the Spencer family home, decorating the gates and fences with flowers and personal messages, and carpeting the grass and roads outside with banks of flowers. Queues stretched for hundreds of yards outside each site of mourning, as people waited to sign books of condolence, and thousands of people simply gathered in the Mall, at all times of the day and night, to be part of the collective grieving. As the week went on flowers were placed outside public buildings across the country and at British embassies around the world, and by Friday evening, the night before the funeral, thousands assembled in central London, to spend the night as part of an informal, unorganised open-air wake. Thousands more filled the capital for the funeral, lining the streets to watch the funeral procession pass, gathering outside Westminster Abbey and in Hyde

Park to watch the ceremony on giant screens; millions more watched the funeral on television in their homes.[1] For seven days, the collectivity of the British nation talked, thought, lived 'Diana', as normal life hung suspended, metaphorically at half-mast, until her body was buried and her passage marked.

The morning after

As dawn broke the morning after the funeral, exactly a week after Diana's death, I came out of a club in Soho with a friend, and we decided to go to Kensington Palace. It had been a strange night in clubland; quiet, calm, contemplative. People were talking more than they were dancing, mulling over the experience of the week. Going to Kensington Palace seemed the obvious thing to do. We were not alone. We had to park half a mile from where the crowds were, although it was six in the morning. Thousands of people were in the gardens, wandering around, looking at the tributes, reading the cards, queuing to sign the books of condolence. The atmosphere was peaceful; people spoke to each other in hushed voices, most were silent. Everyone seemed to be wrapped up in their own emotions. Many had clearly been there all night. Some were clubbers after a night out, like us, others were early risers, with dogs, partners, friends. There were homeless people, sleeping amidst the visitors, keeping watch over their own tributes, or directing people to the queue for the condolence books. There was someone playing the flute. It was a surreal experience.

Kensington Palace Gardens was like nothing I had ever seen before – it was an ever-growing, living installation, composed of pictures, photographs, paintings, arrangements of significant and treasured objects. There were tens of thousands – hundreds of thousands (how could one know?) – of bouquets of flowers, stretching across an area the size of a football pitch in front of the gates to the palace. Roses, carnations, lilies, sunflowers, fresias, expensive bouquets of exotic flowers from high-class florists, cheap bunches from late night supermarkets and garages, flowers cut from country gardens and wrapped in kitchen foil. Floating upwards amidst the flowers, were dozens of helium-filled balloons, in red and silver and gold, swaying in the early morning breeze. Almost every bunch of flowers carried a signed message. Many had poems attached to them, by Shakespeare, Auden, Rossetti, others written by the givers, amateurs moved to write by the experience. There were pictures cut out from newspapers and magazines and mounted on card, photographs scanned into computers and decorated and annotated; there were drawings by children and adults, and multi-media collages, of paper, shells, ceramics, fur-fabric, velvet, mirrored tiles. The crash barriers and fences around the park had been reclaimed, as the outbreak of artistic emotion burst out of all efforts to contain it – flowers and ribbons were woven into the metal, messages tied to the railings. And across the park, trees were decorated with hangings, flowers placed high up in the branches, photos, drawings, pictures, children's toys, messages, poems and lanterns. At the base of trees, and all around the gardens, there were thousands of candles, arranged as shrines, around pictures of Diana, on mirrored bases, in candleholders, on the grass. A rich perfume hung in the air

– the smell of candle wax, and scented candles, of millions of flowers, and incense. It was like Christmas and Diwali and Chanukah rolled into one, a multi-ethnic festival of lights and flowers.

I walked around and read the messages – the ones which caught my eye, a tiny proportion of the multitude. There were messages from classes of school-children, from individual children, from families, from groups of friends and work colleagues, from people who signed themselves as from Persia, Malaysia, Israel, Brazil, India, the United States, Bosnia. There were messages with national flags, and messages signed with English names, Jewish names, South Asian names. Many people identified where they came from – Hendon, Bradford, Brixton, Harlow. There was a card signed by 'David and Colin, on behalf of gay men all over the world', and a huge red AIDS ribbon. There was a floral display in the shape of a London taxi, and a message from London cabbies, and flowers and poems from men in HMP Dartmoor, addressing Diana directly: 'because you saw us as human beings'.

A social drama

In the immediate aftermath of Diana's death, there was a huge amount of commentary and reflection on various aspects of that remarkable week, first by journalists, and later, historians, psychologists, political scientists, feminist theorists, drama, communication and cultural studies writers added their ana-lyses.[2] Much of this has been concerned with Diana herself, and the stories that were told of her, exploring her iconic and celebrity status and the radicalness or otherwise of her self-positioning, as a woman and in relation to the monarchy.[3] Some writers have addressed wider questions about changing attitudes to the monarchy, and about the constitution and governance of the nation,[4] and others have discussed, from a range of viewpoints – left and right, feminist, psycho-analytic, optimistic, pessimistic, agnostic – the question of the meaning of the public's emotional response.[5] A whole book could be devoted to pulling together and evaluating the range of interpretations that has been offered of the Diana phenomenon, and it is certainly beyond the scope of this chapter to do more than point the reader towards the extensive literature that now exists.

Whilst in this era of postmodern challenges to disciplinary conventions, the boundaries between the disciplines which have contributed to this literature are undoubtedly distinctly fuzzy, a sociological lens on the death of Diana has been remarkable for its absence.[6] Yet the collective response to her death begs a sociological analysis, an approach which can conceptualise the power of collective sociality and mobilisation, which can understand the role of symbol, ritual and spirituality in social life and their relationship to morality and politics, and which is sensitive to processes of social and cultural change. Much of the discipline of sociology, in its focus on the analysis the routine, the commonplace and the ordinary, and in its quest for patterns of regularity, does not offer a lens through which to study the unusual and the extraordinary, dramatic moments of collective action, symbolic transformation and epiphany.[7] Yet there is a long tradition within cultural sociology and symbolic anthropology, dating back to Emile Durkheim, through the anthropological work of Victor Turner, to the contemporary writings of Michel Maffesoli, which, I would like to argue, offers powerful conceptual tools with which to make sense of the response to the death of Diana, and it is on this body of work that I draw in this chapter.

It is my argument that this extraordinary week can be seen as a *social drama*, an *effervescent collective performance* which expressed and distilled the *collective conscience*, the *social divine* and the *puissance* of the people.[8] I historicise this neo-Durkheimian cultural analysis and locate the moment as one expressive of various features of the postmodern condition, using the work of Michel Maffesoli to make the link between the Durkheimian tradition and the analysis of postmodernity.[9] I argue that the death of Diana was a moment of *moral remaking*, which enacted a collective reaching, a yearning, for a new moral order, and that it can be read as an instantiation of a *postmodern ethics-politics*. I want to suggest that it is of importance to understandings of contemporary politics, where 'the political' is understood as thoroughly imbricated with 'the cultural', and where cultural politics, performed outside the conventional institutions of 'politics', have at their core a concern with ethics. My approach has its roots in my long-standing interest in collective action and social movements, and my particular fascination with the cultural, emotional and affective dimensions of people moving and acting together, and in the spaces and moments of creative liminality in which experimentation with alternative ways of being and new ethical codes can take place. Whilst not a *social movement* as sociologists tend to use the term, I see the collective response to Diana's death as an instance of collective action and mobilisation which expressed social *movement*, in the sense of social, cultural and political change. Although fleeting, this moment of movement intimated significant features of the dynamic and changing character of the contemporary social formation and offered a snapshot of its changing collective political-ethical imagination.[10]

Moral remaking

[T]here is something eternal in religion which is destined to survive all the particular symbols in which religious thought has successively enveloped itself. There can be no society which does not feel the need of upholding and reaffirming at regular intervals the collective sentiments and the collective ideas which make its unity and its personality. Now this moral remaking cannot be achieved except by the means of reunions, assemblies and meetings where the individuals, being closely united to one another, reaffirm in common their common sentiments.

(Durkheim 1915: 427)

A day will come when our societies will know again those hours of creative effervescence, in the course of which new ideas arise and new formulae are found which serve for a while as a guide to humanity.

(ibid.: 427-8)

In the context of the 'cultural turn' within sociology, recent years have seen a revival of interest in the later work of Emile Durkheim, centring on *The Elementary Forms of Religious Life* and his posthumously published lectures on education, politics, the professions, morality and the law. Jeffrey Alexander proposes that this work developed 'a theory of secular society which emphasized the independent causal importance of symbolic classification, the pivotal role of the symbolic division between sacred and profane, the social significance of ritual behaviour, and the close interrelation between symbolic classifications, ritual processes and the formation of social solidarities' (Alexander 1988: 2). Alexander suggests that the emphasis on ritual and the realm of the symbolic in the work of a number of anthropologists and sociologists has roots in this 'underground wing' (Collins 1988) of Durkheim's writings – for instance, Clifford Geertz, Claude Lévi-Strauss, Edward Shils, Robert Bellah and Victor Turner – though only the latter two, Bellah and Turner, explicitly draw on Durkheim. However, with the publication of Alexander's (1988) landmark collection on Durkheimian cultural sociology, sociologists have now begun to take up again some of the themes of this body of theory, applying them beyond the analysis of 'religion', to explore the 'religious', emotionally charged and ritualistic aspects of the contemporary secular world, such as morality (Shilling and Mellor 1998), mass strikes (Rotherbuhler 1988), revolutions (Hunt 1989; Tiraykian 1988) and politics (Collins 1988).

Let me draw out of Durkheim's theory of 'religion' a number of ideas which are of relevance to my project of developing an understanding of the collective response to the death of Diana. First, *The Elementary Forms* conceptualises religion as being concerned with providing individuals with metaphorical and symbolic ways of understanding the social and their relationship to it: 'Before all, [religion] is a system of ideas with which the individuals represent to themselves the society of which they are members, and the obscure but intimate relations which they have with it' (1915: 225). Religious beliefs are collective representations of the social – the 'social divine' – which, in addition to acting as cognitive maps of social realities, also express and dramatise the social world, 'providing a "flag", a "rallying sign", a set of "dramatic representations" analogous to "games and the principal forms of art"' (1915: 220, 358, 379, 381; Lukes 1975: 292). Religious sentiments are created in and through collective experiences – the *creative effervescence* of people gathered together is a cognitive and emotional experience which produces a sense of, and a belief in, a power greater than the individual.

Key to the use of this work, for the analysis of that which is not ostensibly religious, is Durkheim's own acknowledgement that the role of religion in offering cognitive maps of social reality is in decline in modernity, and his argument that 'there is something eternal in religion which is destined to survive all the particular symbols in which religious thought has successively enveloped itself' (1915: 427). This 'something eternal' is the need for the regular 'moral remaking of society' which is conducted through non-religious rituals: periodic 'reunions, assemblies and meetings' at which people 'reaffirm in common their common sentiments' (1915: 427). Durkheim grants to collective effervescences a decisive role in the formation of the social and its moral order, and because of the transitory and ephemeral nature of the effects of these collective effervescences, he argued that they must be recharged periodically. However, he noted a problematic diminution of their occurrence in modern society. In sum, then, *The Elementary Forms* focuses our attention on the emotional, collective construction not just of religion, but of morality, and on the role of ritual at collective gatherings in distilling the values and ideals of the social group and binding individuals to them and to each other. It is, above all, the spirit of late Durkheim that matters to us here: a *spirit* which sees the sociological significance of the sacred and the symbolic, and their relationship with the social and the moral.

Cultural performance

The work of anthropologist Victor Turner takes up this Durkheimian focus on the role of symbols and ritual in social and cultural processes, and develops a new analytical framework for their study – that of cultural performance.[11] Turner conceptualises cultural performance in its broadest sense – as theatre, music and aesthetic drama, and as ritual and social drama – and explores the continuities between aesthetic drama and the collective dramas and rituals performed in social life. His approach foregrounds process, seeing social process as performative, and performance as process; performance is inherently unfinished, ongoing, open, liminal. He is particularly interested in the contrast between Western, post-Renaissance art as product, hung, framed and complete, and non-Western art, and Western art of other periods, which exemplifies a balance between the ongoing 'being in' of the art – its performance – and it material product (Schechner 1988). Thus his work directs us towards a concern not with the outcome of cultural performance, but to the experience and meaning of 'being in' the performance.

The genres of cultural performance discussed by Turner which are of most interest to us are ritual and social drama. Turner defines ritual as the performance of a complex sequence of symbolic acts (1988: 75), and describes social dramas as isolable units of a harmonic or disharmonic social process which arise in conflict situations (1974: 37). He identifies a characteristic sequential structure within a social drama: first, the breach of regular, everyday, norm-governed social relations, in which affect is primary; this is followed by the crisis phase, in which the cognitive, affective and conative dimensions of human action are engaged, and when the social field is divided into two camps or factions, in which one is ostensibly operating rationally and the other emotionally; after this comes the ritual phase, in which a public redressive ceremony, composed of a sequence of symbolic acts, brings the social field together; finally, normal everyday life is resumed and viable social relations re-established, albeit sometimes by recognition of the existence of an irreparable schism.[12]

Of particular importance to us here is Turner's emphasis on the generative possibilities for social change within cultural performance. In contrast to earlier work on ritual and performance within anthropology, and *contra* western

European and Christian constructions of ritual as rigid and tradition-bound, he stresses the novelty and creativity which can emerge from the freedom of the performance situation: 'the ways in which social actions of various kinds acquire form through the metaphors and paradigms in their actor's heads (put there by explicit teaching and implicit generalisation from social experience), and, in certain intensive circumstances, generate unprecedented forms that bequeath history new metaphors and paradigms' (Turner 1974: 13). The concept of liminality, which he takes from Van Gennep's work on rites of passage, and extends to refer to any condition outside or on the peripheries of daily life (1974: 47), is central. There is, Turner suggests, in all rituals and social dramas, 'at least a moment when those being moved in accordance with a cultural script [are] liberated from normative demands, when they [are], indeed, betwixt and between successive lodgements in jural political systems. In this gap between ordered worlds almost anything may happen' (Turner 1974: 13). In other words, ritual and social dramas are not unidirectionally reflective and expressive of the existing socio-cultural system, and are not necessarily conservative; whilst their symbols draw on cultural precedent, their performance is not necessarily and always determined: 'Without liminality, program might indeed determine performance. But, given liminality, prestigious programs can be undermined and multiple alternative programs may be generated' (1974: 14).

In the liminality of a social drama, outside the patterns and routines of everyday life, people experience a spontaneous *communitas*, as de-differentiation takes place between individuals, and social relations become, if temporarily, more egalitarian, direct and non-rational (Turner 1974: 53). This is similar to the creative effervescence of which Durkheim wrote, during which:

> For a while anything goes: taboos are lifted, fantasies enacted, indicative mood behaviour is reversed; the low are exalted and the mighty abased . . . Ambiguity reigns; people and policies may be judged sceptically in relation to deep values; the vices, follies, stupidities and abuses of contemporary holders of high political, economic or religious status may be scrutinized, ridiculed or condemned in terms of axiomatic values.
>
> (Turner 1974: 102)

Cultural performances therefore 'speak in the subjunctive mood', expressing supposition, desire, hypothesis and possibility, rather than belonging to the everyday indicative mood of culture which speaks of facts, and operates in the realm of cognition, rather than emotion. Performances can be anti-structural, creative, carnivalesque and playful, and often contain, he suggests, a reflexive critique – direct or veiled – of the social world from which they emerge, an evaluation of the way society handles history (Turner 1988: 21-2). They

> are not simple reflectors or expressions of culture or even of changing culture but may themselves be active agencies of change, representing the eye by which culture sees itself and the drawing board on which creative actors

sketch out what they believe to be more apt or interesting 'designs for living' . . . 'Performative reflexivity' is a condition in which a sociocultural group, or its most perceptive members, acting representatively, turn, bend or reflect back upon themselves, upon the relations, actions, symbols, meanings, codes, roles, statuses, social structures, ethical and legal rules, and other socio-cultural components which make up their public 'selves'. Performative reflexivity, too, is not mere reflex, a quick, automatic or habitual response to some stimulus. It is highly contrived, artificial, of culture not nature, a deliberate and voluntary work of art.

(1988: 24)

Performances constitute 'the plural self-knowledge of a group', arousing conscious-ness of ourselves and how we see ourselves, positioning us as heroes in our own dramas (1988: 42). But they do not straightforwardly speak 'the truth' about social reality:

Genres of cultural performance are not simple mirrors but magical mirrors of social reality: they exaggerate, invert, re-form, magnify, dis-color, re-color, even deliberately falsify, chronicled events.

(1988: 42)

In the liminal space of a social drama 'people are allowed to think about how they think, about the terms in which they conduct their thinking, or feel about how they feel in daily life' (1988: 102). They engage a 'ritual metalanguage' which enables them to talk about that which they normally talk. This ritual meta-language is non-verbal as well as verbal, and is as much about emotion, affect and volition as it is cognitive and philosophical:

Since culture is fed by affectual and volitional as well as cognitive sources, and since these may be unconscious in great part, the terms and symbols of plural reflexivity may be suffused with orexis, with desire and appetite, as well as involved with knowing, perceiving and conceiving.

(1988: 103)

Emotional community

More recently Michel Maffesoli (1996) has taken up the mantel of the spirit of late Durkheim and Turner in his *zeitdiagnotische* sociology, which offers an analysis of 'these closing days of the modern era' in terms of their *ambience*, or *aura*, and their characteristic form of sociality: the untidy sociality of micro-groups, or *tribus*. Central to Maffesoli's work is a concern with the collective imagination and sensibility, with *puissance*, the inherent energy and vital force of the people, and *emotional community*, which he understands as sacred, in the way that Durkheim spoke of the *social divine*. He argues that intellectuals have rarely been able to grasp the 'will to live', or *puissance*, the affirmative quality of human life, which nourishes the social body (1996: 31), and he insists on the importance of understanding how *puissance* is always at work, sometimes invisibly in the everyday conviviality of social life, but at other times, bursting forth and expressing itself in the effervescent emotionality of revolts, festivals and uprisings. Maffesoli remarks on the intellectual's mistrust of the masses, of their complexity and heterogeneity, and points to how intellectuals try to 'mould the masses into a "subject of history" or some such commendable and civilised entity', as they measure 'everything by the yard-stick of the project' (1996: 57). He proposes an alternative way of viewing the people: 'It is a shapeless mass, at once mob-like and idealistic, generous and wicked, in short, a contradictory mixture, which like any other living thing, is based on a paradoxical tension' (1996: 57).

Whilst Maffesoli's postmodern mode of theorising rejects simplistic taxonomies, binary oppositions and totalising narratives, he suggests that a distinction can be drawn between rational periods in history, when the principle of individuation and separation holds force, and empathetic periods, characterised by a lack of differentiation, and a 'neo-tribal' loss in a collective subject.[13] He proposes that, as we move from modernity to postmodernity, 'we are witnessing the tendency for a rationalized "social" to be replaced by an empathetic "sociality" which is expressed by a succession of ambiences, feelings and emotions' (1996: 11). The contemporary era has a Dionysian quality, a pleasure-seeking, hedonistic, spontaneous aura, in which there is a resurgence of the qualitative, a re-enchantment of everyday life and a revival of interest in the spiritual, the religious and the magical. In other words, Maffesoli's work suggests that in postmodern sociality, we will, as predicted by Durkheim, 'know again those hours of creative effervescence, in the course of which new ideas arise and new formulae are found which serve for a while as a guide for humanity' (Durkheim 1915: 427-8). Dionysian values take the place of the Promethean values of productivist modernity, and there is a shift from overarching moral frameworks, to a more ambivalent, local, protean ethics which is forged in emotional community. There is a growing detachment from the abstract public sphere and its institutional structures, and people are drawn to the transcendent emotional community of the *tribus*; *puissance* – the vital energy and power of people – takes the place of *pouvoir* – the power of institutional politics and ruling elites. In place of the rational project of the proletariat or the bourgeoisie, and instead of the goals and paths set forth by individual leaders, the Dionysian era places its collective energy in mythical figures:

> Heroes, saints or emblematic figures may be real, however they exist more or less as ideal types, empty 'forms', matrices in which we may all recognize ourselves and commune with others . . . mythical figures and social types that enable a common 'aesthetic' to serve as a repository of our collective self expression. The multiplicity inherent in a given symbol inevitably favours the emergence of a strong collective feeling.
>
> (1996: 10)

So it is that Maffesoli's work leads us back to the subject of this chapter, Princess Diana, a real person who lived and died at the end of the twentieth century, but also a figure as mythical as her namesake the Greek goddess, onto whom the social divine was projected, in death as it had been during her lifetime.

Diana's death

> In our grief for Diana, there is none of that old British reserve. We are united as never before. And we want the world to know it. It is the new British spirit. The spirit of Diana, proclaimed loud and proudly throughout the land.
>
> It isn't mass hysteria. It is perfectly calm and reasoned. It isn't just doing what others do, copying to be part of the crowd. Everyone has their own feeling.
>
> ('The Voice of the Mirror', Daily Mirror, 4 Sept. 1997)

The hundreds of thousands of people who made pilgrimages to and between Kensington Palace, Buckingham Palace, St James's Palace, and Althorp, who laid flowers, made cards, wrote messages, signed books of condolence, were, to draw on Turner, engaging in cultural performances. Most of the individual actions that comprised these performances had their precedent in public responses to deaths of other well-loved public figures – Elvis, John F. Kennedy, John Lennon – and these cultural traces provided the framework within which people acted; like all performances, these performances of collective mourning embedded traces of previous performances, and engaged with cultural stories and traditions. But these traditions were not just the traditions of the British monarchy, or even of the establishment of the British nation. They were an improvised mélange of the traditions of different regions, localities, classes and social groups, of establishment culture and popular culture, as people drew on a wide range of symbols and rituals to invent new ways of showing their grief – the demonstrative floral tributes of working-class East End funerals, the exuberant celebratory memorials of gay mourning in the AIDS era, the shrines of the European Orthodox tradition, the scattering of flowers before the funeral procession of South East Asia, the week-long shiva of the Jewish tradition, the sad, communal celebratory of the Irish wake.[14] These performances were highly mediated by television and newspapers, by almost constant media coverage of the event, but to see them as produced or manufactured by the media would be to ignore the effervescence of the public response, the *puissance* of the people, the way that public emotion constantly broke free of all attempts to contain, name and tame it. The media mobilised, amplified and gave voice to the collective agency of the week, but people were speaking in their own voices, producing and directing their own actions in the public spaces of grief which they created. Rather than seeking to cede agency to the media, as many cultural analysts have done, the public response should be understood as a collective action, in which the collectivity, in its effervescence and *communitas*, took on an energy and strength far greater than the sum of its individual participants, and so generated the power – the *puissance* – which was so remarkable.

The cultural performance of the mourners during that week took on the character of a social drama, as described by Turner: the breach constituted by

Diana's death and the public judgement of the inadequacy of the early royal response gave rise to a crisis situation, in which conflict was enjoined between the people and the monarchy. In the heightened emotion of the period, and with a growing sense of their collective power, people reflected on and questioned the traditions and protocols of the monarchy, demanding, for instance, the lowering of the flag which flew from Buckingham Palace, as a mark of respect for Diana, commenting on and influencing plans for the funeral (the length and route of the procession, the style of the ceremony), and reprimanding the royal family for their aloofness and lack of obvious emotion. In the liminality of the week of mourning, as everyday life was put on hold and people took time out from their routines, normal rules and expectations about modes of behaviour were swept aside: 'the low [were] exalted and the mighty abased . . . Ambiguity reign[ed]; people and policies [were] judged sceptically in relation to deep values' (Turner 1974: 102). Emotion was expressed in public, men cried and carried flowers, deference and respect for the monarchy gave way to explicit public critique, and people took over the streets and parks, so that the customary routes of traffic and pedestrians had to alter.[15] During the funeral, the *puissance* of the people was felt against the *pouvoir* (Maffesoli 1996) of the establishment in the public endorsement of Earl Spencer's oration, with its barely veiled criticisms of the royal family. When, against all custom in funerals, a ripple of applause began outside Westminster Abbey amongst the people watching the ceremony on big screens, it gathered volume and momentum, and spread through the crowds, who rose to their feet, and poured into the Abbey – reversing the centripetal point of the funeral momentarily from inside, where the great and the good were gathered, to the people outside. The tone and form of the funeral were also fundamentally shaped by the aura of the collective mourning; a postmodern mixture of the old and the new, high culture and popular culture, Verdi and Elton John, the funeral served as the public redressive ceremony which brought the social field back together, enabling everyday life to be resumed afterwards, albeit with the question of the future of the monarchy still hanging in the air.

The performances of the week of mourning exemplified Turner's notion of performative reflexivity. People were self-consciously, intelligently, critically, reflexively asking themselves about the actions they were taking, reflecting on their emotions as individuals and on the collective response, on the mediated nature of their relationship to Diana, on what she symbolised to them and to the emotional community of which they were part. They were also, in a 'highly contrived . . . deliberate and voluntary' manner, 'turn[ing], bend[ing], reflect[ing] back upon themselves, upon the relations, actions, symbols, meanings, codes, roles, statuses, social structures, ethical and legal rules and other socio-cultural components which make up their public selves' (Turner 1974: 24). Their actions opened up the space to engage in discourse about discourse, to think about the ways in which public life is normally conducted, about the role of emotions in the public sphere, about the relation between the personal and the public.

But recognition of the reflexivity and critical discourse which was prominent within the mourning should not detract from a more Maffesolian attention to the extra-rational nature of the collective experience. The week was a postmodern moment which illustrated 'the tendency for a rationalized "social" to be replaced by an empathetic "sociality" which is expressed by a succession of ambiences, feelings and emotions' (Maffesoli 1996: 11). It was a week of spontaneous gatherings, uncertain crowd behaviour, in which the modernist desire for order, control and predictability was swept aside, and reason ceded its place to emotion, the emotion, in Zygmunt Bauman's (1992: xi) words, of the 'devalued and demonized "raw" human condition' which modernity seeks to suppress.

As a mythical figure onto whom individual and collective desires were projected, the stories that were told of Diana spoke of a deep-seated longing for re-enchantment, a desire for magic and mystery in a disenchanted world. The tales of Diana in the media, often in the voices of ordinary people who had met her, were tales of enchantment, of her charismatic physical presence, of her charm, her beauty, her captivating smile and seductive eyes, of her clothes, in all their magnificent prolixity, of the way she worked audiences, engaged individuals and lit up those in her presence. People spoke about how she brought smiles to the sick and depressed, giving them new energy and life, and ascribed to her the powers attributed to spiritual healers in pre-modern cultures. In her brother's words, in his funeral oration, she was seen as possessing 'her own particular brand of magic'. And so her death produced a collective moment of re-enchantment – not a happy or joyous one, but a moment when the secular rationality of modernity was cast aside, and a hybrid popular postmodern spirituality was unleashed, in which people invented new ways of showing their grief. The mass outbreak of artistic emotion and creativity outside Kensington Palace, by people whose everyday lives are not engaged in the production of art, mixed symbols and ritual practices from different regional, local, national and religious traditions, from the established Church, from other religions and traditions and from New Age spirituality with symbols from their everyday lives. As if seeking atonement for their behaviour, for having consumed Diana through their relentless interest in *her* private life, people offered tokens from *their* private lives, gifts that were personal and precious to them, as people have traditionally given gifts to their dead ancestors, to saints and to gods.[16] And in their messages to her, in poetry and prose, they expressed sorrow, guilt and regret, and wished her freedom and liberation in death. Through their own improvised rituals, and in the public ritual of the funeral, people engaged with their own moral consciences and with existential matters of life and death.

A new moral framework?

The postmodern sensibility of our time . . . operates in a field of tension between tradition and innovation, conservation and renewal, mass culture and high art, in which the second terms are no longer automatically privileged over the first; a field of tension which can no longer be grasped in categories such as progress vs. reaction, left vs. right, present vs. past.

(Huyssen 1990: 371)

A Durkheimian analysis of the events of the week of mourning suggests that the creative effervescence and emotional religiosity of the gatherings can be seen as expressive of the social divine, as distilling the values and ideals which were in the collective conscience of the people of Britain at that particular moment in time. I do not want to suggest that the collective response to the death of Diana manifested a whole new moral order, but I do propose that it offered, to borrow Bauman's (1992) term, *intimations* of a postmodern ethics–politics, a *yearning*, in bell hooks's (1991) terms, for a new ethical and moral framework for living. Coming as it did just a few months after the New Labour landslide general election victory, which ended eighteen years of Conservative government, many commentators at the time saw both events as expressions of a new, modern, more democratic Britain, in the process of unshackling itself from the yoke of tradition. The 1997 general election was fought and won by New Labour on the basis of the party's 'modernisation', and when Tony Blair captured the national mood, speaking, in the hours after her death, of Diana as the 'People's Princess', he successfully linked her to the general project of modernisation. But to focus on the collective response to Diana's death in terms of the confrontation between tradition and modernity, or to see it only within the context of events on the stage of institutionalised politics is to miss its wider ethical–political implications, and their postmodern character.[17] In asserting the postmodern sensibility of these ethics– politics, I am, following Andreas Huyssen (1990), suggesting a move beyond the modern/traditional, good/bad, progressive/regressive, left/right dichotomies which have predominated in analyses of the response to the death of Diana.

Throughout the week people were interviewed by the media regarding their feelings about Diana, and there was in evidence a strong sense of attachment to and respect for the ethical and moral framework within which she was seen as operating.[18] There was much discussion of 'her causes', 'her work' and 'what she stood for', all of which was placed within the context of her life as a whole, the particularity of the story of her transformation from an innocent young upper- class girl in London, to bride, mother and future Queen, to the unhappy, self- harming bulimic, and through separation and divorce, and, it seemed, out the other side, as a confident, reflexive, independent woman, with a deep love for her children and a passionate commitment to her own set of values. In the aftermath of her death, these ethics seemed to be a source of inspiration and aspiration for those affected by her death, and they can be seen as having been collectively enacted in novel ways during the week of mourning.

Revaluing the non-rational

At the core of Diana's ethical stance was a revaluing of the non-rational; the emotional, affective and intuitive were, for her, legitimate and fundamental sources of knowledge and the bases for action. Her work was, she said, led by the heart; she took up causes that made emotional sense to her – AIDS and the campaign against landmines, for instance – not because she had a rational, strategic political agenda, but because she felt she understood the real emotional problems within society and in individuals' lives. In this she drew quite consciously and explicitly on her own experiences, and on her encounters with the people she met over the years in her work as Princess of Wales:

> I've been in a privileged position for fifteen years. I've got tremendous knowledge about people and how to communicate. I've learnt that, and I want to use it. And when I look at people in public life, I'm not a political animal but I think that the biggest disease this world suffers from in this day and age is the disease of people feeling unloved, and I know that I can give love for a minute, for half an hour, for a day, for a month, but I can give – I'm very happy to do that and I want to do that.[19]

She pursued her causes through an articulate and media-savvy appeal to the emotions, understanding the power of the symbolic moment, such as when, in the early days of anti-gay AIDS panic, she held the hand of a person with AIDS; the visual image, as she met and talked with the victims of landmines in Angola; and the personal, reflexive speech and the soundbite. In stating that she would like to be thought of as the 'Queen of Hearts' she succinctly summed up her personal philosophy and ambition, and exemplified her media literacy.[20] Her approach disturbed the reason/emotion dichotomy, which in modernity has mapped onto the dualism of public/private, as she admitted to personal problems and frailty, and drew upon them to make sense of social problems.

A new relationship to 'the other'

Diana's ethical approach also suggested a reworking and transformation of modernity's relationship to 'the other'. Modernity heightens alterity, in its characteristic obsession with the stranger and his/her difference, and its simultaneous impulse to control the stranger's difference, and to eradicate it. In contrast, Diana's postmodern ethics involved a rapprochement with difference and sought to reassert a common humanity which worked across difference, enjoying it, recognising it and never seeking to erase it. Her values were pluralistic, rather than universalistic, and de-othered the marginalised, bringing them symbolically into the fold of Englishness, which she, from her appearance as Prince Charles's fiancée onwards, came to represent. Much of her popularity with those moved to take to the streets was because of her work with the marginalised and stigmatised – people with AIDS, the homeless, the depressed, drug addicts. She was seen to reach across boundaries of status, class, race, health, nation and sexuality. She was well known to have friendships with gay men – Elton John, Gianni Versace – and to have given much time, often out of the public eye, to AIDS charities such as Lighthouse and Cruisaid. Moreover, the relationship which she was having at the time of her death with Dodi Al Fayed was seen as further exemplifying her ethics of inclusivity and the transcendence of the deep-seated prejudices which have been characteristic of the English nation.

A re-humanising of welfare

Diana's work for charities and 'good causes' took place within the context of the restructuring of the welfare state, which began with the election of the Conservative government of 1979, and which set in train a shift from the post-war welfare settlement's ethic of collective provision and social responsibility for welfare, to one which emphasises the importance of individual responsibility, and in which state provision is combined with an increased reliance on familial, private and charitable voluntary-sector provision. Against a political backdrop in which there was little space to speak about society's responsibility for the welfare of the vulnerable, Diana's well-publicised devotion to her charitable work both chimed with the Conservative emphasis on traditional Victorian philanthropy and at the same time challenged it, by placing welfare issues – particularly unpopular and unrecognised ones such as AIDS, homelessness, drug addiction, victims of landmines and sufferers of leprosy – on the public agenda. The issues with which she chose to engage are significant; they are outsider-issues, not the ones which readily garnered public sympathy, particularly during the victim-blaming climate of the Tory years. Her particular contribution to a new ethics of welfare lay in the way in which she demonstrated the need to re-humanise welfare. Her focus was always on the emotional needs and the humanity of welfare users, the needs that are often neglected by bureaucratised welfare organisations and overstretched paid workers; she was respected and loved by welfare users because she was able to offer an emotional gift of caring which was freely given, outside the nexus of the labour contract. She spent time talking, touching, holding the sick, the dying, the lonely, the frightened, and those who experienced her doing so were clear that she offered something beyond that which paid workers were able to provide. She made 'vulnerable people feel valued, special and not forgotten'.[21] Moreover, she re-humanised the work of providing care, focusing her attention not just on welfare users but on care-providers too, recognising the hidden world of unvalued, underpaid and unpaid carers.

An ethic of pleasure

Diana's way of being in the world also offered a model of the ethical life in which there was a place for pleasure, humour and fun, for the celebration of life. Her life had not been one of asceticism, chastity and material deprivation; for all her good work, she was no Mother Teresa, and that was central to her appeal. Whilst she had revealed some of the pain that she had suffered during her marriage, she also clearly enjoyed life – designer clothes, parties, dancing, spending time with her children, sailing with friends in the Mediterranean, going to the theatre, the ballet and theme parks, riding, swimming, skiing. She often seemed to enjoy inhabiting her body, and was not alienated from the pleasures of the flesh. The public knew that she was in therapy, that she had struggled to find personal happiness and self-fulfilment, and her commitment to the reflexive project of the self resonated with the cultural preoccupation with self-actualisation which characterises postmodernity (Giddens 1991). Diana's combination of commitment to good work with the pursuit of pleasure was thoroughly un-Protestant, and suggested an ethics in which it is possible to combine a concern for others with a concern for self.

These ethics which Diana lived implicitly during her life also guided the collective performance of the week of mourning. The outbreak of emotion which swept the nation constituted a moment of collective revaluing of the realm of the non-rational and the expressive. It saw a remarkable public rupture of the male-rational, female-emotional construction which characterises the modern gender regime, and which has assigned value to the former, and relegated the latter to the private sphere. Men cried in the streets and on television, speaking of their feelings of grief and loss, not just for Diana, but for wives and mothers who had often died long ago, and whose deaths they had not properly mourned; and the ultimate exemplars of masculine dissociation from the world of expressive emotionality, soldiers, cried as they received her coffin at RAF Northholt, and at the funeral. The events of the week also demonstrated the ethic of a new relationship to the other. People were able to express their grief as themselves, occupying the identities that mattered to them – there was space for difference in the crowds in the Mall, Hyde Park and outside the palaces, in the tributes people left to her, and in the funeral itself. Invitations to the funeral included those who would not have been considered suitable guests at previous royal ceremonies: there were people with HIV and AIDS in the Abbey, disabled people, and friends like Elton John and his partner, whose arrival was announced by the BBC commentator in as respectful a way as the arrival of any heterosexual couple. In sharp contrast to her wedding sixteen years before, when taking part in the collective celebrations was to join in the creation of a mythical unitary Englishness of the Establishment, being part of the mourning did not require the suppression of racial, national, ethnic or sexual difference; indeed the diversity of those who mourned was one of the features most consistently and most favourably reported and commented upon in the media during the week. And, finally, through the period of mourning there ran an ethic of pleasure and a desire to celebrate life: there was a creativity and aesthetics in the response to her death which celebrated not just her life, but the beauty of life in general, and the commensality and bonds which were forged between strangers in the public spaces of grief were a truly Durkheimian celebration of collective life, sociability and the social divine.

Conclusion

To understand the collective response to the death of Diana as a moment of creative effervescence and moral remaking, as I have argued in this chapter, suggests an analysis of the politics and culture of postmodernity which is fundamentally rooted in the sociological tradition. My approach takes key tropes from Durkheim's cultural sociology, inflecting them with what is often now conceptualised as a postmodern analytic, in which the political, the cultural and the moral are seen as thoroughly imbricated and mutually constituted, and in which there is a central concern with the emotional, the affective and the realm of ritual and the symbolic. Implicit in this chapter is an assertion of the importance of seeking to understand the collective ethical dimensions of sociality, and, in Maffesoli's words, the ambience and aura, the texture, feeling, energy and emotionality of social phenomena and collective experiences. Thinking in such terms opens up the possibility of an approach to the study of the contemporary which is focused less on the effects and outcomes of an event like the death of Diana, and more on understanding cultural–political phenomena as moments of cultural performance which are expressive of the social in its continuous flow of change.

Notes

Earlier versions of this paper were presented at the Centre for Interdisciplinary Gender Studies at the University of Leeds (November 1997), at a seminar in the Centre for Women's Studies and the Research School for the Social Sciences at the Australian National University (September 1998) and at an ESRC seminar on 'A New Politics?' at the Centre for Sociology and Cultural Studies at the University of Birmingham (September 1999). Thanks to Griselda Pollock, for her provocative paper at the Leeds seminar, to all the audiences for their lively engagement with the ideas in the paper, and to Nicky Edwards, Carol Johnson, Richard Kilminster, Fiona Williams and Sally Wheeler for conversations and cuttings about the death of Diana.

1 The funeral was watched on television by a record audience of 31.5 million in the UK; according to the BBC at its peak 59 per cent of the country was watching the service (and this does not include the millions of people watching on big screens in public spaces in London and around the country). 26.2 million watched the England v. Germany European Championship football semi-final in 1996; 22 million the wedding of Diana and Charles in 1981; and 19 million Winston Churchill's funeral. The funeral was broadcast live to 45 countries and via BBC World to 142 others (*Guardian*, 8 Sept. 1997).

2 In addition to the commentary of all the newspapers and news magazines, there have been whole issues or substantial parts of the following journals devoted to discussions of Diana: *The Nation*, *Granta*, *New Statesman*, *Capital and Class*, *Journal of Gender Studies* (1999), *New Left Review* (1997), *New Formations* (1999), *Anthropology Today*, *Screen* and *Psychology Today*. There have also been books by Campbell (1998), Burchill (1998), Re:Public (1997), Merck (1998), Kear and Steinberg (1999) and Walters (1999).

3 Barcan (1997), Blackmann (1999), Davies (1999), Nunn (1999), Attwood (1999), Cox (1999).

4 Barnett and Bourne Taylor (1999), Gibson (1999), Hey (1999).

5 Rose (1999), Watts (1999), Wilson (1997).

6 A significant exception to this is McGuigan (2000) who offers a sociological analysis of the popular response to the death of Diana as a manifestation of the cultural public sphere – a symbolic space for the emotional expression of democratic participation. There are several possible reasons for this otherwise almost complete silence from sociologists. Besides a certain wariness of the media and a reluctance to be drawn into commenting rashly on current events without time for due reflection, sociologists also tend to share what Nicos Mouzelis has called a 'disregard for macro actors' (Mouzelis 1995), a lack of interest in and attention to the 'great' individual, the people who wield a disproportionate share of power and influence in society. Royalty is more typically the subject matter of history as a discipline, and the popular icon and celebrity the concern of cultural studies, than of sociology.

7 Featherstone (1992) discusses postmodernism's preference for the analysis of 'every-day life' over 'heroic life'.

8 With the voices of sceptics such as Elizabeth Wilson (1997) and contributors to Merck (1998) playing on my mind, it is important to acknowledge that not everyone was caught up in the Diana moment. There were critics from the left and the right, pro- or anti-monarchist, not party to the collective emotion, along with those, like the homeless woman sitting in a doorway in central London, interviewed on Channel 4's 'The Mourning', who were somehow oblivious to the whole event. But, that said, I believe that it is nonetheless possible to speak of 'the collective response' to Diana's death, and to develop an analysis of this which offers insights into the nature of the contemporary. It is my feeling that if it were not possible to allow ourselves to think in neo-Durkheimian terms of the 'collective conscience' in the case of the response to the death of Diana, then we might as well give up on the whole sociological project, for I can think of no better example of this key sociological concept.

9 Alexander (1988) points out that work in a Durkheimian tradition in sociology tends not to provide historically specific analyses of cultural processes, and Davis (1981) makes use of the symbolic anthropology of Clifford Geertz, Mary Douglas, Arnold Van Gennep and Victor Turner, among others, but is critical of their tendency to ignore historical change. Contributors to Alexander (1988) offer a neo-Durkheimian cultural sociology which is very sensitive to issues of historical change and specificity, and which has greatly influenced my approach in this article.

10 My focus is particularly on Britain. For discussions of the commonalities and differences in responses to Diana's death around the world see Re:Public (1997), particularly essays by Sofoulis, Duruz and Johnson, Kennedy and Thomas.

11 The study of performance has become an important part of anthropology and cultural studies, largely due to influence of Turner (1974). For overviews of the performance theory in cultural studies, drama studies and anthropology see Schechner (1988) and Diamond (1996).

12 Diamond's (1996) postmodern take on performance challenges Turner's position for its organic model of culture and the universalism it seems to presuppose; but Turner himself devotes considerable attention to unpicking the problems of organicism in anthropological thought (1974), and is sensitive to the dangers of assuming that his four-phase model of the social drama is universal.

13 Evans (1997) rightly points out that Maffesoli's work retains 'submerged "modernist" periodisations', as in the use of the figures of Prometheus and Dionysus to differenti-ate historical periods, but argues convincingly that he is more successful in producing a postmodern sociology of postmodernity than many theorists of postmodernity.

14 Of course, traditions which appear to be 'pure' and ancient are often recently invented. See Hobsbawm and Ranger (1983).

15 The fact that Diana's death occurred on a Sunday morning, the liminal day of the week, was significant: people had time to think, to absorb the information, watch the news on television, gather in the Mall and at the palaces. It is interesting to consider how events might have unfolded differently had she died on a Monday morning.

16 Many messages left with flowers addressed Diana directly, explicitly speaking of guilt and regret at having been part of the mass consumption of her life.

17 It is beyond the scope of this chapter to explicate in detail the debate between those who characterise the contemporary social condition as modern, those who regard it as late modern, and those who designate it as postmodern. In favouring the notion of postmodernity, I use the concept in a way which sees both continuity and disconti-nuity in the social condition, rather than declaring that the postmodern era represents a complete break with the modernity. Postmodernity is fundamentally rooted in modernity, and modern ideas and practices continue to exist, along with pre-modern traditions and social forms. Postmodernity sees intensifications of the processes which characterise modernity, and new processes and critiques of modernity. It is the time

and space of those who are conscious of living after the metanarrative, when people have lost faith in the possibility of all-encompassing political and theoretical projects, and no longer believe in the inevitability of progress, or accord a hallowed place to rationality. The postmodern state of mind accepts ambivalence, ambiguity, pluralism and variety, embraces contingency (Heller 1989), in contrast to modernity's struggle for order, control, universality, homogeneity and absolutes (Bauman 1992).

18 That the Diana, Princess of Wales Memorial Fund was established after her death to 'carry forward her values' (Joanna Scott, letter to the *Guardian*, 27 Aug. 1999), and that it received £100 million in its first two years, suggests the centrality of her values to the public response to her death.

19 From the 1995 *Panorama* interview, quoted in Begbie (1997: 124).

20 In the 1995 *Panorama* interview.

21 Joanna Scott, letter to the *Guardian*, 27 Aug. 1999.

Part II

New social movements

8   Social movement networks

Virtual and real

Mario Diani

Introduction

The rapidly growing role of 'computer mediated communication' (henceforth, CMC) has attracted considerable attention from social scientists, and generated extensive discussions of its possible impact on social organisation (Castells 1996; Wellman *et al.* 1996; Cerúlo and Ruane 1997). In this chapter I discuss the possible effects of CMC on social movement activity. CMC represents an unusual form of communication, as it does not really fit conventional distinctions between public and private, and direct and mediated communication. It may be expected to affect collective action in both instrumental and symbolic terms, by improving the effectiveness of communication and creating collective identity and solidarity. At the same time, the heterogeneity of social movements prevents us from formulating generic arguments about their relationship to CMC. Accordingly, I briefly discuss the potential consequences of CMC on three different types of movement organisations:

- organisations mobilising mainly participatory resources
- organisations focusing on professional resources
- transnational networks (Tarrow 1998a; Diani and Donati 1999).

The exercise is merely exploratory. As such, it inevitably touches upon very complex issues in a cursory way. Nevertheless, it identifies several general criteria for the investigation of the role of social movements in the virtual space, a topic which so far has seen as much, and possibly more, utopian wishful thinking as systematic reasoning.

CMC, political activism and social movements

We can regard social movements as networks of informal relationships between a multiplicity of individuals and organisations, who share a distinctive collective identity, and mobilise resources on conflictual issues (Diani 1992). This definition identifies several dimensions of social movements that CMC may be expected to shape.[1] These include (a) the behaviour of specific movement actors, individuals or organisations; (b) the relations linking individual activists and organisations to each other (Diani 1995; della Porta and Diani 1999: ch. 5); (c) the feelings of mutual identification and solidarity which bond movement actors together and secure the persistence of movements even when specific campaigns are not taking place (Rupp and Taylor 1987; Melucci 1996). Treating movements as networks also makes the relationship between movements and their spatial location most explicit. Contemporary social movements have developed historically in parallel with the emergence of a public sphere located in specific physical and cultural spaces, namely, in societies defined by national boundaries, specific infrastructures and common cultural traits (Tilly 1978; Calhoun 1992; Emirbayer and Sheller 1999; Tarrow 1998a).

This view of movements broadens our understanding of the relationship between CMC and movements to include issues of networking and identity building. Potential questions include the following:

- how do forms of individual participation change?
- how do social movement organisations (SMOs) modify their ways of operating?
- how do individuals and organisations connect to each other to exchange/pool resources and information?
- how do these actors develop identities and solidarities?
- how do the geographical boundaries of the network change, along with the underlying idea of public space?

This is a massive – and admittedly daunting – research programme; in this chapter I focus in particular on communication between individuals and organisations, and on the spread of collective identities. I pay hardly any attention to individual participation, nor to broader changes in the public sphere. There are good reasons why CMC should affect political activism significantly. The spread of electronic mail may facilitate communication between local and national branches of the same organisation, as well as among the members of local, national and transnational coalitions; it may also strengthen the linkages between individual members and their organisations. Communication technology enables activists to set up discussion groups between individuals interested in a specific issue, thus encouraging interaction and polyadic, rather than dyadic, communication dynamics. Finally, the World Wide Web not only offers the opportunity of making crucial information for campaigners easily accessible from websites; it also allows the independent existence of 'virtual' forms of co-ordination such as that represented by the Institute for Global Communication (www.igc.org) and its different thematic networks (WomensNet, EcoNet, PeaceNet, LaborNet and ConflictNet).[2]

Potential advantages stemming from CMC include the higher speed and the reduced costs of communication among sometimes very distant actors; the persistent accuracy of the original message and the overcoming of the traditional problem of distortion, so common when communication spreads by word of mouth or through summaries by intermediaries; the potential to promote interaction between branches of organisations and/or movement activists; and the opportunity to transform sets of geographically dispersed aggrieved individuals into a densely connected aggrieved population, thus solving one key problem of mobilisation (Myers 1994: 252–7; Bonchek 1995; Rheingold 1993: ch. 8).

These traits of CMC surely increase the possibility of launching campaigns on a scale, and with a speed, previously unheard of; but does this entitle us to conclude that we are witnessing the development of new types of actors, rather than the simple growth in the efficiency of social movement action? In particular, should we expect the emergence of new types of 'virtual' social movements, disconnected from a specific location in space and without reference to any specific 'real' community? To address these issues we need a preliminary – if brief – discussion of the peculiarity of CMC vis-à-vis other, more conventional forms of communication.

CMC and 'conventional' communication

A proper assessment of the impact of CMC requires at least a working typology of communication forms. Mine is based on the distinction between the private or public nature of communication, namely, its accessibility to third parties; and on its direct or mediated form, where 'direct' means any form of communication based on face-to-face interaction.[3]

Private and direct communication includes all exchanges which take place in the course of face-to-face personal interaction between movement activists; occasions range from confidential meetings – for example, of leaders or restricted boards – to discussions within primary groups to all those exchanges where information needs to be restricted within the boundaries of the group.

Private and mediated forms include all the occurrences in which transmission of information and ideas occurs through some technical device, regardless of the level of technical sophistication. Examples range from ordinary mail addressed to members/sympathisers, to telephone calls, to use of e-mail messages. The degree of privacy of these forms of communication may be subject to quite substantial variation: for example, many circular letters addressed to the membership of mass organisations are usually drafted in such a way as to allow for the possibility that the content of the message may become known beyond its original targets. Still, communication here is not primarily designed, nor organised, to reach a public outside given group or organisational boundaries.

Public and direct communication takes place mostly in public spaces, for example on the occasion of public demonstrations or recruitment initiatives. Public addresses, the distribution of leaflets, the very act of marching in a street carrying banners or placards constitute communicative acts which directly (try to) engage the targets of the messages in face-to-face interaction – although the purpose of such activities, and their communicative traits, obviously go beyond direct interaction, aimed as they may be at attracting mass media's attention too. Direct public communication may also occur in those 'semi-public' spaces which constitute the subcultural fabric of social movements: cultural centres, coffee shops, alternative art venues, community associations, etc. (Polletta 1999). I refer to movement free spaces as 'semi-public' rather than 'public' tout court because, while they have no formally restricted access, they are often so heavily shaped by their most regular clients' profiles to discourage people with different persuasions and lifestyles from attending them at all.[4]

Finally, *public and mediated* communication includes all media-related forms. These may consist of press releases, advertising and information campaigns – radio and television adverts, paid announcements in newspapers, etc. – but also of careful strategic 'manipulation' of the media through spectacular activities. The selection of both movement agendas and their leaders or spokespersons on the basis of their estimated potential impact on the media might also be regarded as an example – possibly an extreme one – of 'mediated communication' (Gitlin 1980).

CMC stands in a somewhat ambiguous relationship to these forms of communication. Its private or public nature is unclear. On the one hand, it represents a new version of public communication: not only websites, but also discussion lists or e-mail rosters may be accessed with limited efforts (although access to specialised lists may be easier for those who belong to a specific subculture, search engines make the task relatively easy for outsiders too). On the other hand, as long as access to Internet technology is heavily skewed in favour of better-educated, and/or higher-income groups, then the public nature of CMC may be subject to question (at least by comparison to verbal mass media: printed media in the early, golden – at least by Habermasian standards – age of the public sphere might bear more than a passing analogy to the process of limited access described here).

However, the public nature of CMC is questionable also for another reason, namely, the difficulty of identifying the senders of a message as embodied (individual or corporate) actors, with a specific territorial location. Unless they want to be identified, there is no way to break the anonymity of senders of computer-mediated messages. This breaks with the view of the democratic public sphere as a space where information is exchanged, and opinions debated, between actors prepared to take responsibility for their stances. In itself, there is nothing new in this: after all, especially – but not exclusively – in authoritarian regimes, dissenters of all sorts have always circulated messages without making themselves identifiable by the public (or, most important, by repressive agencies). What is peculiar, however, is the possibility of reciprocity and interaction that CMC offers on a much larger scale than previous forms of communication. While the leaders and activists of underground guerrillas or other clandestine groups could traditionally be contacted only through difficult, uncertain and potentially dangerous negotiations, and subject to the identification of reliable intermediaries, the process is much easier in the case of CMC: that e-mail addresses can be accessed from any location and are located nowhere enormously facilitates dealings with political actors in hiding. The masterly use of CMC by Deputy-Commander Marcos in Chiapas, and the opportunity it gave him to establish regular e-mail contacts to the media, while remaining inaccessible to his opponents, provides an excellent – if frequently mentioned – example (Castells 1997: 68–84; Knudson 1998).

Likewise, CMC is strictly speaking neither direct nor mediated. On the one hand, the technological medium offers a potential for interaction that other mediated forms of communication largely lack. Exchanges of letters between different branches of an organisation require much longer than similar exchanges on the e-mail, to the point of modifying qualitatively the nature of the interaction. Moreover, in contrast for example to telephone communication, which also allows for interaction, CMC – especially in the context of discussion lists – may involve a multiplicity of actors and thus start interactive processes which extend beyond the originators of the exchange. On the other hand, it is disputable whether the warmth and intensity of direct, face-to-face communication may be found in computer-mediated interactions. Although the emotional nature and the depth of virtual experiences and exchanges have been repeatedly underlined (e.g. Turkle 1997; Cerulo and Ruane 1998) it is still unclear to what extent the two experiences can be comparable. This applies particularly to the problem of the sources of trust which are expected to support interaction among people mobilising in social movements.[5] Collective action requires long-term commitments and the willingness to engage in projects that rely upon the contribution of all the parties involved for their success; one has to wonder to what extent virtual interactions are capable of generating mutual bondings of the necessary intensity (Calhoun 1998). Accounts of 'virtual communities' also suggest that most interactions taking place in the virtual sphere actually expand on and reinforce face-to-face acquaintances and exchanges, instead of creating new ones (Wellman *et al.* 1996; Virnoche and Marx 1997). The most successful virtual communities seem indeed to be those where people are expected to disclose their personal identity, and where a core group of committed individuals is willing to engage in some form of 'real' as well as 'virtual' interaction (Tranvik 2000).

CMC, community forms and movement organisations

The capacity of CMC to promote forms of direct communication which transcend the constraints of face-to-face interaction and blur the boundaries between the private and the public sphere may be expected to affect how social movements operate. However, the extent of its impact, and its implications, may differ substantially. We can address this issue by looking, on the one hand, at the efficacy of existing patterns of communication; on the other hand, at the possible creation of new communication channels and the formation of new identities. Beyond the instrumental contribution to more effective mobilisation attempts, the most important question is whether CMC may contribute to 'catness' (Tilly 1978) by transforming mere aggregates of people sharing the same condition into a social network, and thus into a more easily mobilisable group. People exposed to diffused, but in principle individual, grievances may be expected to profit heavily from the opportunities for connection offered by CMC. Permanently ill people, disabled people, victims of road accidents, drug addicts and their relatives experience life conditions which do not automatically entail specific social linkages, and are therefore difficult to turn into collective demands. In such cases, CMC may provide a powerful boost to the establishing of contacts, and thus to the promotion of collective action. The same may apply to groups with specific socio-economic positions and interests, but whose social and geographical isolation discourages co-ordination – think, for example, of the contribution of CMC to the organising of American Midwest farmers (Rheingold 1993: ch. 8).

Any discussion of the impact of CMC has to acknowledge the differentiation in the organisational forms adopted by social movements (or better, by the organised actors operating within them). Although one should not posit a rigid corre-spondence between organisational and communicative forms, still the different solutions that the former offer to mobilisation problems might well reflect varia-tion in the latter. Social movement organisations differ first of all in their *resource mobilisation strategies*. Some of them focus on *professional resources* (in turn made available at times from public authorities or private sponsors, but more frequently from sympathisers' membership fees), others on *participatory resources* (Oliver and Marwell 1992; Diani and Donati 1999).

One should also consider the growing role of what I call *transnational networks*: federations of national chapters (e.g. Friends of Earth International) or coalitions of groups (e.g. the Climate Action Network) mobilising at a transnational level. Although a significant proportion of NGOs operating at this level have individual members,[6] most do not (and even those who do actually recruit largely through their national branches, e.g. Greenpeace). This identifies a different set of organisational problems that CMC may be expected to address.

In order to assess the contribution of CMC to mobilisation attempts by different types of movement organisations, we also need to allow for differences in the characteristics of the population that social movements want to mobilise. A recent typology of real and virtual community forms (Virnoche and Marx 1997) differentiates between situations in which actors share the same geographical space regularly (e.g. members of urban communities), intermittently (e.g. employees of the same firm, students of the same school, or members of voluntary associations), or never (e.g. people sharing some broad world-views, interests, or concerns, but lacking opportunities for direct, face-to-face interaction). The introduction of CMC in such different contexts generates quite different types of virtual social systems. Virnoche and Marx (1997) refer to them as *community networks*, *virtual extensions* (of real intermittent communities), and *virtual communities*, characterised by potentially anonymous and purely mediated patterns of interaction.[7]

Movement organisations mobilising mainly professional resources. Many environmental groups with a participatory profile – for example, WWF or Friends of the Earth – have recently assigned a greater role than in the past to restricted groups of profes-sionals, promoting campaigns funded by passive members' contributions.[8] Other examples may include conservation groups like the National Trust or consumers' protection bodies like Which?[9] On the more radical and confrontational side,

Greenpeace provides the best example of a 'professional protest organisation' (Diani and Donati 1999). Organisations such as these need to mobilise a membership as vast as possible in order to secure the resources to support their professional bodies. All of them address causes which may attract widespread consensus among public opinion and are in principle not especially controversial – although the specific solutions advocated and, especially in the case of Greenpeace, tactics adopted may actually be strongly controversial. Consistent with their emphasis on professional structures, a large section of these organisations' grassroots constituency is dispersed and not organised, as it includes all individuals sharing similar broad views on a given set of related issues. In this case, while it is important to reach potential constituents quickly and at low cost, there is comparatively little need to develop specific strong identities – precisely because members do not need specific incentives to mobilise directly. CMC may increase the effectiveness of communication to ordinary members, and perhaps strengthen their identification by offering some opportunity for a modest involvement in the organisation debate, but with no major impact in terms of identity building and maintenance. The most likely outcome of the introduction of CMC is the conversion of dispersed communities of sympathisers into virtual communities with a slightly higher degree of interaction. The efficiency of the headquarters may also be expected to profit from technological innovation, but no substantial change is likely given the already professional nature of the central bodies. CMC is likely to be most important for organisations such as Greenpeace that combine professionalisation with confrontational strategies. Advanced communication technologies may indeed facilitate dramatically the circulation of news which is so essential to Greenpeace's campaigns.

Movement organisations mobilising mainly participatory resources. Here the picture is radically different. The very existence of these organisations is based on the involvement of the grassroots and on the provision of ideological and solidarity incentives to direct action. Standardised communication from central bodies is usually inadequate in these cases. When mobilisation takes place on a national scale it usually relies upon connecting structures provided either by the local branches of the organisations, or (perhaps more frequently) by other types of organisational infrastructures. These may include other types of associations and informal networks operating as 'transmovement free spaces' (i.e. relational contexts in which activists of different movements may come in contact, thus developing a shared understanding which guarantees the continuity of collective action across time and space); or they may consist of 'indigenous networks' (associational networks of all sorts, not directly related to social movements, but which nonetheless provide the context for social movements to develop – for example, the black churches in the 1960s civil rights movement in the USA); or of 'prefigurative networks', countercultural and/or communitarian settings where movement activists and sympathisers experiment with alternative lifestyles.[10] Whatever the specific form of these networks, CMC may be expected to reinforce already existing ties rather than create new ones.

Sustained collective action is unlikely to originate from purely virtual ties if they are not sustained by previous interaction – as many (e.g. Wellman *et al.* 1996) suggest to be the case most of the time anyway. In Virnoche and Marx's (1997) terms, CMC may be expected to generate community networks – as in the well-known case of Santa Monica, where community virtual networks were behind the successful mobilisation for the provision of elementary facilities to homeless and dispossessed people (Rheingold 1993: ch. 8); or virtual extensions, where ties developed through involvement in associational and other direct networks are reinforced by electronic communication.[11]

Transnational organisations. The impressive growth of movement organisations on a transnational level has been well documented,[12] as has their tendency to operate through coalition and network forms (Sikkink 1993; Smith, Chatfield and Pagnucco 1997; Tarrow 1998b: ch. 11). It is possible to identify several forms of transnational contentious politics. Tarrow defines transnational social movements as

> sustained contentious interactions with opponents – national or nonnational – by connected networks of challengers organised across national boundaries ... [It] is important ... that the challengers themselves be both rooted in domestic social networks and connected to one another more than episodically through common ways of seeing the world, or through informal or organisational ties, and that their challenges be contentious in deed as well as in word.
>
> (1998b: 184)

Other forms of transnational contention include cross-border protest diffusion (where actors copy from each other but then develop largely independently within their own national boundaries), political exchange ('temporary forms of cooperation among essentially national actors that identify a common interest or set of values in a particular political configuration' (1998b: 187)) and transnational advocacy networks. These differ from transnational movements in that they lack the embeddedness in dense networks of face-to-face, daily interaction which is essential to the spread of collective action. In other words, advocacy networks are networks in the sense of connecting structures, but not in the sense of social networks (Tarrow 1998b: 188). While it is possible to identify a few genuine transnational movements (e.g. the peace movement in the 1980s, or fundamentalist Islam), they are outnumbered by advocacy networks on environmental, women's or human rights issues (Porter and Brown 1991: 50–9; Smith *et al.* 1997; Ruth Webster 1998) usually composed of former militants and activist organisations, who connect to promote shared values yet without any form of grassroots structure (Sikkink 1993: 412). Although these networks may promote the resources for the development of domestic social movements (Tarrow 1998b: 192) they should not be regarded as social movements in their own right.

The distinction between movements and other forms of transnational contention is not particularly relevant as far as the practical impact of CMC is concerned.

CMC improves the effectiveness of communication dramatically, and in doing so it often makes the very existence of these networks possible.[13] E-mail increases the co-ordination capacity of groups co-operating on both broad-based campaigns like those on global warming or Third World debt and on initiatives targeting specific companies or governments. Some organisations actually conduct most of their business by e-mail, including decision-making processes (e.g. the Climate Action Network, a coalition of environmental and scientific associations concerned with issues of global warming and pollution).[14]

The distinction is more important from the point of view of identity construction. What Tarrow calls 'transnational social movements' are affected by CMC in a similar way as participatory movements operating within national boundaries and facing the problem of mobilising their own constituencies. As for 'advocacy networks', CMC may strengthen identities and solidarities among their members by increasing the rate of exchange between geographically very distant activists and organisations, and therefore the density of what is, however, a very peculiar constituency. Its peculiarity lies first of all in being an elite of mostly professional campaigners rather than a sector of a 'transnational public opinion' in the broader and more conventional sense of the term. Accordingly this prefigures a pattern of computer-mediated interaction which is proximate to the 'virtual extension' model rather than to the 'virtual communities' one. Although members of the transnational NGO sector do not strictly speaking interact on an everyday basis, they nonetheless have fairly regular opportunities for direct face-to-face interaction on the occasion of international conferences and other related meetings – not to mention the ties originating from previous shared professional or educational backgrounds (McAdam and Rucht 1993).[15]

CMC, social movements and the emergence of virtual society

It has frequently been suggested that CMC will dramatically affect a wide range of fundamental human activities, from work organisation (e.g. through tele-commuting) to democratic procedures (as reflected in the advent of 'electronic democracy') to the multiplication of personal identities and the self (for summaries of the debate: Rheingold 1993; Friedland 1996; Hacker 1996; Wellman *et al.* 1996; Purcell 1997; Turkle 1997). In relation to political and social participation, we may safely expect CMC to operate as a powerful facilitator through 'the maintenance of dispersed face-to-face networks', the development of cultural and 'socio-spatial enclaves', and the technical support to interest group activity (Calhoun 1998: 383–5). However, its contribution to the creation of new types of communities, and to the spread of new democratic practices based on principles of discursiveness and consultation, is far from clear. First of all, most examples of personal interaction in electronic discussion groups actually miss some of the requirements usually associated with the idea of community. Participants in those lists often hide their personal identity, participate only occasionally, are not tied in any sort of committed relationship, and are mostly involved in dyadic or at most triadic interactions (Calhoun 1998: 380; Tranvik 2000). Moreover, examples of community networks such as WELL in the Bay Area or the Santa Monica network suggest that virtual networks operate at their best when they are backed by real social linkages in specifically localised communities, while their capacity to create brand-new ones is uncertain (Virnoche and Marx 1997; Pickerill 2000). Finally, the overall democratising impact of CMC may be severely hampered by two types of resource constraint: while its contribution to networking among citizens' organisations is undeniable, its contribution to the operations of social control agencies, the military, governments and corporations is – at least quantitatively – much greater; and access to CMC is, at least for the time being, heavily correlated to class and status (Norris 1999). In sum, CMC seems to reflect inequality rather than overcome it (Calhoun 1998: 381; Myers 1994; Friedland 1996; Hacker 1996).

The pessimism of some critics (e.g. Calhoun 1998) may be excessive. The speed at which CMC is spreading in the USA and other Western countries leads one to wonder for how long CMC will remain inaccessible to lower-income social groups; nor should one discount the possibility that CMC may affect power-holders' and challengers' opportunities in different ways – by incrementally increasing the former's control capacity, while opening up largely new opportunities to the latter. This would qualify the claim that CMC merely reflects existing balances of power. Still, there are some reasons for caution. The potential to build 'virtual [social movement] communities' seems highest among sympathisers of movement organisations who act mostly on a professional basis and on behalf of causes with a vast resonance among the public opinion – whose radical, if not 'revolutionary', potential is in other words relatively modest. As the collective identity develops in relation to issues (like the environment) which are largely consensual, at least among Western publics, the level of mutual trust required among movement sympathisers tends to be low. A virtual community is therefore more likely to develop even in the absence of direct ties, which are usually regarded as sources of stronger interpersonal trust (Putnam 1995).

By contrast, participatory movement organisations – especially the most radical – are more dependent upon direct, face-to-face interactions, for the purpose both of recruiting members and of securing their commitment. Engaging in what are potentially high-risk activities requires a level of trust and collective identification which is unlikely to develop if not supported by face-to-face interaction (della Porta 1988). Accordingly, the use of CMC may be expected to generate mostly 'community networks' or 'virtual extensions'. Even transnational networks seem to take the form of 'virtual extensions' rather than 'virtual communities', given their reliance on a small elite of strongly connected activists. All in all, the most distinctive contribution of CMC to social movements so far seems to be of an instrumental rather than symbolic kind (see also Bonchek 1995; Pickerill 2000). Existing bonds and solidarities are likely to result in more effective mobilisation attempts than was the case before the diffusion of CMC; it is more disputable, though, whether CMC may create brand-new social ties where there were none.

Notes

Earlier versions of this argument were presented at the 'A New Politics?' conference, CCSS, University of Birmingham, 16–17 Sept. 1999, and at the 'La democrazia nell'era della CNN' conference, University of Padua, Italy, 25–7 May 2000. I'm grateful to the organisers of these meetings, Frank Webster and Gustavo Guizzardi, and the other participants for their critical remarks.

1 Although this view of movements has been proposed as a synthesis of approaches focusing on the Western historical experience, recent research suggests it might well apply to collective action in other areas of the globe (Foweraker 1995; Desai 1996; Kurzman 1998; Rothman and Oliver 1999).
2 Myers (1994) presents a broad overview of these themes.
3 Snow, Zurcher and Ekland-Olson (1980). Cerulo and Ruane (1998) present a sophisticated typology of forms of interaction which goes beyond simple dichotomies like direct vs. mediated.
4 For example, despite their cultural activities being in principle open to the public at large, autonomous youth centres in Italy (Lumley 1990; Dines 2000) or in Germany (von Dirke 1997) may be characterised in this way given their pronounced countercultural profile.
5 Tranvik (2000) presents a general discussion of the relationship between CMC and the creation of social capital.
6 About 20 per cent according to a recent survey (Jackie Smith 1997: 52–3).
7 Another typology differentiates between economic, functional, territorial and extra-territorial communities (Tranvik 2000).
8 Diani and Donati (1999). The extent of the professionalisation of these groups is however a matter of dispute, as the characterisation of Friends of Earth as a 'protest business' (Jordan and Maloney 1997) is at odds with analyses documenting the persistent role of local chapters and grassroots initiatives within the same organisation (cf. Washbourne, Chapter 9 of this volume).
9 None of the examples mentioned totally rules out ordinary members' active participation. But their role is fairly limited by comparison to the role of professional bodies at the centre.
10 I borrow this typology of 'free spaces' from Polletta (1999). For earlier theoretical arguments and extended illustrations see Rupp and Taylor (1987); Roseneil (1995); Whittier (1995); Melucci (1996).
11 Someone could wonder how do phenomena like the use of the Internet by extreme right groups fit this picture, as this seems to generate extensive patterns of linkages between previously isolated individuals (Bonchek 1995). The question is, though, to what extent do these virtual linkages translate into direct action and not simply in manifestations of support. Previous research on recruitment to terrorist activities underlines the important role of face-to-face networks (della Porta 1988). Do virtual linkages operate in the same direction by facilitating the involvement of otherwise isolated individuals in high-risk radical activities? We need more solid evidence to address this question (Bonchek 1995).
12 Using the Yearbook of International Organisations as her source, Jackie Smith (1997: 47) identifies 183 transnational movement organisations in 1973, 348 in 1983 and 631 in 1993.
13 It is worth noting, though, that even transnational forms of campaigning are far from new in absolute terms, as nineteenth-century anti-slavery and Irish nationalist mobilisations suggest (d'Anjou and van Male 1998; Hanagan 1998).
14 Pickerill (2000) offers a broad overview of uses of CMC by environmental organisations, both nationally and transnationally.
15 A very distinctive version of this type is represented by virtual networks of extremist organisations. For example, neo-Nazi groups seem to rely extensively upon the

anonymity guaranteed by CMC to exchange information and co-ordinate violent campaigns across borders. As already noted, we do not have enough evidence to date to assess whether we are facing mainly 'virtual extension' or 'virtual communities' processes.

9 Information Technology and new forms of organising?

Translocalism and networks in Friends of the Earth

Neil Washbourne

Introduction

This chapter considers issues arising from the use of information technologies (ITs) and participative involvement of members in Friends of the Earth (FoE). In so doing it concretises the themes articulated in literature dealing with getting beyond 'simplistic utopian or dystopian views of the future' and the roles of IT in democracy and democratic renewal (Mansell and Silverstone 1997: 3). In taking up these considerations the chapter addresses the capacity of ITs to 'transcend the time and space delimiters of modernist organization' (Loader 1997: 1) and how their participative use in FoE is a demonstration of the limited historical and cultural horizons of a classic of modern organisational literature, Robert Michels's *Political Parties* (1962). This study demonstrates that even a sympathetic attempt to read the reality of FoE national organising and its use of IT through Michels's oligarchy thesis fails, though critical reference to the Michelsian paradigm does sensitise us to changes in society since his time.

The use of ITs in FoE in both local and national contexts gives a detailed example of techno-social restructuring occurring within the real world (Loader 1997: 7) which affects governance at various levels (ibid.: 9) and brings to life again questions of democracy and participation (van Dijk 1999: 84–7).

The construction in FoE of IT's use in translocalist action raises the question of whether 'translocalism' or 'network' is the appropriate formulation for studying FoE collective action and co-operation in relation to ITs, and whether a revamped sociology of organisation possesses the analytical equipment to understand new forms of organisation. This chapter argues that the term 'network', linking non-hierarchical forms and self-organising, is useful but limited for grasping the nature of FoE organising. Further, an exploratory analysis of use of the network term in the social movement literature shows that the term is overextended, possessing less specific explanatory and exploratory value than one might suppose. A transformed analysis of organisation suggests bringing analysis of social movement organisation (SMO) and network operation closer together, yet not allowing the network term exclusive use in understanding non-hierarchical and decentralised forms of organisation. Translocalist and network modes of analysis do not have to be competing formulations but at present the network mode of analysis has not been specified enough to do really useful work.

The transformation of IT use in FoE

Friends of the Earth (England, Wales and Northern Ireland) was studied nationally, locally and regionally. The research was conducted using qualitative techniques: semi-structured interviewing, participant observation, attendance at FoE 'events', and the use of a wide range of FoE publications and documentary sources. The research was conducted between 1993 and 1996.

In the period immediately preceding research fieldwork FoE had some experience of using computers. There was approximately one computer per 1.5 persons at national FoE headquarters and the same in the regional sites managed by national FoE. The computers were slow, and used and developed with no strategy in mind beyond generic support of FoE activity. The predominant use was to support the membership database. Some provision of network facilities had been made through the service provider GreenNet, but these facilities were unreliable and even when reliable of limited use. There were no completely standard software packages on each and every machine.

During the period April to December 1995 the small IT team installed 486 computers throughout national FoE and the seven regional sites to a total of 106 computers, one computer per full-time employee. Each computer was issued with standard software that was Windows based. These included wordprocessing packages, e-mail, Internet access, and fax and voice-mail software. Spreadsheets and databases were loaded for all those who might require their use. Further, a number of new portable notebook computers were purchased and loaded with software for staff or volunteers who might require computer use on the move. All of the computers were linked to an Internet-based computer network, into which all the PCs, Macs and UNIX workstations could be integrated. This task over nine months included the connection of computers at regional sites as widespread as Birmingham, Belfast, Brighton, Bristol, Cambridge and Sheffield. All 'obsolete' computers were disposed of through trade-in, auction to FoE staff, or sale to local groups or aligned organisations.

FoE as an oligarchy

The strong case for seeing FoE as an oligarchy reproduced through the use of ITs would focus on the activities of the FoE national information technology manager. For Michelsians he would be seen, no doubt, as a senior member of the organisation whose activities and interests should be understandable in terms of the promotion of oligarchisation particularly in the light of the massive expansion in IT use, the development of an IT strategy and greatly increased spending on IT. Michels argued that the growth in size of organisations created a technical need for leadership and systems of representation, rather than direct rule by the membership, that could not be addressed by alternative technologies, at least in relation to the technical developments of his day:

> Even if we imagined the means of communication to become much better than those which now exist, how could it be possible to assemble such a

multitude in a given place, at a stated time, and with the frequency demanded by the exigencies of party life?

(Michels 1962: 65)

Does the operation of IT in FoE lead to new ways of resisting oligarchy? Does the availability of different technology from Michels's time have consequences for ordinary members' involvement in organisation?

The IT manager was particularly keen to make IT use in FoE much more proactive, part of FoE's wider engagement with the world, rather than merely part of a support function. In arguing the case for this he was interested in many things: improving the Internet access FoE had been getting from their then suppliers, GreenNet, and expanding this into a bulletin board service, a computer conference facility and an FoE electronic archive. More than this, he was highly critical of FoE's hoarding of information in myriad databases that could not be accessed by all, nor be of guaranteed data quality. His concerns, read in a Michelsian light, would lead one to suppose that myriad organisationally dispersed databases might be a decentralising feature, and that his desire to centralise database access could be understood within a wider oligarchisation of FoE in which technological knowledge becomes a key to social power within the organisation. That might be believed, even though in press releases and articles about the prospective FoENet in FoE newsletters he had focused upon issues more connected to decentralisation in emphasising empowerment of FoE members in general, the creation of new audiences for FoE and the role of new emerging participative information cultures (Longhurst 1995: 16). For a true Michelsian this would be leadership eyewash.

Certainly there was some resistance to the wider use of IT, especially the Internet. This resistance was primarily based upon the expertise FoE members had built up over many years. A senior campaigner, for example, was unsure whether she could trust information she retrieved from the Internet. She was aware that there was no peer review as there was for journals or other information sources she used regularly. The IT manager overcame this limited resistance, but his success did not arise out of Michelsian control over debate. Rather his approach embodied the participative culture of FoE that pre-existed IT use and was carried over in the new technologisation of FoE with renewed energy.

Possible resistance was overcome because others within FoE already felt positively addressed by the informatisation of society in general. This was clearly shown in the meeting and training course attended by seven employed or volunteer members of national FoE. As experienced and skilled members of FoE they already inhabited a rich, hermeneutic world of information sources, contact numbers and so on that they brought together as part of their support activities or for pursuing campaigns. They were enormously positive in encouraging the expansion of FoE's capacities to use these information sources and expand their own IT skills and experience. A member of the Geographical Information Systems (GiS) team planned to use the *mediadisc* software in conjunction with GiS for cross-referencing pollution maps to local press reports, to produce 'interactive workout of pollution incidents'. That everyday informatisation could be easily argued as congruent with FoE's globalist values by the GiS manager is rather important here with regard to the extension of informatisation which until then had proceeded in a piecemeal manner. The GiS manager argued in a series of conference papers on the use of global information systems that many of them were the embodiment of the environmentalists' maxim 'think globally, act locally'.

FoE members, although positive to IT in general, certainly needed persuading that changes to their busy campaigning and informational lives would yield dividends for their ability to connect to each other, help them save time for other valuable pursuits, or give them more leverage in their battles with other powerful social forces (local authority, state, business). If information technologies could help do these things while being congenial to their fundamental values (Friends of the *Earth*; For the *Planet*, for people) they would consider them, use them and judge them.

The IT manager's preferences for FoE worked out because the IT plan and its implementations fitted with members' desires, experiences, values and judgements, not because he held sway over them. It fitted because, in FoE, members' everyday experience of IT helped them carry out the informational tasks so important to FoE, giving them experience of the technology and some awareness of its multiple possibilities. It fitted also because of the futuristic possibilities recognised, say, in the newsgroup meeting (Washbourne 1999: 124–9) that new wider publics could be addressed using the technology while supporting the wider globalist value position of FoE. Thus it was crucial for IT to be interpreted within the wider cultural and social setting of FoE, as the GiS manager argued, and answer to that setting, even as that setting itself was modified by its encounter with IT. This setting I have called the moral order of FoE, a negotiated and negotiable ordering of practical and value relevance which is an order of accounts (cf. Washbourne 1999: 87–90).

Translocalism against oligarchy

A significant defence against oligarchy has been the translocalist, empowered action of, in particular, local groups and group members. Translocal action in FoE has proved itself open to global or any other linkages that it can actually make and uses a variety of resources to do so. IT particularly has been used by local groups in order to aid translocal linking. The importance of translocal and trans-localist action is that it is decentred, connects to other places without having to go via centres, whether of power or geography, and is both pragmatic and embedded within translocalist value positions.

In making sense of translocalism within FoE we necessarily draw away from Michelsian analyses. Translocalism is decentralised action (which can nevertheless, out of its own interest, concern or need, take part in more centralised action). Translocalism is both a new reality in contemporary organising, and points towards a different mode of attention to what was there already in many kinds of organising. Translocalism points towards the construction of action via resources, accounts and other social materials. It suggests that Michels's belief that social action and institutions can only be constructed in certain kinds of way with hierarchical authority relations and domination by elites is not true and that its untruth is not revealed by a changing interpretation of organisations but by an empirical analysis of organising on a translocalist basis. Translocalism in FoE has its foundations in the local and regional group situation of skilled and know-ledgeable actors. This can be seen empirically in the campaigning, publishing, researching, networking 'origin' of translocalist action (Washbourne 1999: 116–41). If there are boundaries to such action, they are boundaries of choice and their own making, not the boundaries of authority.

FoE local groups have also taken on board informatisation independently of national FoE; one might even say ahead of national FoE, as if being near what might be called the centre made it harder to see the congruence between values and IT. This itself has become an arena for new local and national group rela-tions, most notably through the regional action of the Local Group Networking Project (LGNP). This tied together regional campaigning and e-mail and Internet support to carry action and campaigns out across the separation by both space and time of FoE local and regional group members.

The appropriate frame of reference for the LGNP is the attempt within FoE to support local groups much more fully than has been done in the past, and to be seen to be doing so by other local groups. Thus it is for the longer-term reordering of local–regional–national relations, as well as the recognition that they were already in the state of being reordered, that national FoE funded it. The project arose out of early 1990s Local Groups' Annual Conference calls from local groups for more support for them from national FoE. This led to open competition for funding for projects. Eight West Yorkshire local FoE groups joined company to bid for money to aid regional campaigning and e-mail linkages to enable regional campaigning by aiding communication. The groups were awarded £20,000 in order to 'put in place the conditions which would help a sustainable, effective campaigning network within West Yorkshire to grow'. This project plays with the ambiguity of the term 'networking', meaning either engaging in human relationships on the one hand, or a developed 'web' of computers and electronic linkages on the other.

An FoE local group member in the West Yorkshire region explains it thus, particularly to any other FoE members, on the national FoE local group pages:

> Our pilot [scheme] has two main aspects. One is to experiment with electronic wizardry . . . to increase communications between [local groups] . . . by linking them up with computer networks . . . The second element . . . is to employ a part-time co-ordinator for the County. There is a huge potential for County-wide campaigns . . . For voluntary groups to be employ-ing a person is going to be interesting, and management structures have been the subject of many a meeting![1]

This upbeat message – available to the rest of the FoE network so long as they have Internet access and available to any other Net surfer – misses out the pain and agony of actually constructing a new enterprise of this type. For a start the smooth relations that hold in the final report between the objectives of the project – transformation to regional campaigning; to communicate effectively by infor-mation technology; development of the human network; increase the level of fundrais-ing; increase the membership and community links – are not necessarily without contradictions and different levels of emphasis even within the West Yorkshire group, let alone between national and local FoE.

The focus of the original bid (October 1994) was to employ a part-time cam-paigns co-ordinator to enable regional campaigns and to 'expand and manage the existing electronic network'. Significant involvement of the Local Group Development Officer (LGDO) was envisaged, as was the joint management of the co-ordinator by 'Underwood Street [national FoE headquarters] and the eight local groups'. The concluding paragraph of the bid shows the balance between local group and national FoE interests in the project:

> The West Yorkshire groups would like to contribute to the development of FoE and its aims by taking part in this pilot scheme. We believe that the experiences that could be learnt from such a scheme would benefit not only the environment in West Yorkshire but also the FoE local groups network as a whole.

The actual bid submitted was a larger document, the result of a further two months' discussion. In it more detailed targets were articulated as well as a better worked-out rationale of why national FoE should be interested in this particular 'local' group bid. These included the notion that it would prove 'that such a regional campaigning network can work with mutual benefit and effectively with UWS [Underwood Street] – in campaigning, financial and technological terms'. Further the generality of this project was stressed since it would 'provide evidence to allow FoE to assess whether it is possible to replicate the project elsewhere'. It was intimated that a result of this might be increase in membership not only at the local and regional level but also at the national level, and fundraising increases in both. The electronic link was preferred to the development of a central office to facilitate information access by greater numbers of West Yorkshire members, allowing communication without the need to travel, to allow communication between local groups, regional groups and Underwood Street, and to allow the co-ordinator the same access. This last proposal had the co-ordinator managed from Underwood Street.

The transformation in bids allows us to see the regional grouping's responses to 'getting real' about the bid. They recognise the interest of national FoE and try to address it in concrete ways. At the same time, although identifying with a wider FoE identity, they are perfectly clear who they are and what they wish to get out of this project. Further they were on the way to incorporating many of these changes into their own activities before the success of the bid. Their trans-localism was in existence before the project and was able to be elaborated and encouraged by access to greater resources and minor formalisation of thinking that involvement in the project encouraged.

This was recognised in the original bid. The human and electronic networking had already starting taking place. Since October 1993 the groups had 'work[ed] closer and better together as well as providing meetings to discuss TPPs, water catchment plans etc.'. They had also started using e-mail though this was very much the minority: three groups linked via only five activists with access. Mostly this access happened through work. One activist worked in computing, others had access via professional employment.[2] Thus independently of the bid and the project links that had been made across local groups, translocalism was in operation linking skills, knowledge and energy across the region. Some members of the regional grouping felt that they were more members of the regional grouping than of local groups.

This 'free' sociality, a development of unconstrained social relationships linking like-minded well-resourced members across physical distance, existed prior to the project or even the e-mail links in the groups but was greatly aided by both the project and the e-mail use. It is what I call translocalism.

E-mail use between local groups in itself is only an aspect of translocalism, an indicator, rather than its defining feature. E-mail use within the groups became deep if not widespread. Seven of the eight groups were using e-mail regularly for information dissemination, co-production of reports and communication. Access caused minor problems because of the low number of computers per group membership. Although all groups 'acknowledged that this was a big issue in their group' this did not stop a high level of communication between those who did have access. Typically members sent in excess of 200 messages in a few months. These included messages to arrange meetings, messages in lieu of meetings, the organisation of campaigns, sending reports, etc. The activists who did have access were able to cut down on the number of face-to-face meetings. Symbolically access to e-mail was a crucial feature in identification with the West Yorkshire grouping. Some even feel more identified now with that grouping than their local group. This version of their translocalism supplemented local group identity with a regional identity.

Translocalism was elaborated in co-operative writing and sharing of local–regional expertise. The use of e-mail and computer disk to pass copies of 'report writing in progress' around the network asking for comments, suggestions and improvements was felt to be key to the quality of booklets produced out of the regional grouping and an important elaboration of non-oligarchic relations. There was no one expert telling the others the answer to environmental ills but rather a shared group writing, incorporating the talents of the many while contributing to their own skilling up and education. This was most keenly felt with regard to writing the booklet *Road Traffic – Stemming the Tide*. A similar process of deliberative and direct participation went into this as goes into many reports of national FoE (Washbourne 1999: 92–115). The drafting of sections, reading and writing, the combining and shared proof-reading of a booklet allow for a strong sense of involvement, achievement, identification and development of knowledges and competencies in addition to identities. As the LGNP co-ordinator states: '[t]his seems to expose a huge area for development of the representation of regional expertise'.

The report highlights (quite literally) that where e-mail is not being used then this may be more due to lack of certainty about the need for wider networking rather than about using e-mail. Thus for the future FoE may need to address the question: Is it that groups currently 'aren't used to being part of a *network of local groups* but are more used to communicating only with Underwood Street'? (emphasis in the original). This of course raises the issue of how happy national FoE would be to be bypassed. The claim made in the report on the LGNP by the co-ordinator immediately after the sentence cited above is 'E-mail has the potential of making the local groups into a real *network*, with groups and activists working more closely together without the need to go through Underwood Street. This has been borne out in the Pilot Project, albeit on a smaller scale, with group members being directly in touch with each other's campaigns' (emphasis in the original). This suggests that the translocalism of the LGNP and of the West Yorkshire grouping and local groups may be in advance of its development in some other local groups. Translocalism as achievement may be unevenly developed and depends upon available time and commitment, as well as the skills and knowledgeability of members.

The future for that regional grouping looks likely to include more time and energy spent on the IT side of regional co-operation. Local groups see IT as supporting translocalist action of local and regional groups within the moral order of FoE and this is a key reason why they have embraced it. Translocalist action is action transcending particular places; practical action using the skills, resources and knowledges of local groups as they exist. This action doesn't just belong to a specific location, and can be expressed as far as the groups and members wish to express it. Although the concept of translocalism has been developed to understand FoE organising we need now to consider the concept of network which was referred to in the LGNP and is seen as a key notion in understanding contemporary organisation.

Translocalism or networks?

The issue of the conceptual and real importance of networks and networking has been raised not only in the LGNP but also in key texts in contemporary social science. Networks, they have argued, are the new forms of organisation of our times, in capitalist corporations, global criminal organisation and social movement organisation (cf. Castells 1996, 1997, 1998; van Dijk 1999). The operation of networks in both Castells's and van Dijk's accounts is crucially related to the strategic utilisation of ITs. 'Networking' as a way of understanding organising in FoE clearly has some useful points – the focus on lack of hierarchy, the role of informal connections and the emphasis on self-organising. Thus FoE can easily be read as possessing network elements. However, the word 'network' can commit us to assertions and distinctions we do not wish to make. As I have argued, this research instead focuses upon translocalism as key in restricting oligarchy in FoE, and its impact upon organising such that organisation becomes different, looser, impacted by informal organisation and more able to respond to the exigencies of the world.

The use of 'network', where positive, seems to benefit from the idea of networks as forms of organising that easily span space, and are self-organising and non-hierarchical. Thus the idea that FoE's 'original' origins are in transnational friendship networks articulates the first point strongly, the second only slightly less so, but the third only a little since Brower, the originator of the FoE idea, chose the other network members and dominated the construction of the network (Washbourne 1999: ch. 2). The distinction between human networks and computer networks, as evidenced in the LGNP discussed earlier, seems to revolve around the distinction between actual linkages and the mere capacity for linkage. The distinction between 'real' and 'apparent' networking, articulated in the LGNP, points to the value of the term network as the self-organising deliverer of goods rather than a quiescent potential for the same.

In order to make sense of the term 'network', distinguishing theoretically valuable or essential elaboration from merely speculative ones, we need to investigate the use of the concept of network in social movement theory, where social movements, such as the environmental movement, the object of my research, are understood as networks.

Organisations, networks and social movements

I shall use Donatella della Porta and Mario Diani's (1999) comprehensive guide to social movements, in particular focusing on chapters 5 and 6 concerning 'Movement networks' and 'Social movements and organizational form'. This volume is perhaps the most comprehensive introduction available to the social movement literature.

In my own analysis of FoE as an organisation I have emphasised the importance of translocalist and informal organising as part of the grounds for resistance to oligarchy. FoE's organisation includes both more and less formal elements. Contemporary analysis of organisations confirms this more broadly (Law 1994; Grant, Keenoy and Oswich 1998). No longer are organisations seen merely as rational, single-goal-oriented hierarchies but rather the product of performance, discourse and multiple decentred forms of organising. This marks both a change in mode of analysis and a change of actual organisation in the world.

In her chapter on 'Social movements and organizational form' Donatella della Porta sees this change as a result more of changes in actual organisation than changes in modes of analysis as such. The rise in modes of participation in the student movement of the 1960s arose, she argues, out of a critique of 'the traditional left's bureaucratic structures' (della Porta and Diani 1999: 137). Eventually, though, a need was felt to go beyond merely spontaneous structures. However, rather than Michels's (1962) single, big oligarchic organisation this led to a panoply of organisational possibilities: local nuclei; umbrella organisations; parties; public interest groups; movement associations; and supportive associations (della Porta and Diani 1999: 144–6; cf. Doyle and McEachern 1998: 62). It is accepted in her analysis that there is no single model of organisation for social movements and also no predetermined organisational evolution. Both conclusions deny the claims of Michels's 'iron law'. Nevertheless she also recognises that modes of analysis are important. She rejects old-style theories of bureaucratisation and oligarchy for organisation study (della Porta and Diani: 147) arguing that the iron law of oligarchy was only ever 'valid for certain kinds of organization and environment' (ibid.: 151). In accepting change in the world and in modes of analysis of organising she is open to analysing the adaptive and creative transformation of models of organisation in social movements, even allowing for alliances with institutional actors which allow them to maintain 'a more informal and decentralized structure' (ibid.: 164). Specific forms of organisation are compromises with the dilemmas of any possible forms of organisation. Searching and innovating among organisational possibilities members try to satisfy demands for both participation and efficiency (ibid.: 163) (cf. Doyle and McEachern 1998).

Seen in this light translocalism in FoE local and regional organising can be seen as the latest attempt to satisfy efficiency and participatory demands. Network-type organisation places perhaps more emphasis on participation than most but networks must surely also answer to members concerning effectiveness.

In his chapter on 'Movement networks', however, Diani (della Porta and Diani 1999) maintains a rather stronger distinction between networks and other types of organising even if that organising is relatively non-hierarchical. Diani is particularly keen to conceptualise the connection between actor relationships in social movements and broader social dynamics (ibid.: 112). He uses the idea of 'network' chiefly to understand recruitment to social movements. Networks are seen as important for the recruitment of activists and the mobilisation of supporters as various studies have shown that between two-thirds and three-quarters is a product of network membership (ibid.: 113), the density of links being positively related to the likelihood of sharing inspiration, convictions and points of view. This notion has not been accepted without a challenge (ibid.: 114–15). The most significant problematisation has come from the claim that as social network membership is ubiquitous it will always be potentially possible to point to prior social network commitments and involvements as the (potential) cause of mobilisation. Although Diani takes this objection seriously, the way he deals with it is not completely satisfactory. He has committed himself to networks alone as the mode of organisation and mode of analysis appropriate to social movements.

In another publication (Diani 1992: 13) offers us an interesting and illuminating definition of a social movement in terms of networks:

> a network of informal interactions between a plurality of individuals, groups and/or organizations, engaged in a political or cultural conflict on the basis of a shared collective identity.

Diani has it in mind to make a concept that can do the useful work of differentiating the social movement from related phenomena such as political parties, interest groups, coalitions and protest events (ibid.: 3) and by doing so articulate a specific area of investigation for social movement research. Diani makes a fundamental opposition between social movement and forms of organisation which is actually concerned with the question of structure versus flux: '[t]his concept takes into account the greater organizational rigidity and the more hier-archical structure that these organizations display by comparison with social movement networks' (ibid.: 14). Diani is concerned that if this distinction is ignored this might 'foster . . . the application to social movement analysis of concepts borrowed from organization theory, that only partly fit the looser struc-ture of social movements' (ibid.).[3] As I argued at the start of this section, and as della Porta also recognises, organisational analysis now has incorporated as central to its activities taking into account the *fluidity and discursivity* of organisation, thereby fostering a mode of analysis much more suited to understanding looser forms of structure. Thus the claim that Diani makes, that the concepts ' "public interest group" and "sect" ' don't really capture the interaction processes of moulding shared systems of beliefs way beyond the boundary of any particular organisation (ibid.), does not exclude the fact that the conceptual equipment of contemporary organisational sociology might be precisely appropriate to this task. Newer forms of organisational analysis are more discursively based and the boundaries of the organisation are not assumed from the start but must, rather, *be established* (Law 1994; Grant, Keenoy and Oswich 1998; Albrow and Washbourne 1997; Washbourne 1999). The boundaries of FoE, as understood in my research, had to be established by a procedure rather like an analysis of networks of involvement. Not to have engaged in this procedure would have been to cut off many angles of the research that established the performance of FoE from multiple centres in relation to shared identity. My own approach integrates *newer organisational analysis* with an appreciation of the looseness of structuring of much organising. The fundamental opposition between networks and organisa-tions is not, I consider, helpful. Nor is it the case that the network concept is the only appropriate one for analysing such looser structuring.

Both empirical and theoretical considerations are at issue here, of course. Diani is prepared, conceptually, to concede membership of social movements to organ-isations that are open to interactions with other actors, and that are characterised by conflict and collective identity. Thus openness to interaction and charac-terisable by conflict and collective identity might hold, for him, for 'bureaucratic interest/groups, and even political parties' (della Porta and Diani 1999: 15–16). However, this judgement is in fact quite a tough one. How open to interaction and how far characterised by questions of conflict and collective identity? If the interest in asking these questions of organisations is the concern to address the fluidity and flux of reality then the change in mode of analysis of organisations, exampled earlier, deals with that consideration more successfully than the judge-ment adjudicating membership of a social movement to an organisation on the basis of demonstrable interactional, conflictual and identitarian factors. Wasn't it always rather that membership or not of social movements was a question about whether members of social movement networks considered other bodies to be a part or not? In this way clear demonstrability gives way to perspectivism since members of networks will have differentially considered organisations as members. Surely it is preferable to see networks and formal organisation and all forms in between as linked. They are all *forms of organising*, each of which has different characteristics and consequences to its use. In this light della Porta's analysis of organisational forms each articulating the dilemmas of organising in different ways is suggestive and most appropriate (della Porta and Diani 1999: 163).

This organisational plurality seems to me to be the strength of social movements (cf. Dalton 1994: 246) and at the same time causes both a problem and creates an opportunity for social movement analysis. First, if, with Diani, we do not consider organisations part of the movement *per se*, then analysis of organisational forms, though necessary, and of some importance to understanding stages of social movement history, will always be seen as peripheral to the 'real thing', analysis of the movement *qua* movement. Second, these organisational forms should not be separated from an analysis of the movement as embedded within and carried by networks when there is less reason now than before to see organisations merely as stable, crystallised end products of movement rather than part of movement themselves. To focus on networks to the neglect of (other) social organisational forms forces social movement analysis into distortion.

Further, it is the case that many of these so-called networks are in fact other forms of association (groups, teams, cliques, pressure groups, parties, sects, churches, etc.) and should be analysed as such, not merely to understand mobilisation, but the whole activity of social movement organising. The opportunity for social movement research is to integrate analysis on the basis of networks with that of organisational forms. By which I do not mean that they should be treated as if they were simply the same but rather they should be seen as being built out of the same human activity – forms of organising. This appears to be the approach endorsed by some social movement researchers (Tarrow 1998b: 123–4; Doyle and McEachern 1998: 62, 101).

Network is a useful and often unavoidable concept. So long as it is not over extended, analysing as networks what are other organisational forms, and so long as it is not used merely oppositionally to the concept of organisation then it can be an invaluable analytical tool (cf. Doyle and McEachern 1998: 63–5). In transforming our analysis of organisations integrating looser non-hierarchical conceptions is essential. However, analyses may not always require the network concept.

The examples we have seen of the empirical operation of translocalism in FoE demonstrate the absence of hierarchy and fluidity of organisation. In this respect it does much the same work of the term network. However, unlike the concept of network, translocalism draws upon a variety of forms of organising to articulate itself, both networks and more formal organisation. As such, translocalism is a more substantive conception for analysing organisational life and encourages us to engage with the messiness of organisations as well as their dominant organisational forms.

Conclusion

IT use in FoE has grown greatly in the 1990s in terms both of expansion of the amount of IT used and its intensification. Michels would have understood this within wider claims about organisational concentration, centralisation and oligarchy. In FoE this is not the way IT use has expanded. At both national and autonomous local group level there was a participative discussion about the benefits, pragmatic and ideal for FoE, arising from IT use. The expansion of IT use arose in relation to a widely shared conception that IT could not only help FoE influence public policy and environmental debate but also was congruent with FoE's globalist values. I call that action, arising in specific, local circumstances but able to mobilise resources to go beyond the merely local, *translocalism*. Although it has the benefits of loose and non-hierarchical structure the term 'network' does not express the specificity of translocal organisation. Nor is 'network' used in the wider literature with the clarity which could make its use more than a perspectival marker for non-bureaucratic administrative and organisational modes. Diani's use apparently takes 'network' to be pure flux yet the social world can only resemble flux more or less. Any determinate action, idea or meaning reaches out of flux into some form and mode of ordering. We need conceptions that enable us to grasp both flux and ordering and at present 'translocalism' has much more to be said for it than 'network'.

Notes

I wish to thank Kate Nash for careful reading and insightful comments on earlier drafts of this chapter, and two anonymous referees for careful criticism.

1 http://www.foe.co.uk/local/news/north/loc-gp.htm
2 This raises a central issue which I discuss in detail elsewhere. The backbone of the 'limits to oligarchy' (see Washbourne 1999: ch. 4) is the knowledgeability and skill of FoE members, in particular of local group members as members of autonomous local groups.
3 Doyle and McEachern (1998: 65) share this concern and also relate it the 'biases of the organizational sociologist at work'. They, though, also relate organisations more closely to the wider social movement since to neglect to do so 'gives a one-sided account of the dynamics of their actions' (ibid.: 85).

10 Weaving a Green Web

Environmental protest and computer-mediated communication in Britain

Jenny Pickerill

Introduction

Environmental organisations, groups and individual activists have been utilising computer-mediated communication (CMC) for several years to facilitate their political projects. CMC is more than an extension of existing forms of communication. It offers an enormous variety of opportunities to environmental activists to which they have not previously had access and, as such, activists have utilised CMC in many ways. The British environmental movement is diverse and factionalised, and yet CMC has been adopted by the majority of groups within the movement. This ranges from the more institutionalised non-government organisations (NGOs) such as Friends of the Earth and Greenpeace, to the informal, looser networks of individuals involved in groups such as Earth First!, Reclaim the Streets and McSpotlight.

The potential benefits of CMC appear to be particularly suited to the activities of, and are being extensively utilised by, environmental activists (Castells 1997; Young 1993). Primarily, CMC offers new potential for *organising* and *mobilising* cross-nationally more quickly and cheaply than previously. Second, it is distinguished from other forms of media by having *fewer editorial constraints* upon it, providing editorial control to all users (Atton 1996). Third, environmentalists have in the past used new technology *quickly* and *innovatively*. Often they utilise it in ways that challenge existing doctrines and exemplify alternatives (Warf and Grimes 1997). Thus an examination of environmentalists' use of CMC provides insight into how such technology can be used in ways that differ from corporate or government use and possibly indicate future trends. Finally, environmental activists take up, with alacrity, the very technologies that are pioneered by their opponents, and the same technologies that are facilitating the processes that many are opposing, for example, globalisation. This dynamic poses challenges to the activists as well as to their corporate disputants. As technology has historically been viewed with scepticism by environmentalists, their utilisation of CMC seems paradoxical in that CMC requires the use of advanced technology whose production and use have extensive environmental and social consequences. Environmentalists have negotiated this paradox, by recycling equipment, using renewable power sources, or asserting their role in maintaining the freedom of the Internet from corporate control.

Social movement theories offer an instructive framework through which to examine the British environmental movement. In particular, the social movement processes provide concepts through which detailed analyses of the implications of CMC are possible. Of these processes three in particular highlight the potential of CMC. First, CMC enables a *greater audience* to be reached and thus potentially increases the number of those who could be *mobilised* into environmental protest. Second, CMC facilitates *increased interaction* between *dispersed individuals* who may exchange information which will aid others in their campaigning, or simply encourages others to continue. Each scenario is likely to impact upon the identity of environmental activists, which in turn is important to the cohesiveness of the environmental movement. Third, CMC can be used to develop *new tactics* of environmental protest and thus add to, or change, the repertoire of action. This chapter considers how CMC use has influenced the organisation and mobilisation of participants, identity formation and changing repertoires of action in three environmental groups in Britain. These are Friends of the Earth UK, Save Westwood, Lyminge Forest Campaign and McSpotlight. They were chosen as each represents a differing style of organisation, location, ideology and tactics, and each has utilised CMC for multifarious purposes.

Using these case studies, the ways that environmental groups use CMC differently and for alternate purposes will be demonstrated. It will be argued that participants are still mobilised most effectively if they are within existing movement networks, rather than non-integrated individuals. This is despite the potential of CMC to reach a wider audience than previously contacted by social movement literature. However, groups such as FoE, who do not require the physical presence of activists, are able to stimulate on-line activism by individuals not necessarily politically active in other ways. In terms of organisational structure, all groups can benefit from the speed and relative cheapness of CMC. Those organisations which are less hierarchical, smaller and more flexible are particularly able to take advantage of the technology as they are not restricted in their CMC use by bureaucracy or protocols. In particular, e-mail enables activists to keep in touch from dispersed or transitory locations (as some direct action environmentalists find themselves peripatetic). Similarly, all groups can benefit from on-line encounters that strengthen their feelings of solidarity. This could be most keenly felt by those involved in a small physically isolated campaign, such as at Lyminge, or those involved in a group which has limited resources to produce regular newsletters or magazines. Finally, despite potential to use CMC to develop new forms of protest tactics, its use is often restricted to that of an additional communication tool. Relatively few instances of on-line activism or electronic civil disobedience are practised by British environmentalists, though CMC is still used in many innovative ways.

Environmental politics, environmental movements

Social movements emerge as combinations of individuals join and project their opinions into the political arena. Social movement theory offers a framework through which the workings and events of movements such as the environmental scene can be analysed. Such an approach seems preferable to those that consider organisations only in terms of 'interest groups' or 'pressure groups' and their effects on the political system in the context of political science methods, or descriptively as part of a 'DiY counterculture' (McKay 1998). In contrast, social movement perspectives such as those advanced by Melucci (1994, 1996), Castells (1997) and Diani (1992) enable a greater depth of analysis into the actions of the diverse social movement participants. These actions occur on several levels (personally, culturally and politically), all of which need to be examined in order to understand fully the processes which produce the tangible products of social movements in, for example, non-violent direct action, protest events, or political lobbying. Many of these processes remain hidden using other approaches, but are vital in the constitution of the social movement's functions.

Diani (1992) has attempted a synthesis of the numerous social movement perspectives in order to produce a general definition of what constitutes a social movement, irrespective of the different theoretical perspectives. He proposes that a social movement is a network of informal interactions between a plurality of individuals, groups and/or organisations the boundaries of which are determined by the collective identity shared by those involved, whose 'actors are engaged in political and/or cultural conflicts, meant to promote or oppose social change either at the systematic or non-systemic level' (Diani 1992: 11). Finally, that social movement action occurs within and outside the institutional sphere[1] (cf. Doyle and McEachern 1998).

Social movement analyses are increasingly being applied to the British environmental movement. Wall (1999) utilised many of the concepts in his examination of Earth First!, and Chesters (2000) has argued that such theory is the most appropriate way to probe the underlying processes that result in the actions of the British radical environmental movement. The British environmental scene is vigorous and vibrant and yet diverse and deeply factionalised. It is composed of many elements that have a variety of ways of being politically active. The environmental movement is the sum of all the different structural forms that exist within the environmental scene: the individual, network, group and organisation. The movement thus encompasses all the assorted eco-philosophies and positions held by these actors. Many of the individuals involved in networks or informal groups, or groups such as Earth First!, do not believe in taking part in formal traditional politics (Rüdig 1995). They consciously abstain from electoral politics and instead promote do-it-yourself (DiY) politics, normally through direct action, for example against the Newbury bypass or a Reclaim the Streets event (Doherty 1997). In contrast, organisations tend to be more formalised and are involved in both the politics of non-institutional social movements and the institutional politics of government. These are often defined as non-governmental organisations (NGOs) – permanent, and well defined with a constitution. They are by and large autonomous from government and operate at local, regional, national and transnational levels.

The British environmental scene can best be conceptualised as a social movement. It has a tendency towards informal participatory democratic modes of organisation, a fluid structure of networks, and a mix of non-institutional and institutional politics. Combined with its counter-hegemonic aim towards changing societal values in a paradigmatic battle with the dominant model of society and concentrations of power, it fits within Diani's, and many other theorists', definitions of a social movement.

Communication in social movements

Having established that social movement theory can offer valuable insights into the workings of the environmental movement, it is time to consider how such theories can relate to the way environmental activists are utilising CMC. Despite the wealth of literature that has examined the potential implications of CMC upon society (see e.g. Jones 1997), there has been relatively little attempt to place such discussions within the social movement perspectives.

Social movements contest and create cultural patterns in contention with the prevailing model of society. In order to express their views communication is vital, both within the social movement itself and out to other movements, political decision-makers, the media and the public. Accordingly, social movements historically have been concerned with access to, and use of, communication technologies such as the printing press, television, radio, CB (Citizen's Band) radios, mobile phones, photography and video. In this context the use of CMC could be viewed as simply an addition to the other forms of communication technologies utilised. However, CMC is more than just an extension of existing media and potentially may trigger fundamental changes in social movement processes. In addition, Melucci (1996: 194) suggests that the use of CMC could develop into a general conflictual issue of its own since it

> concerns the control of programming languages and of the various media relating to computer assisted communication. On the one hand, there can be observed a concentration of power, with very few core centres that control the world in terms of the world-wide transmission and distribution of ideas, languages, programmes, and the like; on the other hand, we can see emerging symptoms of resistance to this trend, manifest in, for example, the action of hackers, information pirates, self-managed networks, and so on.

Furthermore, Melucci's concept of the production of codes can be considered in terms of CMC. In this programmed/technocratic world much of society revolves around the production of information and communication resources. Conflict arises around these issues and social movements form to challenge the apparatuses that govern the production of information (principally their opponents, the government and corporate interests) in order to reveal that the dominant system of meanings is not neutral but reflects vested interests and unequal forms of power. Thus the social movements are seeking to 'recast the language and cultural codes that organise information' (Melucci 1994: 102). This is achieved through a number of channels, with some groups attempting to use mainstream media, while others prefer to project their own message through alternative media and CMC. Codes are also challenged culturally by exemplifying alternative lifestyles and through street protest. CMC potentially increases social movements' participants' ability to communicate because it is low cost, offers editorial control, and promises an international audience.

In this respect then even the most basic-level advances and changes in the form of communication technology which are adopted by movement activists may well aid their capacity to form and project alternative codes to the wider public and their political adversaries. Whether their adversaries will benefit to the same extent from communication technology advances and thus out-rank any movement advances has yet to be seen.

Internet, e-mail and social movement processes

Internet and e-mail use has the potential to impact upon many social movement activities and its influence can be examined in detail by considering these processes separately. Thus, the way in which CMC may alter how social movement participants are mobilised, its networks and organisations, identity, opportunity structures, repertoires of action, movement intellectuals, and how space is created for debate can all be appraised in order to determine the effects of Internet and e-mail use on the social movement as a whole.

Most obviously there is likely to be increased efficiency of operations. CMC use offers speed in terms of response, information gathering and networking ability to social movement organisations (SMOs), which in turn might alter their organisational capabilities. There is also a potential for an increased diffusion of ideas and tactics across social movements and geographical areas. Use of CMC may enable less hierarchical forms of organisation to exist more effectively than previously and thus reduce the pressure towards professionalisation that many SMOs face. Technology use may also create divisions within the movement between users and non-users, increasing the risk of exclusion and divisions within the movement. At the same time, CMC offers opportunities for new forms of tactics to be developed using the technologies, such as flooding a company with e-mails, or overloading a website with too many requests for information. Movement intellectuals' ideas may be able to be distributed more freely and consumed within the social movement and thus aid their ability to stimulate protest. At the same time, however, CMC also enables vast numbers of other individuals to distribute their ideas more freely and critique existing intellectuals, and thus may enable new intellectuals to develop, and the movement to move further towards 'participatory democracy'. In this way activists could use CMC to create a space for debate between themselves, or with the public and government. Let us examine more closely some of these processes.

Participant mobilisation, networks and organisations

Movement networks are often viewed as the cornerstone of any attempts at mobilisation (della Porta and Diani 1999). Research so far has concluded that recruitment and mobilisation is reliant upon inclusion and integration within social movement networks (Wall 1999; McAdam 1988). Initial inclusion in social networks is reliant upon face-to-face interaction. However, Jasper and Poulson (1995) have been able to identify that 'strangers' can be recruited into collective activism in the absence of social networks, through 'moral shocks'. Moral shocks refers to a public event, individual experience, or generated condensing symbols. It is suggested that movements use both mechanisms for recruitment: the existing social networks and moral shocks.

CMC could contribute to these forms of mobilisation in a number of ways. It may serve as a useful technology through which to articulate moral shocks to a wider audience than previously possible. There remains doubt, however, as to whether participation is likely to occur without previous interaction (Wall 1999). In this volume Diani has argued that the usefulness of CMC in mobilising participation is dependent upon the types of resources that organisations are attempting to mobilise. Those mobilising professional resources (such as FoE) are expected to gain in terms of efficiency of communication at headquarters, to members and to the media, but this is not likely to impact upon identity building as there is little need to mobilise direct action.

For those mobilising participatory resources (such as direct action groups) mobilisation remains reliant upon existing linkages. Thus, Calhoun (1998: 383) argues that CMC may facilitate actors' participation through 'the maintenance of dispersed face-to-face networks', but that these networks would have to pre-exist for meaningful virtual interaction to take place. In this way it is unlikely that purely virtual ties will result in sustained collective action. What is of particular interest is whether CMC might be able to replace the importance of face-to-face interaction.

SMOs link to each other through both official consultation channels and the multiple affiliations of their activists. CMC use is likely to improve the effectiveness of this communication in terms of increased speed, reduced costs, persistent accuracy of the original message, increased interaction between branches of organisations and the possibility of connecting a geographically dispersed set of individuals into a united aggrieved population (Myers 1994).

Use of CMC may also affect the 'strength' of movement networks in that communication becomes simultaneously both easier and more fragmented. Those who are connected are able to communicate with others connected more quickly, easily and cheaply than before. For those who are not, the use of CMC by other groups can actually begin to exclude them as they become left out of conversations, and communication with them without using CMC appears to become relatively harder. Although clandestine groups have long existed effectively within many social movements, CMC facilitates not only their anonymity, but also their connections to other SMOs without revealing themselves. CMC use may increase communication between the different types of groups by providing yet another form of communication.

Technological development is likely to change the forms of organisation (Tilly 1978). CMC use offers speed in terms of response, information gathering, networking ability to groups and reduction of co-ordination costs, which in turn might alter their organisational capabilities. The utilisation of CMC may reduce the requirements for a highly structured organisation, in that it is now possible for a 'lightweight' one to get a message across. Although the use of CMC requires some technical proficiency,[2] it also affords more flexibility to groups who can benefit from the lack of editorial control. This once again reinforces the proposition that CMC may facilitate the development of less rigid and formal organisational forms (and reduce the push towards professionalism), enable smaller groups to voice their views more successfully and perhaps trigger mobilisation. However, although in principle evolution towards institutionalisation may be challenged by the use of CMC, it is more likely that the process would have been challenged anyway by wider forces calling for greater accountability and democratisation (Washbourne 1999).

In summary, the way that groups are currently structured and their ideology will significantly affect the way they choose to utilise CMC and thus its potential for change. For example, the more radical groups may embrace the technology more enthusiastically as a new resource for change, while a well-established group may feel less inclined to risk a potentially expensive venture into new territory.

Identities

The creation and shaping of identities within social movements is vital to the successful mobilisation of collective action and to the maintenance of the movement through latent periods (Johnston *et al.* 1994; Castells 1997). CMC could facilitate the building of collective identity and solidarity, by increasing the ability of individuals to communicate with other like-minded activists, in a form of 'direct' communication, strengthening feelings of identity even across dispersed networks. Whether virtual interactions have a similar capacity to formulate identities as face-to-face interactions needs to be examined.

A key aspect of this may be the requirement of mutual trust, which is essential for mobilisation purposes. The problem is how mutual trust is created through virtual interaction (Tarrow 1998b: 193). In virtual interactions activists seek some form of validation of the individual or group, for example through word of mouth or through the linkages from websites that activists approve of. This validation and approval of sources has also been sought in social movements from printed media and alternative media sources.

CMC use may also enable a cross-movement, cross-cultural interaction and thus change an individual's view of their identity. For example, s/he may move from being primarily concerned with local environmental issues and through Internet use begin to view themself as a political activist with wider concerns. Similarly, an environmental activist may begin to interact, through CMC, with for example computer hackers. As a result each could acquire new skills and develop a new identity. Finally, CMC use may affect their identity perceived by their opponents and critics as being modern, non-Luddite, pro-progress and innovative by using a technology with which many of the mass public are not adept.

Repertoires of action

The repertoires of action of a movement refer to the set of strategies, tactics or forms of protest which are employed by its participants. Repertoires of action are likely to be strongly influenced by historical traditions, diffusion of ideas from other social movements or cultures, movement leaders' choices and political opportunity structures (Doherty 1999a). The repertoire of action is also finite, limited by both time and space, such that techniques of protest evolve slowly, limited by tradition, adapted from previous forms, and this in turn might actually limit innovation to the margins (Wall 1999).

The use of CMC clearly extends the existing protest repertoire in terms of providing another tool to be utilised during protest organisation and campaigning. In particular CMC use will affect the need to gain media attention. Trying to gain media attention is particularly difficult, primarily because moderate actions are not newsworthy, yet extreme acts will be condemned and, even when coverage is given, actions are often represented without explanation of the proposed message. The use of CMC could radically alter this search for media representation, by enabling self-representation to a wide audience. Traditionally many choices of repertoires of action have been based on the assumption that their actual action will be mediated by the media and more powerful actors. The use of CMC challenges this assumption as it enables the activists themselves to mediate their message.

In addition, the use of CMC enables the development of radical new forms of action which were not previously possible, such as the use of electronic civil disobedience, and could aid the diffusion of information about the construction and operation of tactics, which previously would have had to be distributed through underground publications and word of mouth.

Overall, the use of CMC may do more than simply enable new forms of action to be developed at the margins of existing repertoires, such as adapting existing notions of civil disobedience to the electronic sphere. It may also enable the merger of previously distinct sets of action into new forms, such as the use of on-line tactics simultaneously with street tactics, and change the focus and characteristics of the repertoire of action more fundamentally.

Case studies

Although it is evident that Internet and e-mail are having an influence on social movements and their activities, to date there has been little empirical analysis of the situation. Currently, much of the commentary is anecdotal and/or speculative. The following addresses these shortcomings by reporting research undertaken between 1997 and 1999 for case studies of Friends of the Earth UK, Save Westwood Lyminge Forest Campaign and McSpotlight.

Friends of the Earth UK

Friends of the Earth (FoE) UK is one of the biggest and most influential of the UK environmental groups (McCormick 1991). FoE UK has attempted to initiate radical changes in government policy and societal behaviour. Its strategy has been five-pronged. Primarily, it has concentrated upon lobbying government, giving evidence at public inquiries and increasingly consulting on Parliamentary Select Committees. FoE also works with businesses to improve environmental practices. Second, its concern has been to collate or generate accurate infor-mation and research about environmental problems and disseminate this to the public. Third, FoE has employed the media as a tool to stimulate public debate. Fourth, in order to empower individuals and communities to take action locally FoE has expended resources into the support and formation of a network of local groups. Finally, FoE has pledged to co-ordinate with other groups to effect change. These tactics are operated through the FoE UK network which is composed of the national office, regional campaign co-ordinators and 250 local groups. It has attempted to reflect its desire for participatory democracy within its internal dynamics (notably by the national office overseeing campaigns but not determining local group activities), but is simultaneously critiqued for being too hierarchical and bureaucratic.

The transformation of FoE UK from a small number of enthusiastic people in the 1970s to a large organisation in the 1990s has altered its internal dynamics (Rawcliffe 1992). FoE has had to respond to the tension between the centralising forces of UK politics and the decentralising demands of local activism by developing a regional structure of FoE comprising of the election of regional board members and eight regional FoE offices (Maynard 1998).

The FoE UK website was launched in 1994 and e-mail was simultaneously installed across the organisation. The website was begun by IT staff, supported by the enthusiasm of Andrew Lees and Richard Weatherley. Originally an IT project, as it developed campaign teams began to take control of sections and development policies were designed. Now there is one full-time Web producer who co-ordinates the website and another who co-ordinates the Intranet. By 1998 their website was attracting over 20,000 visitors a week (*FoE Annual Review* 1998).

At FoE UK headquarters most staff have access to a computer and their own e-mail accounts. All the regional offices are also connected to HQ by permanent ISDN lines, which allows them access to the Intranet. The pattern of access by local groups is more chequered as they have to fund CMC themselves and rely upon volunteers to set it up. Although FoE's original concept of FoEnet included extending its facilities to the local groups, this vision was never realised due to an estimated and unfeasible expense of £500,000 (Lamb 1996). Also few have an office space so access was restricted to a computer in one member's own home.

Despite these problems many local groups have their own websites and many co-ordinate campaigns via e-mail (Ritchie 1999).

Save Westwood, Lyminge Forest Campaign

The Save Westwood, Lyminge Forest Campaign is an organic direct action protest that was not the by-product of a particular organisation or pre-existing group. Situated in West Kent between Canterbury and Folkestone, the forest was occupied by protesters in March 1997 in an attempt to stop the Forestry Commission sale to Rank for development into a private holiday complex (Newsome 1997; Garner 1997). Between ten and one hundred protesters have lived on site since March 1997 (Daly 1997). They built tunnels, towers, tree houses and hanging lock-ons in a number of camps spread across the wood in an attempt to raise the cost of their eviction and disrupt Forestry Commission plans to sell the wood (Goodwin 1997).

In order to prevent this development they (as in the loose networks of individuals associated with the campaign) have employed a number of tactics.[3] Primarily their occupation of the site is an act of resistance to any attempts at clearing the wood to build the development. Through this act and associated media attention they have also sought to raise the public profile of the proposals in order to gain mass support to pressurise the local council and Forestry Commission. They have also undertaken other acts of direct action in attempts to persuade Rank to change policy. Notably a group of forty protesters occupied the boardroom of Rank HQ on Wednesday, 13 August 1997 (Krinks 1997). Finally, on some of their publicity flyers they have encouraged writing to MPs to support the on-site protesters' action.

The campaign has had several websites and there have been requests for support and eviction alerts sent out over e-mail networks. Only one of these sites was under the direct control of the on-site protesters and was started by Merlin and Sef in early 1997. Its format has altered significantly since, but the content has remained relatively the same. It held information about the purpose of the protest, contact details, a wish list, map and Rank's plans. It included colourful graphics and photographs. Overall the website is extensive, detailed and designed to appeal to a wide variety of audiences.

Within this protest only a few individuals actually had access to CMC and influence upon the website. CMC was used to provide information to other activists and sympathetic individuals in order to encourage them to visit the forest in person, give their support and to generate interest at a national and inter-national level. Use of CMC relied upon the enthusiasm of certain individuals for the technology and thus its use was of a personal nature as opposed to the structured work nature of FoE use.

McSpotlight

McSpotlight was a website launched on 16 February 1996. It was established in conjunction with the McLibel trial of two members of London Greenpeace for allegedly distributing libellous material ('What's Wrong With McDonald's?' pamphlets) about McDonald's (Vidal 1997). Although created as a separate venture from the trial and involving different individuals, the website supported the case of the defendants, posted up the original leaflet that was classified as libellous, and had notes from the two-year-long trial.

The McInformation Network, a loose coalition of individuals, created the website (George 1999). Many people joined in to do a small section of work or a specific task and then left, while others continued to be involved through the height of the website, between February 1996 and the end of the appeal in March 1999. McSpotlight was a collaborative but ad-hoc effort with a core of volunteers who did not overtly attempt to dominate decisions about content. The aim of McSpotlight was threefold. Primarily, it was to gather all the critical information it could about McDonald's and to make this publicly available, attempting to shame McDonald's and to challenge corporate bullying. Second, it acted as a support network for all those aiming to expose what was disguised by the public relations campaigns of multinational corporations. Finally, it was to demonstrate that attempts at censorship and silencing critics will not only fail, but also backfire, that rather than dampen dissent, it would be inflame it because CMC provides a forum in which activists no longer need to rely upon the attention of the traditional media to distribute their message, but are able to distribute their own information (George 1999).

The McSpotlight site gained an international reputation as a hugely popular site. It won many awards (for example, the NetGuide gold site and EuroCool site of the day), was often referred to in Internet magazines as an example of a great activist site, and gained significant mainstream media attention (see e.g. Neuborne 1996), which itself raised the profile of the McLibel trial (Reed 1999). McSpotlight website contained over 20,000 pages with many different sections, several mirror sites[4] around the globe, and international contributions. The site contained sections about the McLibel trial, campaigning tools, a debate area, and further information about the issues. It also contained a 'Beyond McDonald's' section which illustrated that it was not just McDonald's whose business practices needed to be questioned, but those of many other multinationals. There was also a large press-cuttings section that collected information that had been written about McDonald's or McSpotlight and it contained court transcripts and transcripts of interviews with key witnesses and the defendants themselves.

The use of CMC was crucial to the McSpotlight campaign. It was the unregulated and uncensorable nature of the Internet that enabled the activists to publish the libellous documents and also to publicise the case and the cause to an international audience. Such publication was technically breaking British law, but as the site was hosted in the Netherlands the legal situation was unclear, providing a loophole which McSpotlight utilised. The website and e-mail enabled them to update readers regularly on the trial situation without printing newsletters and having to distribute them. A discussion forum was also set up on the website where participants could swap ideas and arguments.

Mobilising new forms of protest?

These case studies have all utilised CMC for various purposes and in alternate ways. Each has a different organisational structure and contrasting resources. I want now to examine in detail each of the social movement processes which were outlined above with respect to CMC use in these cases.

Mobilising activists and encouraging new participation

There are a number of ways in which FoE UK's use of Internet and e-mail has the potential to mobilise participation and strengthen movement networks. One of FoE's main sources of local participation is through its network of local groups and CMC has been seen as a valuable addition to existing communication methods between the national office and local groups (Lamb 1996; Pipes 1996). However, while the head and regional offices have CMC access, local group access remains marginalised and uneven across the country, and despite an increasing number of local groups utilising CMC some are still wary of its usefulness. Ian Welch, former co-ordinator of Newcastle FoE, commented about the amount of time that creating a website takes:

> I'm trying to be careful about the amount of time I spend on it . . . it hasn't had a huge number of hits . . . and you don't want to be spending hours on it when you could be out there handing out leaflets which will actually get to a wider range of people.

Burt (1999) suggested that CMC has facilitated FoE's networking imperative and has enabled local groups to become 'information hubs', sharing their knowledge and experience throughout the FoE UK network. This appears somewhat optimistic. First, local networking has always been practised by FoE and has been specifically aided by the presence of regional campaign co-ordinators. Intranet, Internet and e-mail are just extensions to such efforts (Washbourne 1999). Second, although aspects of CMC, such as the e-mail-based campaign networks discussion lists, have facilitated information sharing, there are still significant barriers to effective inter-group communication. Rather than facilitating nationwide networking, CMC has enabled local groups to be better able to utilise the information available from head office, but not necessarily from each other. E-mail is still rarely used for intra-group communication (though there are a few exceptions; see Ritchie 1999) and less so for inter-group dialogue. Its main purpose appears to be to communicate with, contribute to and use the information from head office.

Information provided by one local group would eventually be utilised by another once it is on, for example, the Wild Places website.[5] However, this use of CMC, rather than encouraging the formation of a national non-hierarchical network across FoE groups, actually reinforces the importance of a central head office. The central office remains the hub of the network, the focal point through which most information passes, just as it has always been. In this sense the hopes that CMC might aid FoE UK's attempts to disperse more power to the regions and local groups seem unlikely to materialise. Regional campaign co-ordinators are increasing in importance as the focal hub of regions, though at this level co-ordination is still preferred face-to-face or by telephone.

What CMC has enabled is the localisation of information that can be specifically utilised by local groups to aid their campaigns. Although FoE has often placed an emphasis upon mobilising participation at the local level, many of its campaigns have been run at a national level, using national data. Websites such as Wild Places and Factory Watch[6] have enabled data to be provided at the local level, a task that had previously been prohibited by cost. Placing databases of information (about wildlife or factory pollution statistics) on the website has enabled local groups to create their own specific maps or data charts according to their interests rather than relying upon general national data provided by staff at the national office. This has shifted the task of providing information from the staff at the national office to the local groups themselves. Local groups have benefited from greater access to this specific information, which in turn is likely to have helped mobilise them to launch local campaigns.

FoE also attempts to recruit and mobilise individuals through its website, though few new members have been so recruited[7] and other forms of communication retain their importance. However

> the Web is beginning to be considered as a comparable mechanism to print, in terms of numbers, of getting in front of the public. This is new, and the balance is set to tip in favour of the Web over the next few years.
>
> (Web producer)

The Midlands regional campaign co-ordinator also believed that CMC was not particularly useful in mobilising local support around an issue, but that it had

> added to our ability to campaign, but the fundamental way that we are going to carry on campaigning is by engaging people on the street and talking to people and putting our message over through local media, and the Internet just adds another medium through which we can get our campaigning message across.

Information on-line, especially data local to individuals' residences (such as Factory Watch), may act as a form of 'moral shock' and trigger individuals' involvement in FoE campaigns. FoE has also begun to utilise e-mail to encourage on-line activism, mobilising environmental activism without the need for face-to-face contact. The Climate on-line campaign, launched in August 1997, was an e-mail network of individuals who, at the command of FoE, sent out personal e-mails to world leaders attending the UN Climate Change Summit in Kyoto urging them to protect the environment. The response was disappointing for campaigners:

We should get 50,000 people involved in theory, but we have got 2,000 so far. But a lot of these are very active . . . when we ask them to do something about 85 per cent of them do it, which I think is really quite a high percentage.

(Web producer)

Apart from networking within the FoE channels, CMC has been used as an additional channel through which FoE can communicate with other SMOs. The Real Food campaign was co-ordinated extensively with non-FoE groups mostly via e-mail. Simon Festing, FoE's housing campaigner, set up a new website called URGENT (the Urban Regeneration and Greenfield Environment NeTwork). It was an autonomous site, but funded by FoE, and had information from a variety of different organisations:

we've [FoE] provided the money for this website to be set up but it's being managed externally by this network URGENT . . . so while I'm having input, so are the other people. It's just about co-operation.

(Simon Festing)

Distinct from participant mobilisation, CMC could alter the organisational structure of FoE. As illustrated, Internet and e-mail have facilitated new and quicker forms of communication within the FoE national network, especially to the local groups. The Intranet has also aided information provision and discussion within the core of FoE UK (the head and regional offices). Such use has not been without its organisational problems, however, as there were tensions between what campaigners desired electronically and IT resources and capability:

A number of related problems have further limited the role of IT, staff demanding unrealistic, open-ended, nebulous systems and ignoring technical limitations of information systems, poor forward-planning from users, with sudden and unrealistic demands on IT staff . . . technical staff ignoring real-world organisational problems and concentrating on esoteric issues.

(Richard Weatherley, former IT manager)

Also, although public enquiries were increasingly arriving via e-mail, response tended to be via post, as much of the requested information was not available in electronic form. There were also criticisms about the lack of overall co-ordination of the website, a task that has since been taken up by a newly created post. The size of FoE as an organisation and the sheer amount of information available sometimes impairs its ability to update information quickly. Like other FoE publications, in order for new information to go on the website the information must be cleared through a procedure and a set of channels. FoE has had to impose rules on the use of CMC, establishing an e-mail etiquette and protocol, effectively enforcing boundaries on its use and encapsulating it within policy guidelines. This can restrict its potential or effectiveness in use and means that FoE UK is unable to benefit fully from the speed and interactivity CMC offers.

The Save Westwood, Lyminge Forest Campaign used Internet and e-mail on a much smaller scale than FoE UK. The main aim of the Lyminge website was primarily to attract participants to the forest and to encourage them to bring supplies. It was also to raise public concern and generate media coverage by publicising the protesters' existence and activities to as wide an audience as possible. In order to mobilise participation the activists spread the news through word of mouth, underground literature (such as *SchNEWS* and *Earth First! Action Update*), press releases and telephone trees.[8] CMC was used in parallel to these methods, both through the website and by sending out requests for participation to several e-mail distribution lists. Although activists were attempting to reach a wide audience and encourage general support, they were also trying to reach those already within, or sympathetic to, the movement. This could be achieved through the existing network ties and communication structures, but more quickly and cheaply through CMC, which is faster than newsletters and more able to reach a wide audience than word of mouth:

> it helps a lot having the website because you are just reaching people, people who are like-minded and doing the same kind of thing . . . basically they are activists.

(Blue)

It is likely that potential participants would hear about the protest through several of these channels. Furthermore, even if individuals had only heard about the protest through CMC and then visited the forest, they may have already been integrated into movement networks. It is hard, and probably impossible, to tell whether CMC actually mobilised participation of a previously non-integrated individual.

Of those on site only a few had even heard of the website before they had arrived in the forest. While some questioned its usefulness, arguing that word of mouth was the main way of getting information out, some, such as Merlin, argued that the Internet had been a useful mobilising tool: 'I know of quite a lot of people who visited the forest because they had heard about it over the Internet.' E-mail was used as a tool for regularly updating people about the protest situation while the maps on the website were used by some visitors to help locate the forest. International attention was attracted through their website publicity, and visitors arrived from Canada, Poland and Germany. One of the main problems identified by the website designers was the inability to update it regularly, and the lack of information on it. Mike felt that if it had been more dynamic and interactive then users would linger on the site longer and perhaps be intrigued enough to get involved in the campaign.

The use of CMC at Lyminge did not particularly affect the organisational structure of the protest. As the protest was based on site in the forest the majority of the participants undertook autonomous tasks of their choice based within their specific camps. Few on-site protesters had seen or contributed to the website. Of those interviewed the majority were aware of its existence, but did not particularly want to become involved and seemed happy to leave its responsibility to someone else. The lack of permanent office space also meant that there were limited opportunities for new participants to become involved in using the Internet. The result was that there were effectively just a few 'gatekeepers' to the website and despite their attempts to encourage participation it became the preserve of a select set of enthusiasts. This was in contrast to other site activities, as Ben told me: 'When we write leaflets people tend to go round the site asking if anyone wants to help or put stuff on it, but not for the Internet.'

In contrast to the Lyminge protest, the Internet was central to McSpotlight. McSpotlight encouraged the public to inform themselves and to use this information to demonstrate against McDonald's. The site was designed as a resource for a variety of people, and included campaigning materials and the original libellous leaflets translated into twenty languages to print off and hand out. The website was specifically structured to be accessible and easy to use by the public, using a fresh and innovative design, with site maps, an introductory tour and a search engine to help new users around.

The site received a large number of hits (over 70 million by February 1999), but also the most mainstream media coverage of any website in the world (George 1999), stimulating its notoriety and spreading the information further. E-mail was also a valuable technique for information dispersal, where list servers were used to keep people up to date. 'The global McLibel list server now has nearly two thousand people subscribing to it,' said McLibel defendant Dave Morris. Overall, the McSpotlight site, coupled with the McLibel trial, received so much attention that it has triggered a general media critique of McDonald's:

> We've got massive amounts of attention . . . feedback from people around the world, massive amounts of hits on the information, the leaflets have been distributed to millions of people world-wide . . . so we definitely feel like we achieved out aims.
>
> (Devin, McSpotlight volunteer)

It is obviously difficult in such situations to determine precisely what mobilising consequences McSpotlight had. The anti-McDonald's campaign had been in existence for ten years prior to the website and means other than CMC had been used to distribute the information. Dave Morris counselled that

> you can over-exaggerate, a website doesn't replace direct distribution of information to the public and in this country alone three million leaflets were handed out during the case direct to the public.

The media attention McSpotlight received was indeed large and in many ways the campaign achieved its aims. It prevented McDonald's being able to silence its critics, raised the profile of the McLibel case and illustrated the potential of CMC for activist campaigning. McSpotlight served as a blueprint for many other activist sites. Its high profile and success at outwitting McDonald's have mobilised others to use the Internet for environmental campaigning and illustrated how CMC can be used to link together previously existing networks into new forms, and on an international scale. One of the outlets from the McLibel trial was the film 'McLibel: Two Worlds Collide'. It was banned from national television and so a global screening was planned using e-mail to market the idea:

> From just one e-mail message, 104 screenings in 19 countries were held and we estimate that about 8 million people watched the film. Which kind of makes me think that there's a lot of untapped potential in e-mail.
>
> (Franny Armstrong, McLibel film producer)

McSpotlight was able to utilise CMC to mobilise huge media and public interest in its campaign, and also stimulate others into distributing the information further. Without CMC doubtless the campaign would have continued, but CMC enabled them to reach a wider audience, develop a large support base, stimulate local actions, and, as their use of CMC was in itself novel, stir up media attention. CMC was also obviously essential in the organisation of McSpotlight. The contributors to the site were spread internationally, with fifty people from across the globe, and e-mail was used to help co-ordinate these efforts:

> There are now people from fourteen different countries working on the project, using any equipment they can get their hands on. We tend to communicate using e-mail, most of us have actually never met.
>
> (John, McSpotlight volunteer)

The use of CMC has altered the way in which these three case studies attempted to mobilise participation and structure their forms of organisation. FoE UK has been able to encourage on-line activism and for new members to join via its website. It has also facilitated local participation through the provision of local data. Those at Lyminge succeeded in raising the profile of the campaign, attracted some new visitors and established international links through CMC. Finally, McSpotlight attracted international media attention, generated participation of others in its attempts to distribute information and reached a wider audience than its pre-CMC methods had achieved. All have benefited from the speed and relative cheapness that CMC offered, whatever forms of organisation they had chosen. In particular the less hierarchically structured Lyminge and McSpotlight campaigns appeared to benefit especially from CMC. Its flexibility suited their organisational structure. Many activists do not have office space or a permanent address (which causes access problems to CMC), but e-mail enables many to keep in touch from whatever location they are in. This facilitation of networking strengthens the ties that bind the movement together.

All cases did to some extent attempt to mobilise non-integrated individuals. The 'moral shock' tactic was invoked by websites such as FoE's Factory Watch, and McSpotlight's facts about McDonald's, trying to alert people to their local situation. Significantly, though, both Lyminge and McSpotlight attempted to use CMC to reach those sympathetic to and already within the environmental movement in order to mobilise their participation. Specific targeting through e-mail lists facilitated this. As illustrated, it is possible to mobilise, without face-to-face contact through CMC, those who are already within the movement networks (or similar movements). CMC is simply a quicker, cheaper and more global method of utilising these networks. CMC has also strengthened existing network ties by easing the passage of communication between dispersed individuals. In all cases, although a wider audience, not previously linked into the networks, was also contacted, there was no evidence that participation resulted, only that it was easier for such individuals to grasp the information. FoE has been able to create a virtual community of individuals who will act electronically when requested to do so, but it did not attract as many participants as was hoped and the potential for off-line collective action seems limited.

Such findings appear to be supportive of Diani's assertion that groups such as FoE will be able to create virtual communities whereas those requiring direct participation do not require on-line communities or desktop activism – they require physical presence. Their main focus of campaigning remains to mobilise others to take to the street or forest or picket line to voice dissent physically and publicly. To attract such presence they rely upon the existing network ties while simultaneously attempting to inform the general public of their campaign.

Identities on- and off-line

FoE UK's presence on the Internet added to its existing image as a provider of information. It has also aided FoE's interaction with some of its critics. During the early anti-road protests FoE was accused of not giving full support to the more radical direct action protesters (Lamb 1996). In recent years, however, the provision of the field locations for the testing of genetically modified crops, which were then used by direct action protesters to locate and destroy the crops, led to the accusation that FoE was encouraging such action (Barber, quoted in *The Times*, 1998: 11). E-mail has enabled interaction between FoE and more radical protesters, as they can co-exist on the same e-mail distribution and discussion lists. The campaign networks on-line and e-mail discussion lists centred upon specific topics have also enabled interaction across dispersed networks nationally, perhaps contributing to those involved feelings of solidarity. Finally, the use of CMC by FoE helps challenge the stereotype of anti-technology environmentalists. The IT technical and support manager commented, 'I think it has probably changed our image as not Luddites, not against progress, not automatically against technology.'

Activists at Lyminge Forest also created a powerful image of the modern-day protester, quashing the stereotype of the anti-technology environmentalist, when media attention focused on their use of wind turbines and solar panels to recharge car batteries. These were then used to power CB communications, computers, radios and tunnel ventilation systems (Newsome 1997; Nuthall 1997). One participant, Matt, also felt that distributing information to the public through CMC might help dispel inaccurate assumptions about the protesters:

we've always got to be seen in a good light [for the protest to change public opinion], so putting it on a website sees us in a more acceptable light. It's no longer underground subversive eco-warriors, it's like everyday environmentalists having tea with the local parish, stuff like that.

CMC also served to boost the morale on-site at Lyminge. By making contact with groups internationally and receiving supportive e-mails activists felt a sense of solidarity with others, even when on-site numbers were low. This correlates with Warf and Grimes's assertion that CMC will 'reduce activists' feelings of isolation' fostering 'the sharing of useful ideas and strategies' (1997: 268). Through initial CMC contact international visitors came to the protest and had skill-sharing sessions, further enabling a cross-cultural interaction.

McSpotlight was about challenging the threats from multinationals and the British legal system. It was not the first time that an international network has been established to criticise the workings of a multinational (for example, Nestlé has also been targeted by an international campaign for several years). However, CMC enabled interaction between individuals across the globe and a rapid exchange of information. It served as a point of amalgamation for all the information individuals had been collecting for years. In this way individuals were able to feel part of something bigger, they were able to feel solidarity with each other. It drew together individuals from a range of movement backgrounds, further facilitating cross-movement and international interaction. In the words of one volunteer, Devin:

> It's making protest movements feel like they are international . . . it's really being felt within activist circles that we are part of a global movement against capitalism and neo-liberalism and it's enabled boundaries to be crossed over.

Identity is a fluid construct that alters with new interactions. CMC enables numerous new interactions between people who may even be within the same movement but who have not worked together before, and it facilitates international, cross-movement, collaboration. All case studies benefited from such encounters that aided their feelings of solidarity and of being part of something bigger than their own campaign. Environmentalists' use of modern technology helps crack the image of them as primitive hippies living in a past age, 'These people are media-friendly, technology-literate and unencumbered by outdated ideological baggage' (Conor Foley, quoted by Brass and Poklewski 1997: 98). Environmental activists are increasingly being perceived as very innovative, adaptable, skilful and armed with an array of technology to help them communicate and co-ordinate (Chesters 2000). The potential of CMC is still largely unknown and as such the users in the case studies felt optimistic of their chances at success. They felt better prepared to fight for their cause, as Devin says:

> The Internet is the first time that grassroots activists have had a media where there is a level playing field with the multinational and all their millions of dollars.

Environmental activists' innovative use of Internet and e-mail has also helped determine how their potential is viewed. Their use is shaping the way the technology is likely to be used in the future by illustrating, through success stories such as McSpotlight, that political activists can benefit from its utilisation.

Tactics

FoE UK has utilised CMC to facilitate most of its tactics: political lobbying, accurate information provision, a proactive approach towards the media, developing local networks of activists and co-ordination with other environmental groups. Use of CMC has not altered FoE's main aim – that of providing information about the environment to stimulate change in societal attitudes, but it has opened up new techniques through which to achieve it.

FoE has utilised CMC to develop several innovative websites providing interactive access to its databases using Geographical Information Systems on-line. For example, its Wild Places site provided an interactive map illustrating the UK's Sites of Special Scientific Interest and the threats to them. Factory Watch also enabled users to create their own local maps and rank factories according to several criteria. It took official government pollution data and tried to make it clear and accessible to the public. This is a new tactic in information provision which enables locals to campaign more effectively in their area. The launch of the Factory Watch campaign triggered an increase of 500 per cent of people accessing the website, an indication that people were actively seeking the information. Its launch also appears to have stimulated a response from the Environment Agency, which a week later launched its list of top ten polluters (Nuthall 1999). FoE has also utilised CMC to push legal boundaries it might not otherwise have challenged (as it officially does not endorse illegal actions), by placing its banned mahogany advert[9] on its website and was one of the main sources for the on-line lists of locations of test sites for genetically modified organisms, crops which were subsequently destroyed by direct action protesters. Thus, FoE has utilised CMC as an additional channel through which to distribute information in innovative ways.

The media is crucial to FoE both to spread its message and marshal support for its demands. It uses the media to advertise the information on its website, and uses its website campaigns (such as Factory Watch) to capture the attention of the media. CMC is used by the Media Unit at FoE to aid their collection of information, but the mainstream media 'are reluctant to use it and ignorant about it' (Ian Willmore, Media Unit). CMC is also used to bypass the mainstream media and give direct contact with the public, 'allowing the real facts to be read without our message being distorted through the media prism' (Pipes 1996: 63). The result of this may be a change of emphasis in FoE from attracting media attention to ploughing resources into the Internet in order to distil its message. However, use of the media was never purely to spread environmental information, but also to bring pressure to bear upon politicians. The Internet is unlikely, in the medium term at least, to have the same effect as a damning headline in a national paper in forcing the government to react.

The use of CMC by Lyminge Forest protesters was primarily as an additional tool to the media they already utilised. It was not utilised as a new technique of protest. This was not due to a lack of ideas (Mike voiced many future plans for the site: 'you could have an interactive trail on-line which takes people through the forest and highlights all the wildlife . . . We have unlimited space on the Web page which we are not utilising at all'), but instead reflects the many constraints that hinder political action: commitment, time, money and expense (Warf and Grimes 1997). Not surprisingly, activists living in the forest had problems gaining access to a computer with an Internet link. There were also pressures on the time required to write Web pages; 'with so few of us here all the time . . . so few constants . . . and so many different places to point ourselves' (Mike) it was hard to justify their time spent using CMC. At the end of the day, if the defences were not built then eviction would have been much easier for the Forestry Commission.

The website itself did not encourage any form of action using CMC. It asked for donations, encouraged visitors, suggested boycotting or writing a letter of objection to Rank, and was used as an additional tool to aid the traditional forms of action, publicity and information distribution. The protest was centred on a physical location and was very much about physically protecting that 'real' place and space. That those in control of the website were eventually living on site full time and thus clearly believed in on-site direct action probably contributed to their emphasis upon physical participation.

McSpotlight's existence was in itself a new tactic. They were pushing at legal boundaries, and created several innovative features on the website:

> an awful lot of what we did was ground-breaking stuff and it was using the media in ways it hadn't been used before, for example frames . . . to hijack the McDonald's website and deconstruct it.
>
> (Devin, McSpotlight volunteer)

McSpotlight encouraged action in a number of ways. Volunteers were requested to help construct and maintain the site, give donations (both financial and equipment), adopt-a-store (an attempt to leaflet every UK McDonald's), or join a mailing list. The McSpotlight Kit was available to download to help prevent the site ever being shut down and several mirror sites were established. A key feature of the site was the Debating Room that encouraged uncensored discussion about McDonald's with an international audience and participation. A guided tour was developed of McDonald's own website pointing out inaccuracies and untruths (mixing two sites into one was innovative at the time) and the McLibel film was also available on-line. One of the key tactics for McSpotlight also aimed to make the information available internationally and this was achieved mostly easily and quickly through CMC (Lubbers 1996). These were a combination of actions to preserve the site from any legal challenge by McDonald's and also practical ways to get its contents out to as wide an audience as possible. McSpotlight did not actively encourage on-line activism, apart from their guided tour of McDonald's website:

we were the first to do a critical tour of someone else's website and we found and published their e-mail addresses which they did not make public. We also wrote a new version of their 'comment' form so that people could send their opinions to them. As a group, we did not use any forms of electronic sabotage against them . . . mailbombing is just 'Net abuse' and hey, we're not the ones trying to suppress freedom of speech by shutting one side up.

(McSpotlight volunteer)

All the case studies utilised CMC to aid their repertoire of action. FoE and McSpotlight used CMC to extend their tactics and were both innovative in their design. Only FoE actively encouraged on-line activism in the form of e-mail petitions, while McSpotlight used the technology to bypass the mainstream media, a media which environmental activists have in the past had to rely upon for coverage. Lyminge utilised CMC less to extend their tactics, and more as an additional communication tool. So far there has been little evidence of the use of on-line activism, such as the use of electronic civil disobedience, in Britain by environmental activists. Electronic civil disobedience is a 'form of mass decentered electronic direct action, utilizes virtual blockades and virtual sit-ins' (Wray 1998: 5). Recent examples include the demonstrations in Britain on 18 June 1999, where company targets received thousands of e-mails which crashed their computer systems, and in April 2000 the electrohippies collective distributed denial of service attacks on specific companies believed to be harming the environment (electrohippies collective 2000). However, although some participants of the case studies privately supported the idea of electronic civil disobedience, each group rejected the possibility of utilising such tactics because they broke Netiquette, were deemed to damage the functioning of the Internet, were thought to lead to reprisal attacks and were seen as being tantamount to blackmail rather than encouraging positive change for the environment.

The use of CMC has enhanced some of the environmental movement's cohesion and ability to co-ordinate campaigns. CMC has been used as a supplement to the many media already employed and environmentalists have transferred much of their information onto the new media, using e-mail networks in much the same manner as they utilised word of mouth and networks of telephone trees. Despite innovative use of CMC they have yet to utilise fully its possibilities of being more than simply a communication tool. They have only recently begun to challenge their techniques of campaigning and explore the potential of on-line protests, and use it as a tool for organising simultaneous global demonstrations, such as during the 18 June 1999 protests and the anti-WTO (World Trade Organisation) actions in November 1999 (Chesters 2000).

Conclusions

E-mail has been an absolute revolution in terms of communication. It is the method of communication among environmentalists and it has made an awful lot of difference to who can be an activist, how well connected you are, how quickly you can react to events. You could be an activist and live on your own in the middle of a desert if you are connected to the Internet.

(Devin, McSpotlight volunteer)

As with other technologies (such as mobile phones and video cameras), CMC has facilitated the development of new ways of campaigning for environmentalists. However, it has wider implications than these. Its speed, cheapness, interactivity, and relative freedom from government or corporate control have enabled significant changes in the way campaigns are organised and advertised and goals are achieved. Social movement perspectives serve as a useful analytical tool with which to examine the different processes that result in collective action and as a framework to consider the influence of CMC use by environmental groups.

Close analysis of the way in which three environmental groups have utilised Internet and e-mail has revealed the wide array of uses for the technology, and subsequent different implications of its use for each group. It has been illustrated that it is possible to mobilise those who are already within the movement networks (or those who are cognate), using CMC without face-to-face contact. CMC is simply a quicker, cheaper and more global method of utilising these networks. More people can be contacted more quickly than through traditional forms of communication such as word of mouth and underground publications, and this contact is also on a much larger scale, with both the Lyminge campaign and McSpotlight benefiting from international collaboration. In the light of recent global protests such as the anti-WTO campaign (centred upon Seattle) in November 1999, it seems likely that there will be growth in the global radical environmental movement through such use of Internet and e-mail (Chesters 2000). It is also these groups (the non-hierarchical, flexible and often radical) which are best able to benefit from CMC's ability to aid organisation. CMC enables groups to co-ordinate campaigns without the need for a central office, newsletters, or the physical presence of activists, as such groups are unrestricted by bureaucratic organisational procedures. Furthermore, all groups benefited from interacting with members of other movements internationally, aiding their feelings of solidarity and being part of something bigger than their own campaign. Environmentalists' use of modern technology also helped challenge the stereotype of the anti-technology, anti-progress protester.

In terms of tactics each case study utilised CMC to facilitate a repertoire of action, and to some extent extend it into new territories. Despite many of these uses being particularly innovative, such as Factory Watch on FoE's site and the guided tour of McDonald's website by McSpotlight, these were extensions to the existing repertoire, rather than new additions. There is little evidence, as yet, that CMC was being used to constitute radical new forms of protest. Although the lack of evidence of electronic activism is partly due to its illegal and secretive nature, and the reticence of companies to highlight any attacks, such acts also require considerable technical ingenuity which may not yet be prevalent in the British environmental movement. Recent examples, such as the e-mail bombardment of companies during the 18 June demonstrations in London, have yet to be practised by large numbers of environmentalists. Much debate is occurring within the movement as to the validity of such techniques and many remain critical of their use (electrohippies collective 2000).

The implications of CMC use upon social movement processes have been examined using the experiences of these three British environmental groups. In doing so it has been demonstrated that while CMC holds the potential to provide a new method of recruitment, mobilisation remains reliant upon integration into existing networks. Perhaps only once CMC use has become further integrated into individuals' daily lives will on-line interaction be able to replace the current importance of face-to-face interaction for initial inclusion into social movement networks. Thus, in the future it may be possible for whole new networks to be generated on-line which could trigger physical direct action off-line. At present CMC is resigned to act as a strengthener (in terms of reducing the importance of the elements of time and space in communication) of the existing networks.

Analysis of the way in which CMC may alter movement identities has confirmed the social movement perspective view that cross-movement and cross-cultural interaction affects identities and individuals' feelings of solidarity. It has also highlighted the possible implications of the wider trend towards globalisation, indicating that protests are increasingly becoming global and individuals are able to identify, and communicate with, like-minded activists spread across dispersed global networks. Both CMC and these global processes have the potential to alter dramatically individuals' notions of their role as environmental activists. Finally, in relation to repertoires of action, CMC use is located among the variety of influences to which tactics evolve and respond. The role of CMC in this is significant, in that it is a technology which holds great potential for the development of new tactics, but it is also just another step in the process long since identified by social movement analysts.

CMC use will continue to evolve and be utilised by environmentalists, modifying and being modified by social movement processes. The new inter-actions triggered by CMC have significantly altered each of the environmental groups considered here, and are likely to produce new collaborations and new forms of environmental protest, particularly in the global arena. Although problems and restrictions remain in its utilisation, environmentalists continue to weave a green Web.

Notes

1 Thus, a social movement can include both institutional bodies and loose structures of organisation, can simultaneously be attempting to gain access to power structures and challenging their existence.

2 The extent to which skills are still required is debatable with the simplification of web-site design and increasing usability of software packages. However, actual Web design has developed into a competitive commercial business which is increasingly employing new software, the development of new languages and new Web standard formats, such as JAVA, which are not easy for non-professionals to acquire. The result is that Web pages produced using the simpler languages such as HTML are increasingly unable to

compete with the newer designs, or to keep pace with demanding Internet audiences. It is especially notable that many of the larger NGOs now use languages such as JAVA and hire commercial Web-page designers.

3   Here I am referring only to the methods used by the protesters, not by the locals who had fought the development through political lobbying of MPs and through the legal system.

4   Mirror sites are exact copies of the McSpotlight website located on different servers around the world.

5   A website with an interactive map illustrating the UK's Sites of Special Scientific Interest and the threats to them. Its aim was to give public access to FoE's unique database and help generate support for the Wildlife Bill.

6   An interactive map of polluting factories. Provides a search engine for the dataset and an ability to rank local factories based on several criteria. The aim of the site was to provide such local environmental information to the public and press the government for a Community Right to Know Act.

7   So far 50–100 people have joined per year through the website. However, the joining pages have since been redesigned in an attempt to increase these numbers. Between April 1998 and April 1999, 207 new people have joined over the Web.

8   A telephone tree constitutes a list of individuals' telephone numbers arranged in a branch-like manner. It has a hierarchical structure in that a trigger phone call from the 'bottom' contacts a few individuals who in turn each contact a few further individuals. In this way the original message is relayed up the branches of the telephone tree.

9   In October 1995 the Advertising Standards Authority banned FoE's 'Mahogany is Murder' cinema advertisement. Their judgement was based upon two complaints by the Timber Trade Federation and the Brazilian Government.

11 Grassroots environmental movements

Mobilisation in an Information Age

Alan Dordoy and Mary Mellor

Introduction

In the Information Age, argues Castells, key social movements will become the agents of social change, the new historical subjects, replacing traditional political action based on industry and the state. Environmentalists, together with feminists, fundamentalists, nationalists and localists – a motley crew – will engage in politics in a different way, and their politics will be of a different kind.

The different way of engaging in politics is exemplified by the Zapatistas and their use of the Internet which leads Castells to describe them as the 'first informational guerrilla movement' (1997: 79). Greenpeace is the exemplar of a global environmental movement that has used highly effective media communications to achieve its aims (ibid.: 118). Use of the new technologies of communication for publicity purposes will also be accompanied by new political structures based on networking and decentralisation.

The new social movements will also produce a different kind of politics more in tune with the Information Age. This is particularly true for the environmental movement:

> I propose the hypothesis that there is a direct correspondence between the themes put forward by the environmental movement and the fundamental dimensions of the new social structure, the network society . . . that there is an implicit, coherent ecological discourse that cuts across various political orientations and social origins within the movement.
>
> (Castells 1997: 122)

The themes that provide these linkages are the dominance since the 1970s of science and technology resulting in the transformation of space and time. More specifically, the transcendence of space/time frameworks and limits and the domination of a real virtuality of abstract flows of information, wealth and power over material forces and conditions. Central to Castells's theoretical model is the distinction between two spatialities, the 'space of flows' and the 'space of places' (1997: 123–4). The dominant processes of network society are organised in the space of flows. Social practices at a distance can occur simultaneously in the space of flows via telecommunications; locality is irrelevant to the flows of information and wealth and the process of concentration of power. Human experience and meaning, on the other hand, are still locally based and this is a source of the identity problems in network society as political processes are removed from the sphere where the average citizen can have any control. Political struggle will therefore have to follow the new power structure:

> The new power lies in the codes of information and in the images of representation around which societies organize their institutions, and people build their lives, and decide their behaviour. The sites of this power are people's minds.
>
> (Castells 1997: 359)

The struggle is to be around cultural codes through information flows and symbol manipulation (Castells 1997: 362). For Castells, environmental groups have a key role to play as the oppositional groups of the network society. They have the ability to bridge the gap between the local and the global, the space of places and the space of flows. They will combine adopting the new communication-based mechanisms of power with the creation of a new politics attuned to the Information Age. The task for the green movement is to create a 'green culture' and the new mode of political action is linked directly to the achievement of such a culture:

> their most striking initiatives often result from 'turbulences' in the interactive network of multilayered communication – as in the production of a 'green culture' by a universal form of putting together experiences of preserving nature and surviving capitalism at the same time.
>
> (Castells 1997: 362)

Although stressing the environmental movement's integrative potential, Castells recognises that at present it embraces a range of groups: conservationists, NIMBYs (not-in-my-backyard), counter-culturalists, global campaigners, green politicians. Some operate almost exclusively within the space of places and others within the space of flows. At the grassroots are those whose motivation is their own politics of locality. Within the space of flows are those who either unite through their access to the media or who use the media to make their case. These two groups range from major environmental organisations such as Greenpeace whose campaigning style is based on media-orientated activities that trigger responses in the audience such as the Brent Spar campaign, or the various anti-whaling exploits, to high-profile direct-action campaigners. The ability to communicate widely and at speed is obviously effective both in terms of gaining public support and in mobilising activists, as in the campaign against GM foods.

Much excitement has been raised by the use of the Internet to co-ordinate environmental direct action. For John Vidal of the *Guardian*:

> the ecological-inspired critique of democracy is now exploding and the crop pullers should be seen as part of an international movement that, thanks to

E-mail and the web, watchdog groups and increasing networking is throwing up new issues, philosophies, ethics and legal arguments.

(Guardian, 17 Aug. 1999)

Notable examples of the use of a global networking to co-ordinate political action are the anti-World Trade Organisation action in Seattle, November 1999, and the earlier worldwide campaign against the Multilateral Agreement on Investment (MAI). If implemented MAI would mean that no investment could be opposed on environmental or social justice grounds. Although this initiative is stalled, it will doubtless return.

Central to his elaboration of the Information Society is Castells's concern that the loss of identity associated with industrial society and the nation-state will not necessarily be replaced. He hopes that it will be, but the choice lies between identity based on communities of resistance, resting on place or pre-existing identity (ethnicity, gender), or identity based on a project such as a new religion. His hope is that the environmental movement can provide a link between communities of resistance and an identity-creating project. Within the environmental movement, Castells identifies environmental justice as the ecological 'new frontier' (1997: 131). He sees environmental justice as 'an all-encompassing notion that affirms the use value of life, all forms of life, against the interests of wealth, power and technology' that 'is gradually capturing minds and policies as the environmental movement enters a new stage of development' (ibid.: 132). He looks forward to the emergence of 'a new international of good-willing generous citizens' (ibid.: 133) who will supersede the exhausted political movements of industrial society.

Castells here is drawing evidence from two levels. One is the emergence of an 'ecological approach to life' that appears to represent a new holistic way of thinking. More specifically, he points to particular developments within environmental campaigning, the linking of environmental conditions with wider social questions particularly of poverty, racism and neo-colonialism. The latter linkage has been fuelled by the 'new grassroots movements' which have been emerging since the mid-1970s as movements of ecological resistance (Taylor 1995). Grassroots campaigning has always been part of environmental campaigning, but it has taken different forms. NIMBYism has tended to be dominated by middle-class communities opposing environmental or social change that would affect the amenity value of their neighbourhood. Grassroots direct action has also been carried out by activists who support local issues such as forest or road campaigns, but not necessarily because they are part of the local community. The importance of campaigns for environmental justice is that they are based in poorer communities where environmental problems are seen as another aspect of their social inequality. The question we would wish to ask here is whether environmental justice is likely to be the 'new frontier' of the ecological politics of the Information Society or are the barricades of the old politics re-emerging?

The environmental justice movement

Environmental justice sees environmental problems as issues of social justice. While the poor of the cities oppose threats to their health, those in rural communities campaign against the loss or dereliction of their land and the resources on which their livelihood depends. While the rural movements of the South such as the Indian Chipko (tree-hugging) movement have been described as the 'environmentalism of the poor' (Guha and Martinez-Alier 1997), the origins of the environmental justice movement lie in the struggles of the urban poor of the North. Although the commonality of these campaigns is increasingly recognised, the history of the environmental justice movement has been dominated by the US experience and oriented to 'toxic struggles' within poor, black and minority communities (Hofrichter 1993; Bullard 1994; Szasz 1994; Hartley 1995; Heiman 1996).

Toxicity represents a political bridge between the health and safety issues of the old industrial society and the new issues of information rights. It emerges through industrial production (including the new technologies) but can remain hidden until revealed by epiphenomena such as ill-health. One of the first cases to gain widespread media attention was the campaign led by Lois Gibbs against toxic contamination in the blue-collar private housing estate of Love Canal in Niagara Falls, New York State in 1978. Her concern began with the failing health of her children and others in the local school. Persistent questioning revealed (with the help of friendly scientists) the existence of an old chemical dump underneath the school. However, the articulation of an environmental justice movement grew from the more immediate and obvious questions of social justice in the location of toxic waste dumps of which the local, usually black or minority, community were well aware (Szasz 1994).

The link between racism and the siting of toxic waste emerged in the 1982 Warren County protest over the location of a landfill for PCB contaminated soils in a predominantly African-American community in North Carolina. This was followed in 1987 by a report on toxic waste and race by the United Church for Christ Commission on Racial Justice (Heiman 1996). The First People of Color Environmental Justice Leadership Summit was held in 1991 in Washington, DC. While racism is central to the environmental justice movement, issues of class and gender are also important. Bullard has argued that although race and class are central to the toxicity struggle, the environmental justice movement is much wider:

> Environmental justice activists have not limited their focus to toxics or racism. Their movement is inclusive, cutting across race, ethnicity, class, religion and political affiliation.
>
> (Bullard 1994: 123)

Given the location of the campaigns within local communities, women were at their heart (Bettercourt 1996). Networking was also very important. The campaign at Love Canal led to the formation of the Central Clearing House for

Hazardous Waste which by the end of the 1980s was supporting nearly 5000 local campaigns.

Castells's optimism about the potential of the environmental justice movement is shared by Brown and Masterson-Allen (1994: 282) who see the toxic waste campaigns as the basis of a 'new global movement' linking local experience to a critique of wider industrial processes. Szasz and Meuser (1997) also see environmental justice as potentially replacing worker solidarity as the source of a new politics, reaching across race and gender lines and bringing together issues around work and community. It embodies the new politics of empowerment and direct action and challenges the elitism of the traditional (middle-class) environmental organisations. It is not unexpected, then, that the environmental justice movement would be seen by Castells as the basis of a new politics for the new society.

Are the new grassroots movements part of the Information Society?

Information is certainly essential to grassroots environmental campaigns, for publicity for their cause, to gain relevant information and to build coalitions with other groups. Evidence from grassroots groups on the Internet attests to the importance of developing links with similar groups and sharing experience and expertise in achieving success (e.g. www.ran.org/victories/index.html). For Bullard, finding independent sources of information and expertise is vital for local campaigns (1994: 132) and the use of information is important for a variety of reasons:

- to counter the media bombardment that emphasises powerlessness
- to provide positive feedback on protests to build confidence, particularly news of victories
- to provide information flows within communities to highlight the community's strength and potential
- to enable inter-organisational communication
- to link to wider information systems to gain a wider context and to overcome NIMBYism.

(Bullard 1994: 137)

However, whether the new grassroots movements obtain these benefits in practice is doubtful. Bullard found that the environmental groups in black communities were small and understaffed, with a very limited operating budget (1994: 133). It is hardly surprising, given what we know about power structures in society, that grassroots movements in poor communities would not be the first or main users of new technologies. The more interesting question is what is the potential for future development? Will there be a trickle down of information technology access? The evidence is less than convincing. While the lived experience of those in low-income and minority communities can overcome their disadvantage and lead to resistance to toxic production or disposal decisions this is often despite, not because of, information technologies. As Goldman (1996) has pointed out, even where information has been collected and disseminated, it does not fall on neutral ground. Well-intentioned attempts to empower local communities through on-line access to chemical release information, local health-risk assessments and Geographical Information Systems mapping have had the effect of alerting better-off communities to these dangers, who may then act to keep the waste out of their own areas, often at the expense of those in poorer locations. Goldman found that from the mid-1980s to mid-1990s the chances of minorities living near hazardous sites in the United States had actually increased. This led him to conclude that 'increased public awareness of toxic hazards may contribute perversely to even greater environmental disparities by race and class' (1996: 128).

Emphasis on the link between social inequality and environmental issues may also be counter-productive. Shibley and Prosterman (1998), in their study of the politics of lead poisoning in urban areas, found that if the specificity of the groups mainly affected (low income living in industrial areas and near major roads) was stressed, then wider political concern lessened. They argue that environmental justice organisations have to maintain the fiction of a widespread 'silent killer' epidemic in order to attract public expenditure, even if this meant that expenditure was not targeted in the areas that most need it. They saw the failure to target expenditure as an environmental justice issue in itself.

Even getting media attention has become increasingly difficult since the early days of the environmental justice campaigns. Tokar (1995) found that between 1989 and 1995 environmental coverage on US TV network news fell by 60 per cent. This is the medium by which most US citizens receive information, where the battle for coverage is vital and TV stations tend to rely on packaged reports from outside agencies. Anti-environmental groups are increasingly competing for this space. Tokar presents evidence that timber companies are paying workers to attend anti-environmental rallies that will claim media attention. The companies are also better placed in the information struggle and have launched an anti-environmental counter-movement which promotes the 'wise use' of resources in which the importance of maintaining employment figures highly. Goldman (1996) points to the doughnut model of siting of hazardous activities. Adjacent to the toxic site are the white employees sacrificing health for work. Beyond them are the unemployed black/minority communities. Well away are the white middle class.

In political terms, Goldman argues, the environmental justice movement is a 'gnat on the elephant's behind'. Far from increasing in effectiveness over time, problems of securing resources means that 'the environmental movement has been downsizing faster than corporate America as "wise use" activists gain public support for their defense of private property and jobs' (1996: 130). The Central Clearing House for Hazardous Waste is one organisation that has seen a marked decline in its resources. Epstein's (1997) review of the grassroots movements involved in the struggle for environmental justice also found most to be short-lived, based on a few participants with only a small number of people committed in the longer term.

Even the claim that environmental justice struggles transcend social difference is questioned. Common experience of inequality does not necessarily bring unity around environmental issues. A particularly interesting piece of research by Pulido (1996) raises fundamental questions about the environmental justice movement's ability to unite around environmental issues. Looking at the specific example of Los Angeles she found that racial and ethnic identities prevented a multi-community and class politics emerging. Suspicion between the African-American and Latino communities was compounded by language barriers. Often the different communities had independent campaigns around the same issues. The building of campaigns around identity meant that leadership often came from outside of the areas affected (for example, from the black Churches). These leaders tended to blunt the political demands of the local community and to prevent a politics of class emerging. Pulido concludes:

> the conventional wisdom . . . concerning the formation of a broad-based movement must be reconsidered. The notion that if only linkages were properly articulated, then various oppressed groups would find common ground is weak at best and denies the power associated with different forms of oppression.
>
> (Pulido 1996: 185–6)

From Pulido's evidence identity politics is working against the emergence of a network society and a new politics. It is hard to share Castells's notion that environmentalism 'is the only global identity put forward on behalf of all human beings, regardless of their specific social, historical or gender attachments or their religious faith' (1997: 127). Such a universalist view of political identity is contradicted by the evidence from the environmental justice movement. In the USA the new grassroots movements often express frustration with the mainstream environmental groups, the so-called 'gang of ten' (Kamienieki *et al.* 1995: 321). Greenpeace, one of the most international of the environmental groups, is a supporter rather than a membership organisation, and therefore cannot organisationally link the local with the global. It certainly operates on a global networking basis, as Castells envisaged, but it does not as yet have an analysis that can enable it to link with the social issues raised by the environmental justice movement. Environmental campaigners whose aim is to preserve nature do not necessarily see any solidarity with poor communities campaigning over health and resource use. Green notions of population control also conflict with the interests of poor nations which are inevitably the main target of such measures. Poor people often find themselves driven to invade wilderness or areas of indigenous population to secure a livelihood. While the environment movement in general, and the environmental justice issue in particular, would seem to be an appropriate politics for the Information Age they bring with them many of the political features of the old industrial/capitalist order, particularly around issues of power and inequality.

Novotny (1995) sees approaches like Castells's as exhibiting a 'postmaterialist' environmentalism which fits poorly with the experiences of the grassroots groups which come under the general banner of the environmental justice movement. These groups do not tend to see the problems they confront as 'environmental' but rather as 'poverty, housing or community problems'. Industrial pollution and toxic waste dumping are experienced not as abstract green issues but as aspects of class position and racial injustice. One of Novotny's examples makes this especially clear: the polluting petrochemical industry around New Orleans is built directly in the setting of the old slave plantations. They affect life not in a cultural, but in a directly material way, through housing conditions, employment, health-care or impact on children's education. A similar point is made by Epstein (1997) in her analysis of the environmental justice movement.

If Castells's optimism about the environmental movement seems to be some-what misplaced where does that leave political action in the Information Age? In the rest of this chapter we argue that developments within the technologies of the network society are unlikely to see the emergence of a new mode of political mobilisation that will benefit the new grassroots movements before returning to the question of the politics of the environment.

Politics and the Information Society

If the network society is to change the face of politics it will need to overcome the structural inequalities of the old industrial society. There is little evidence that this is happening. The use of information technology by grassroots groups does not necessarily increase their overall power, as a study of a residents' group campaigning around the redevelopment of their housing estate in Wilmington, North Carolina, shows (Mele 1999). The poor, black and predominantly female group found that access to information technology did allow them to link up with other groups and to gain advice from planners and architects. It enabled them to draw up their own plans and gave them a voice to challenge the housing authority officials. On the other hand, having access to information and expertise did not guarantee a victory. As Mele points out, the fact that this group had access to Internet resources at all was largely accidental, the result of an adult education computing course having been put on for estate residents and a networked PC having been provided in the estate resource centre. If the facilities and expertise necessary to gain access to the Internet are only accidentally available to grassroots groups (which is often the case), whereas they are structurally available to the institutional forces they face, the use of information technology becomes just another example of structural inequality.

Castells notes that a computer-literate elite may be increasingly necessary to give voice to grassroots movements, in the same way that artisan printers did for the early labour movement (1997: 129–30). However, this may be highly problematic for the development of such groups, especially as the elite is likely to be male and white while many of the groups involved will be predominantly female and black. The role of expertise within the environmental justice movement is a highly contentious issue (Epstein 1997). A core principle of the groups campaigning under the heading of environmental justice is that 'we speak for ourselves'. As the dumping of toxic wastes is most likely to be attempted in areas which are poor, non-white, female-led and largely powerless, the split between the campaigning groups and Castells's 'computer-literate elite' will exactly mirror that between those groups and the corporations doing the dumping.

This leads to the wider question of how egalitarian the new communication technologies are likely to be. In recent years a huge amount of discussion has been generated around the political possibilities of network technologies, the flexible identities that can be constructed in the new cybercommunities, the potential for a new civic realm, a Habermasian ideal speech situation or an Athenian-style direct democratic forum on a mass society scale (Leadbetter 2000). The latter analogy is apt as the participants in each type of forum would seem to have the same profile, being not of the class that does the labouring (Cudmore 1999). Ethnographic research also demolishes the idea of the cybercommunity being non-gendered (Cushing 1996; Ward 1999; O'Brien 1999) or non-raced (Burkhalter 1999).

The potential for development of a global environmental network is undermined by the huge global inequalities in the distribution of Internet access. The Internet does not provide a means of communication for the vast majority of the world's population. In 1998, only 0.75 per cent of the world's Internet users were in Africa; and of these 85–90 per cent were in South Africa (Chivhanga 1999). By March 2000, the African proportion had increased only to 0.85 per cent (derived from estimates from NUA Ltd – http://www.nua.ie/surveys/how_many_online/). Obvious restrictions on access include the need for an electricity supply and telephone lines as well as to funds to purchase equipment. Even if these are overcome, the costs of use for those in the South can be prohibitive. Walch (1999: 55), for example, describes how for one Indian development group 'a whole month's salary was spent merely on the connection costs for picking up the huge volume of e-mail sent from a (well-meaning) US support group'.

As the Internet advances across the globe it is being increasingly dominated by commercial interests. As a result a sea of 'sludge' is steadily drowning out the free-information exchangers, as anyone looking for details of environmental or other radical campaigns on the Net will find out. Of the top twenty search terms for April 2000, seven were sex related, three chat or Hotmail, five computer music or games related. No search term that might relate to political discourse appears in the top 100 (www.searchwords.com). Twenty-five per cent of pages visited from home and 20 per cent of those visited from work are estimated to be sex related (*Guardian*, 6 May 1999). In a similar vein, the most hit websites show a massive bias towards the commercial Web providers, on-line shopping and porn (www.pcdataonline.com/reports/). Even in those sites which have a theme of political discourse, questions relating to the nature of the Web itself dominate – privacy, encryption, censorship, etc. Jordan points out, for example, that the key real world civil rights issues of 'gender, race, class and ecology' find little echo in the work of the Internet civil rights organisation the Electronic Frontier

Federation (Jordan 1999). As Streck says, it is as if 'discussion in the salons of eighteenth-century England and France concerned only the status of the salons as salons' (1998: 43).

An additional problem for effective political use of the Internet is the increasingly pressing one of information overload. As Walch argues: 'As in the realm of material production under capitalism, the problem of cultural overproduction in cyberspace arises. It is not a wasteland, but a jungle grown so thick that all overview is lost. In this thick undergrowth, the power to inform (and to become informed) implies the ability to cut a path' (1999: 73). The fact that information has been posted on the Web does not mean it is going to be found by those who may need it or be able to respond to it. Access will imply existing group links from outside of cyberspace or will rely heavily on tools such as the search engines. These play a major role in controlling access to information. However, they index only a small proportion of the more than 800 million pages of the Web (from Lycos's 2.5 per cent up to Northern Light's 16 per cent), their commercial interest is in keeping users locked in, and so reading their adverts, rather than providing a full index (Schofield 1999).

Political uses of the Web are likely to be further weakened and drowned out in the next phases of its commercialisation. Access will increasingly be via the new-generation mobile phone, the TV and the games machine rather than the PC. All of these will have limited functionality in terms of using the Web in an interactive way, in any sense other than chat or shopping. Mobile phone access in particular means increasing channelling of that access through menus predefined by the service provider. On the other hand, the commercial importance of the Web is amply demonstrated in the huge legal battle with Microsoft over the inclusion of its Web browser in the Windows operating system, by the huge investment in unprofitable Internet companies and by the increasing competition between Internet service providers over 'free' Web access.

From an environmental point of view there is also the materiality of the PC industry itself. The language of information and communication technologies tends to draw attention away from the sheer scale of white-goods shifting involved. The rate of increase in computing power means that a new PC will be redundant in three years' time. As Callister and Burbules (1998) point out, this redundancy is not like that of a new car. It will not just have gone a bit out of fashion and not incorporate the latest goodies but it will lack the functionality to run the software needed to view the vast majority of Web pages satisfactorily. It is as if a three-year-old car would no longer work because the roads had been totally redesigned since it was built. At the same time, this increased power means larger boxes (bigger fans, more peripherals), bigger monitors (more windows to run at once) and so on; the PC that once sat in the corner of a desk now dominates it completely. The scale of the problem of pollution in production and disposal of PCs is hard to quantify.[1] As Harpold and Philip (1999) point out: 'It is one of the ironies of the high-tech economy that the manufacturing technologies which support it are equally or more destructive of the environment as those of traditional industrial practices.' A clear expression of this irony can be seen by visiting the website of the

SouthWest Organizing Project (www.swop.net/). This is an umbrella organ-isation for grassroots groups around Albuquerque, New Mexico. A major focus of its campaigning is the electronics industry: 'The land, air, water and public infrastructure has been threatened by the industry which has taken advantage of the limited economic development of the region as well as the willingness of state and local authorities to relax environmental regulations' (Novotny 1995: 72). SWOP, however, are using the very technology against which they are protesting to make their case. This is as if anti-car campaigners organised actions that had to be driven to.

The problems of access and the changing nature of the Internet would seem to argue against the emergence of a radical new politics through the new technology. Even the best examples of information technology use for political means are not conclusive. Reports about the 18 June 1999 Carnival against Capitalism action, for example, claimed that it was 'planned on the web' (where) 'ranks of protesters . . . can be recruited into action just by setting up a handful of websites' (*Guardian*, 24 June 1999). This might be true, but there were also fly posters all over our city centre here in Newcastle – one of the oldest methods of political communication – writing on walls. This raises the question of whether the use of new technology represents a qualitatively new form of political communication; that is, does it alter the nature of communication fundamentally and/or will it have a markedly broader reach than existing methods of communication? Is the Internet any different in essence to William Cobbett's *Political Register* which spread news of 'Captain Swing' in the 1830s or the telephone trees that supported the Greenham Common protest? All were difficult to infiltrate and had the benefit of being 'leaderless'.

It is also not clear that effective manipulation of communication networks is a new phenomenon dependent on Internet technology. For example, as Anderson's biography of Guevara shows very clearly, meetings with foreign journalists and staged media events were crucial to the success of Castro's uprising in Cuba some forty years ago (Anderson 1997). At the same time effective use of the new systems of communication does not necessarily lead to success. Castells has high-lighted the effectiveness of Zapatistas' manipulation of the communication net-works in raising the profile of this initially obscure group, but their struggle carries on unresolved. Their opponents are similarly able to manage information and stage-manage events to counter their efforts (e.g. Michael McCaughan, *Guardian*, 9 Aug. 1999). Even more importantly, the Zapatistas do not directly communicate with the world. Their websites are hosted by several US universities[2] and they thus appear courtesy of the university authorities and the liberal values of academic freedom that justify tolerance of what elsewhere could be defined a misuse of bandwidth. They also appear courtesy of all of the surveillance apparatuses of the US state (Carracedo 1999).

A similar point can be made about most if not all of the websites which publicise a range of grassroots issues and movements from around the world. There are some very useful websites[3] but these are not directly the property of the groups whose views they communicate. The problem of access to servers by groups in the

South means that much of their material has to be hosted by sympathetic organisations (and individuals with access to university servers) in the North. While such support may be well intended, it raises problems – 'the wariness of being dominated by support, with knowledge being a tool of control'. A risk is that 'information is put into a hierarchy and the agenda set through the selection presented' by the host organisation. The 'info-overload of the North overshadows any possible counter-agenda presentation by movements in the South' (Walch 1999: 131). An additional problem here is that of language. English is not just the main language of the Web but that of the operating systems, programs and manuals. 'With linguistic dominance comes cultural dominance. Many in the South are beginning to fear that the spread of ICT might mean McCulture strengthening its hegemonic grip' (ibid.: 52).

The above arguments indicate that, as the amount of information on the Internet increases exponentially, the early promise of its open-ended and egalitarian use retreats. The Internet may have been started by the US military and evolved into the plaything of computer hobbyists and academics; but its time as a liberal, free-information (although predominantly male, white, middle-class) vehicle is rapidly changing. The process of the social (re)shaping of the Internet is visible before our very eyes as adverts pop up or down in virtually every site visited. Universities may increasingly expect their Web space to be used for commercially marketable distance learning courses rather than for the free exchange of academic ideas and knowledge or the support of grassroots networks.

Given the way in which the new information technologies and particularly the Internet are developing it would seem that the promises of the new informational politics are not being met. As Webster has argued, Castells's (1997) optimistic assumptions have been driven by a technological determinism, underestimating the importance of older structures of power. Undoubtedly environmental organisations and increasingly the new grassroots movements will use new technology as use of the telephone or the television spread to poorer communities, but this is only within the context of political 'business as usual' where existing power structures retain their dominance.

There are areas where the 'space of flows' has created a qualitative difference, in the ability of capitalism to de-materialise itself. Ninety-five per cent of all international transactions in money terms are non-substantial: there is no material trade. Increasingly stock-market investments are being linked to a new wave of financial speculation that Chancellor (1999) has described as bubble.com. These changes can, however, be analysed within traditional critical frameworks and do not escape the 'old politics' (Dordoy and Mellor 2000: 41–61).

Castells hoped that the environmental movement would be able to bridge the gap between the space of flows and the space of places. He hoped that by being at the cutting edge in terms of manipulation of the media, by stage management of events and in terms of use of the new communications technologies, in particular the Internet, that environmental groups could both have a local focus and act globally at the same time (1997: 128–9). While the green movement does operate both globally and locally, it is not yet as an integrated movement and as we have shown the battleground of the new technologies does not escape from the old political struggles.

Justice, politics and the environment

Despite the qualifications and reservations we have expressed about Castells's optimism at the emergence of a new politics around the environment and environmental justice, the grassroots movements and struggles that are taking place worldwide do express the centrality of the environmental issue to the politics of the late twentieth century. There is also a growing body of 'good-willing' people. A major international conference of academics and activists on environmental justice was held in Melbourne, Australia in October 1997. There is a growing field of political ecology that explores the distribution of ecological goods and bads. At the same time there are political divisions. The Western public is moved more by issues of nature preservation and consumer safety than by the problems of health and resource access of poorer communities. Concern about climate change does not diminish the desire for overseas travel or the expectation that mangetout from Kenya will come fresh each day. Concern about genetically modified foods is not necessarily accompanied by awareness of the growing global disparities of the resource rich and the resource poor. Castells looks to a cultural change with the emergence of a 'green culture' (1997: 127). We would want to argue that the continuing existence of the old politics of class, seen more broadly in the uneven distribution of ecological resources and dangers, is still a more likely source of political change around the environment.

What the Information Society has revealed to the human community is the vulnerability and interconnectedness of ecological processes. While Castells's core ideas are about cultural/technological change and his 'frontier' lies in environmental justice, his notion of 'green culture' is rooted in a cosmological view of the physical world. He criticises the transient and superficial nature of human life in clock time and timeless time (the electronic instant) in favour of what Lash and Urry (1994) have called 'glacial time' – the time of the cosmos. It is worth quoting Castells at length here:

> Ecological thinking considers interaction between all forms of matter in an evolutionary perspective. The idea of limiting the use of resources to renewable resources, central to environmentalism, is predicated precisely on the notion that alteration of basic balances in the planet, and in the universe, may, over time, undo a delicate ecological equilibrium, with catastrophic consequences. The holistic notion of integration between humans and nature, as present in 'deep ecology' writers, doesn't refer to a naive worshipping of pristine natural landscapes, but to the fundamental consideration that the relevant unit of experience is not each individual, or for that matter, historically existing human communities. To merge ourselves with our cosmological self we need first to change the notion of time, to feel 'glacial time' running through our lives, to sense the energy of the stars flowing in our blood, and to assume the

rivers of our thoughts endlessly merging in the boundless ocean of multiformed living matter.

(Castells 1997: 125–6)

Rather than looking to the emergence of a green culture from human consciousness and the development of a shared identity, Castells is sharing the deep-ecology notion of cosmological knowledge coming from the outside in, i.e. from the natural world as 'Nature', an idealised notion. This becomes even more clear in a later statement by Castells:

Environmentalism shifts from the defense of one's environment, health and well-being, to the ecological project of integrating human kind and nature, on the basis of the socio-biological identity of the species, assuming humankind's cosmological meaning.

(ibid.: 358)

Such a statement begs many questions. It is not clear how human actors will move from their own specific problems to the 'ecological project of integrating human kind and nature'. The notion of the socio-biological identity of the species is a contentious one and deeply problematic for feminists as women are often seen as being closer to nature (Mellor 1997). The notion of 'assuming humankind's cosmological meaning' is both idealistic and teleological. How are we to know what this cosmological meaning is? Why should there be one?

Despite this excursion into the rhetoric of deep ecology, we would want to support Castells's view of the centrality of the environmental issue to political developments in an age in which the contraction of space and time in global life has shown the limitations and interconnection of the global environment. The globalisation of production and consumption is pressing up against ecological limits. The main benefit of the speed of contemporary communications is that awareness is growing of these issues, although the global political response is less than overwhelming.

The environmental movement is an important factor in raising ecological awareness and it is developing elements that Castells identified, but as we have pointed out not in a way that can qualitatively overcome existing power relations and interests. Rather than Castells's universalised cultural politics of the Information Society we would argue that a materialist analysis that stresses the ecological framework of human existence would be more fruitful. The emphasis we would place is not on the agency of cultural change accompanying the dematerialisation of the social in space and time, but on the continuing agency of the materiality of human existence in terms of human–human relations (class, 'race', gender) and human–nature relations (the ecological framework of human life). These ideas are set out in more detail elsewhere (Mellor 1997; Dordoy and Mellor 2000; Mellor 2000a; Mellor 2000b).

We would argue (as does Castells) that the natural world itself is an actor in this process. This view would see humanity as necessarily embodied in the materiality of its physical needs and embedded in both the local and global environments. Our understanding of the dynamics of ecology would embrace what Mellor has described as social materialism (class, 'race' and gender) and physical materialism (biology and ecology) (Mellor 1992). Our analysis focuses on the dynamics between social and physical materialism, what Mellor (2000a) has called deep materialism. It is in these dynamics that the inequalities of political ecology emerge. Dominant groups accumulate resources, space and time at the expense of other peoples and species. This pattern of exploitation can be understood within expanded versions of existing materialist frameworks of analysis (Benton 1996). In particular, Marx and Engels's analysis of the interaction between humanity and nature in terms of class can be expanded to include sex/gender, racism/ colonialism and speciesism.

Far from a transition from a materialised industrial world to the dematerialised world of the Information Society, material processes are still the central dynamic of human existence. All human processes leave an 'ecological footprint' (Wackernagel and Rees 1996). What is important are the social inequalities that affect how that footprint is distributed. The ecological footprint of London for instance is calculated as equivalent to the whole of UK cultivable land. The rest of the UK can survive because most of this impact is distributed across the globe. An analysis of the Information Society that stresses its transcendence of space/time without taking account of the ecological consequences of that transcendence is telling only half the story. (Some) human activities may evolve and change but human bodies are always grounded in the biological and ecological cycles of birth, growth and death. Equally, the network society is still based on social inequality and the dynamics of capitalism.

As long as the Information Society is supported by a productive infrastructure and does not live as ephemerally as it thinks, then the problems and mechanism of (re) production and their consequences still exist. Castells agrees that under the new 'informational' form of capitalism there is 'a specially close linkage between human culture and productive force, between spirit and matter' (1996: 18). The question is the balance in this linkage. We would argue that capitalism remains capitalism, whatever specific form it takes. The new informational and communications technologies serve to intensify the classical processes of the capitalist form, processes of commodification and exploitation, rather than to shift us into a new social form. As the experience of the grassroots environmental justice movement shows, it is the real struggle of people in real situations that matters. Communication technologies can be both an aid and a barrier to those struggles.

Notes

1 The Silicon Valley Toxics Coalition gives some indications. It is estimated that over 315 million computers will have become obsolete by 2004. Only a small proportion of these are recycled. Others are dumped, incinerated or just stored. All of these options, including recycling, are hazardous (http://www.svtc.org/). Another estimate, from the National Engineers website, is that the PCs being dumped in landfill by 2005 will fill a one-acre hole 3.5 miles deep (http//www.eweek.org/2000/News/Eweek/acers2.html).

This is on top of the pollution caused in production itself, particularly air and water pollution.

2   Zapatistas in Cyberspace, for example, from the Univesity of Texas (http://www.eco.utexas.edu/faculty/Cleaver/zapsincyber.html). The EZLN site is hosted from a private account of a University of California academic (http://www.ezln.org/fzln/index.html).

3   Examples would be the Nepalnet, hosted from Canada (www.panasia.org.sg/nepalnet/) or the Rainforest Action Network, hosted from San Fransisco (www.ran.org/).

12 Globalisation, citizenship and technology

The Multilateral Agreement on Investment (MAI) meets the Internet

Peter (Jay) Smith and Elizabeth Smythe

Introduction

For over three hundred years politics has been a state-centred activity revolving around the institutions of states and relations between states. Since the eighteenth century who we are as citizens was defined, and given meaning by, states. Culturally, beginning with the French Revolution, people identified themselves as citizens of particular nation-states. Moreover, the territory of states not only provided the public space in which politics occurred, but also the primary space for economic activity as markets tended to be located within and regulated by states. In sum, there was a considerable overlap of economic, political, and cultural space (Shields and Evans 1998).

Today, political, economic and cultural spaces are said to be becoming increasingly separated. Economic activity is becoming globalised while politics is still defined by the shrinking confines of the nation-state. The cultural question of 'who am I?' is being separated from its association with civic nationalism. For economic elites there is a growing identification with capital and economic globalisation. For many others, however, identity is being reattached to homogeneous ethnic communities (Shields and Evans 1998). The driving force behind these changes is, observers claim, globalisation. Globalisation is commonly defined in economic terms as an increasingly integrated system of global production involving a transnational division of labour organised within a single linked group of corporations. As part of this process capital, unlike labour, moves fairly freely, facilitated by rapidly changing technology. Increasingly open national economies, as a result, have become integrated into, and dependent upon, networks of international exchange.

As states open themselves up to the global economy they expose themselves to a loss of political and economic authority. Indeed, much of the recent popular discussion of globalisation has centred on the extent to which it has constrained states, undermined sovereignty and created an international system where global capital dictates state policies (Greider 1995). Susan Strange (1996: 4), for example, contends that:

> Where states were once the masters of markets, now it is the markets which, on many crucial issues, are the masters over the governments of states. And the declining authority of states is reflected in a growing diffusion of authority to other institutions and associations, and to local and regional bodies, and in a growing asymmetry between the larger states with structural power and weaker ones without.

As the state retreats and becomes less relevant the implications for the politics of the state are profound. According to Brodie (1997: 7), 'the ascendancy of the market *over* the state and *inside* the state . . . atrophies the public, closes political spaces, and further marginalizes the already marginalized'. The atrophy of the public and the problematising of the state, territory and sovereignty have, in turn, profound implications for citizenship. Lipschutz, for example, argues that there is a 'crisis of citizenship' which arises, in turn, from a crisis of the nation state, itself in trouble largely as a consequence of globalisation (1998: 3).

Globalisation thus poses serious questions to both the future of the state and the citizen. If there is no sovereign people can there be a state? How can citizenship have any relevance in a world in which national borders are becoming porous and even disappearing at least for capital, if not for labour? This is, no doubt, a pessimistic interpretation of the impact of globalisation on the state, politics and citizenship. In our opinion it is too pessimistic. We argue that globalisation is contestable and that as capitalism globalises, so do its opponents. In both instances information technologies are playing a key role. In other words, the flip side of economic globalisation is political globalisation and mobilisation, both made possible by the information revolution. As Higgot and Reich argue, 'We are not going to have a global information economy without a global civil society' (1999: 20). In the newly emerging global civil society new political spaces arise both within and outside the borders of the state. For example, global social movements and NGOs have shown a capacity to contest the actions of corporate capital directly at the global level even as they simultaneously seek state action at the national level (Low 1997).

In the first section of this article we argue that this alleged 'crisis of citizenship' is based on an overly narrow definition of citizenship which does not sufficiently address alternative means of acting politically, other than those involving domestic state institutions. Moreover, we argue that globalisation has involved new processes and means of communicating and organising which have provided the capacity for new forms of expression and connection among groups and citizens which are not easily controlled by states and ruling elites. As a consequence these means of communicating have provided an alternative voice and capacity to mobilise to those often excluded from the increasingly narrow spectrum of public discourse.

The second section of the chapter uses the case study of the failed attempt to negotiate the Multilateral Agreement on Investment (MAI) at the Organisation for Economic Co-operation and Development (OECD) in the 1995–8 period to develop this argument. This is a particularly good case since the agreement to develop binding rules on how states treat foreign investors was based on a set of core liberal values, widely shared among state elites of the twenty-nine OECD member countries. Despite having virtually no access initially to mainstream media and limited resources (in comparison with multinational capital) a broad coalition of NGOs was able to organise an effective opposition to the MAI and to articulate an alternative vision and critique of globalisation which challenged the prevailing discourse in a number of OECD countries.

We do not take the simplistic view that these NGOs were solely responsible for defeating the MAI, but rather use this case to examine how Internet technology contributed to the capacity of groups to communicate, to quickly mobilise and widely disseminate critical information, outside the control of national elites. While many observers have commented on the proliferation of websites and their importance in bringing the draft agreement to the public, especially in the absence of media attention, little systematic research has been undertaken to look closely at these websites. In contrast we both analyse those websites and interview a number of NGO representatives about their use of the Internet. In the concluding section we argue that the speed and ease of dissemination of large amounts of information, and the lack of control over the Internet have helped create new forms of community which are not spatially defined and thus will have a longer-term impact on political action and on the policy-making process, including foreign policy.

The crisis of citizenship

Citizenship in an era of globalisation

In order to better appreciate this crisis of citizenship it is necessary to outline the view of citizenship that held sway in political theory for most of the postwar period. The most influential exponent of this view was T. H. Marshall who saw citizenship almost entirely in terms of the possession of rights. According to Marshall, citizenship rights could be divided into three different groups – civil, political and social – all of which we were entitled to as citizens and were embedded in the post-war, liberal-democratic welfare state. Each of these rights, according to Marshall, emerged sequentially in the modern era. Civil citizenship, which is rooted in liberalism, embodies the rights that secure individual freedoms, that is, 'liberty of the person, freedom of speech, thought, faith, the right to own property, to conclude valid contracts, and the right to justice' (Marshall 1964: 17). Political citizenship is composed of the democratic rights of participation – 'the right to participate in the exercise of political power as a member of a body invested with political authority or as an elector of the members of such a body' (ibid.:72). Finally, social citizenship refers to the rights to a minimum standard of welfare and income: 'the whole range from the right to a modicum of economic welfare and security to the right to share to the full in the social heritage and to live the life of a civilized being according to the standards prevailing in society' (ibid.).

While Marshall notes that civil and political rights emerged at different times in the modern era, both are rooted in the ancient world. Political citizenship, for example, draws upon the Aristotelian view of citizenship as participation in self-rule, the freedom to participate in public decisions. Civil citizenship is rooted in Roman jurisprudence which conceived individuals as equal rights-bearing creatures. As citizens all were equally entitled to the due process and the equal benefit and protection of the law – in essence, a very private, personal and economic view of citizenship. Of the three groups of rights only social citizenship was new.[1] For Marshall, individual freedoms and the right to participate meant little to citizens if they were shackled by the constraints of poverty.

Today, Marshall's vision of citizenship is under attack. All three elements of citizenship, which formed an integrated whole, are becoming lost, separated or challenged. Social rights are eroding. The welfare state is being hollowed out, as states abandon any notion of redistributing wealth. States are now the midwives of globalisation, radically altering their governments and spending, particularly social spending, as part of an effort to conform to the perceived demands of a global economy.

However, it cannot be said that all elements of citizenship are in equal difficulty. The ideological handmaiden of globalisation, neo-liberalism, is, in effect, a restatement of classical liberalism, where civic citizenship, particularly the protection of property rights, trumps social and political citizenship. In the neo-liberal model, the market replaces the state and the individual, the community. Rather than accept citizenship as a political and social status, neo-liberals reassert the role of the market, rejecting the idea that citizenship confers a status independent of economic standing (Kymlicka and Norman 1995). The ascendancy of markets thus erodes the political dimension of citizenship and becomes a substitute for political decision-making, narrowing the scope of the public and collective decision-making.

The result, it is claimed, is a crisis of citizenship. As the state reduces 'the welfare role of the state and casts citizens out on their own . . . its citizens lose interest in the well-being of the state and the political activities meant to legitimate it' (Lipschutz 1998: 1). Moreover, argues Lipschutz, if the national community

> ceases to exist, or is transformed into something different, what becomes of citizenship and common notions of civic virtue? More specifically, what do citizenship and civic virtue mean in a world in which national and societal borders are becoming permeable, and, in some instances, disappearing?
>
> (1998: 1)

In this view globalisation is an inexorable and unstoppable force destined to leave in its wake the husks and shells of nation-states, empty of any substantive authority and reduced largely to symbolism. The future of citizenship would thus look bleak. We contend, however, that this is too simple a view of globalisation. Globalisation, we argue, is a contradictory and contested phenomenon that both disempowers and empowers states and citizens and is by no means homogeneous in its effects.

The other side of globalisation

To understand how globalisation might empower citizens we must recognise that the information revolution made globalisation possible. As Kobrin notes, 'the emerging global world economy is electronic, integrated through information systems and technology rather than organisational hierarchies' (1998b: 362). We are witnessing what has been described as a third industrial revolution 'characterised by the intensive application of information and communications technology, flexible production systems and organisational structures, market segmentation and globalisation' (Cerny 1995: 607). Financial markets were one of the first economic sectors to globalise by capitalising on the creation of private electronic networks. These networks have facilitated orders of magnitude and concentration far exceeding anything that had been seen previously in financial markets (Sassen 1998a). The consequence has been that the global capital market now has the power to discipline national governments – whether it be the Mexico 'crisis' of December 1994 or the Asian 'crises' of 1997 and 1998. The power of currency traders now exceeds that of central bankers in the determination of foreign exchange rates.

The information revolution is thus reshaping capitalist market economies. In particular, it is disintegrating the vertically integrated 'Fordist' firms which had previously dominated industrial production. However, the information revolution is a contradictory process. While it breaks down hierarchies it creates new power structures. It redistributes not only economic, but also political power. Where economic globalisation appears to be closing public spaces for state-centred citizenship, it may be opening them up elsewhere. For example, in the field of international relations there once was a time when diplomats were the sole interlocutors between countries. Now, however, through the means of the Internet, 'unmediated dialogue and information exchange between citizens from around the world occurs 24 hours a day' (Rothkopf 1998: 3).

Information technologies are thus transforming not only the economy but politics as well, offering new alternatives to citizen activity. The Internet, argues Holmes, breaks down hierarchies whether they be political, economic, class, race or gender (1997: 13). In doing so, 'by allowing the construction of oppositional subjectivities hitherto excluded from the public sphere, the Internet's inherently decentralized form is heralded as its most significant feature' (ibid.). Others such as Rowland go further, describing the Internet as anarchic in nature. By anarchy Rowland is referring not to the absence of government which creates chaos but to a 'vision of an alternative libertarian society based on cooperation as opposed to competition' (Rowland 1997: 340). 'The Net', claims Rowland, 'is public space that is shared by millions of citizens but lacks a government.' While the physical structures of the Net – copper and optical fibre lines and other machinery – may be owned and controlled privately it is the space created when these lines are filled with data – cyberspace – that must be seen as public space. Concludes Rowland:

> The Net exists in that space and is, by definition, owned and controlled by millions of users. It was designed and built to be that way, the design works. The public nature of the Internet is lodged deep in its defining technologies.
>
> (1997: 337)

Thus the Net as a decentralised, if not anarchic, communication system instantiates new forms of interaction and permits new kinds of relationships of power participants. While Rowland views the Net as public space, others see it as permitting a multiplicity of communities, for example, environmental, human rights, to speak to one another, thus, in effect, creating a multiplicity of public spheres existing outside the confines of the state. The Net decentres and continues citizenship in a different form.

The Net possesses other features that promote its use, for example, its accessibility, low cost and ability to disseminate large amounts of information quickly. The result is that 'there is little doubt that the Internet is an enormously important tool and space for democratic participation at all levels, for strengthening civil society and for the formation of a whole new world of transnational political and civic projects' (Sassen 1998b: 546). The public nature and global reach of the Internet means, in effect, that globalisation is contestable. Furthermore, the Net's fundamental change of the economics of long-distance interaction and association encourages the emergence of many more global organisations, by broadening national and regional organisations and as well the formal structuring of relations between individuals worldwide (Koweck 1997). The Net thus encourages the growth of a global civil society. Finally, if globalisation is contestable then the struggle between states and markets is not necessarily over.

Global civil society

Before discussing global civil society it is necessary to specify what is meant by civil society. This is no easy task as there is no single, static definition of the concept. It has a long and contested conceptual history. At its most basic it could be defined as 'that arena of social engagement which exists above the individual and yet below the state' (Wapner 1995: 312–13). While this definition is relatively uncontroversial disagreement arises when two questions are asked:

- Who is included in civil society?
- Is civil society political or apolitical?

In regard to the first question, the fundamental division is between those who include the economy as a part of civil society and those who do not. Earlier eighteenth- and nineteenth-century thinkers – Hegel, Marx and de Tocqueville – all included the economy as a part of civil society. In *Democracy in America*, de Tocqueville distinguished between the state, or more particularly government, and civil life. The state, or government, included legislatures, bureaucracies, courts, the police and the military. Civil life referred to the public life of citizens, that is, their life outside the household. Civil life in America, thought de Tocqueville, was characterised by an abundance of associations of which there were two types, civil associations and political associations. Civil associations are part of the capitalist economic sphere and consist of private economic associations of commerce and industry. Political associations are concerned 'with the public and formal support of specific doctrines by a certain number of individuals who have undertaken to cooperate in a stated way in order to make those associations prevail' (de Tocqueville 1969: 190). Political associations, thought de Tocqueville, were free schools of democracy providing lessons in the art of association. It is important to point out that de Tocqueville included both private bodies, such as churches, and public bodies, such as interest groups, political parties, juries and town councils, among his political associations. Civil society, then, for de Tocqueville, is very much a space for public action; the good citizen operates in and develops politically within civil society. Civil society, thought de Tocqueville, constituted a formidable barrier against a potentially tyrannical or paternalistic state.

Recently there has been a tendency among neo-de Tocquevillian analysts such as Robert Putnam to omit the political and/or economic element in civil society.[2] Putnam argues, for example, that largely apolitical associations that crosscut the major lines of conflict within a society will help produce the moderation and compromising spirit necessary for democratic self-government (Putnam 1995). Putnam thus leaves political associations, such as political parties and social movements, outside of his version of civil society. Putnam also leaves the economy outside of civil society, as do others. We do not.

We argue that both the political and the economic variables must be included as part of civil society. The political variable includes those organisations, parties and social movements that mobilise citizens around particular social and economic issues. Each provides critical sites of civic engagement for citizens. Similarly, the economy cannot be omitted from the civil society. By leaving the economy outside of civil society we neglect to analyse ways in which the economy can be seen as a despotic force as prone as the state to coerce civil society (Axtman 1996). We also potentially neglect the conflict between capital and labour on who should pay the price for, and reap the benefits of, a global economy. This approach does not reduce the economy to one pluralist force among many. Rather, we argue, the economy, or the market, is the most potent force in civil society rivalling, if not superseding, the state in terms of importance. Thus we favour a more inclusive approach to understanding civil society and the emerging global civil society. Global civil society consists of the myriad groups and networks of action and knowledge that can, but do not necessarily, extend across state borders.[3] It includes local, national and global actors. It also includes the economy as well as the family.

The emerging global civil society is highly political. For example, the pressure market forces put upon states throughout the world to reduce spending and the welfare state is well known. Less observed has been the growth of non-profit organisations, primarily NGOs and transnational social movements, that challenge the globalisation process. What constitutes an NGO, Higgott and Reich tell us, is not a discrete science. They note that their numbers, both nationally and internationally, have expanded rapidly. NGOs may be large organisations such as Médicins sans Frontières, Care and Oxfam, but there are many smaller NGOs as well. In addition groups may vary in the extent to which they challenge or are beneficiaries of the status quo (Macdonald 1994). Increasingly some NGOs and social movements are taking positions vis-à-vis economic globalisation. Cecelia Lynch, for example, notes that 'there is a developing understanding among some "progressive" contemporary social movement groups that economic globalization poses the primary obstacle to the fulfillment of their goals' (Lynch 1998: 149).

In effect, as capitalism is globalising so are its opponents.[4] In both instances the information revolution is playing a key role. According to Higgot and Reich (1999: 16):

> The information revolution, especially Internet technology with its speed and reduction in cost in the transfer of information, is perhaps the largest factor at the disposal of NGOs in an era of changing international diplomacy. In addition to the flows of information that have traditionally been controlled by state or corporate actors, now a vast array of other non state actors, with access to a computer and modem, can become international communicators. The rise of NGO networks is the classic example of the emergence of new foreign policy actors who can now have a vastly increased number of channels of cross border communication.

The result is that it is becoming increasingly difficult to limit access to international trade and investment negotiation processes. Those opposed to the neo-liberal policies of economic globalisation – unions, church groups, environmentalists, national-cultural organisations – have found that the Internet has empowered them as international actors. The information revolution once feared by many is now being used as a democratising force to pressure groups to articulate their positions to ever wider and more demanding publics, domestically and internationally. In effect, the top-down globalisation process, driven by economic, political and state elites, is being contested as new voices in civil and global civil society emerge to challenge it. One of the most cited recent examples of how forces in civil and global civil society have combined to resist the traditional closed-door, top-down, multilateral process is the defeat of the Multilateral Agreement on Investment.

The MAI, NGOs and the Internet

Why the MAI? Making the case for this case

Why use the MAI as a case study to examine empirically the argument about globalisation's impact on citizens, democracy and states? First, many have argued that the root of many of the constraints states currently face in their capacity to make policy is globalisation, especially in the form of integrated globalised production, increasing economic interdependence among states, and the enhanced mobility of capital. As a consequence capital has increased its power over both labour and states. In order to insulate this liberalisation of exchange rules from domestic political processes, Gill (1995) and others have argued, efforts have been made to create international rules designed to further limit state intervention in markets, erode state policy autonomy and thus indirectly erode democracy and citizenship. Nothing, one could argue, better epitomises these trends than the effort launched, in the spring of 1995, to negotiate a multilateral agreement on investment at the OECD.

The agreement, as originally proposed, was clearly designed and intended to limit state discretionary authority to discriminate between domestic and foreign investment in regulation and to provide a high level of certainty to investors by ensuring transparent domestic processes and high levels of compensation for investors, in the case of either direct or indirect expropriation. In the initial draft of the agreement corporations, like states, were given recourse to dispute resolution procedures in the event that states were seen to violate the agreement. The intended effect of this provision was to enhance the protection of foreign investors from changes in state regulations which might hurt their interests. Thus discriminatory state regulation of foreign firms, or regulation that could be seen as indirect expropriation, would be prohibited unless states negotiated specific exemptions, which negotiators at the outset, at least, intended to keep to a minimum. Thus the MAI reflected, it could be argued, the growing power of capital and the resulting limits on state policy discretion. At the same time the process of negotiating these rules was very much an inter-state one and thus subject to, and embedded in, domestic political processes within the twenty-nine OECD member countries.

The second reason for choosing the MAI is the even more obvious one, that this was the first major inter-state economic negotiation where the media (Drohan 1998; De Jonquieres 1998), the negotiators, the NGOs opposing the agreement and academics (Kobrin 1998) all seem to agree that the Internet was a key tool, used effectively by opponents to prevent an agreement. Thus examining this case should shed some light on the question of whether new technology, as part of the process of globalisation, has opened up alternate public spaces that may be able to counteract the constraints on the state. It may indicate whether, or to what extent, these new public spaces which have been opened to civil society can compensate for the loss of some aspects of citizenship which arise as a result of globalised production, by generating new forms and ways to articulate a challenge to the market. In order to evaluate the extent to which this was, or was not, the case we need to begin with an overview of the MAI negotiations, the role that NGOs played in the process and where the Internet fits in. We then need to look in more detail at the MAI and the Internet, specifically how organisations and individuals used it.

The MAI negotiations

The MAI negotiations were drawn out over a three-and-a-half-year process which ultimately resulted in the cessation of negotiations on 2 December 1998. The negotiations had been formally launched in May 1995 at the OECD ministerial meeting, largely as a result of a US-led, and business-supported, initiative. The idea was to create a binding, free-standing agreement, thought to be easier within a smaller, like-minded group of wealthier economies. Non-OECD states would then accede to the agreement on a negotiated, case-by-case basis.

The OECD ministers' decision to launch negotiations in May 1995 was not a secret, although it received almost no press attention at the time. The negotiations began in earnest the following autumn in 1995 and appeared, at first, to make rapid progress on agreeing to the main principles, such as national treatment and strong investor protection, including investor–state dispute resolution processes. The key political issues of which economic sectors or state policies would be exempted from these general obligations were not really addressed until the winter of 1997. Within the negotiating group of member countries there was already some discontent with the process, especially the role of the secretariat and the chair in putting forward draft texts that were not regarded by some members to represent a consensus. This discontent and the real political divisions began to emerge in March and April 1997 as member states lodged their reservations to the obligations contained in the text.

Around the same time a draft of the February 1997 text was leaked and ended up very quickly in the hands of, and on the websites of, two public policy advocacy groups in North America. These groups pointed to the text as proof of a secretive process which threatened state sovereignty and had major implications for citizens. Until that point there had been almost no media coverage of the negotiations (Preamble Center 1998). The agreement had been portrayed as 'technical' and entirely in keeping with the rather mundane economic work for which the OECD was known. With the leak of the draft text and the dramatic pronouncements of critics came an increase in media coverage in some countries, just at the point at which the process was becoming bogged down and more political.

As domestic attention to the negotiations grew in a number of member countries, the pressures on negotiators increased, as did the number of state reservations lodged against the obligations of the agreement. Legislative committees, again reflecting public pressure, began hearings, starting with Canada in the autumn of 1997, followed in 1998 by Australia, France, the UK and the European Parliament, among others. Recognising that the likelihood of an agreement which would bring real gains in liberalisation for global capital was slipping away, negotiators attempted a high-level political meeting in February 1998 designed to break the logjam. When it failed it became clear to a number of key players, especially the USA, that whatever limited agreement might ultimately emerge from the process was unlikely to be worth the political costs of trying to get it ratified. As enthusiasm for the agreement waned, a number of states under the most pressure, including France, pressed for a hiatus in the negotiations, which was agreed to in April 1998. Opposition continued to mount and when the negotiations were due to resume in mid-October the French Government, under pressure from the Greens and Communists within its coalition, withdrew from the negotiations (Riché 1998), thereby ending any real hope of agreement, a fact acknowledged by the rest of the negotiators in December 1998.

What this brief summary clearly indicates is that no set of opponents, even ones armed with Internet technology, can take credit for the failure to agree at the OECD. However, the political delays and disagreements created an opportunity which these groups were able to exploit effectively to mobilise domestic opposition in a number of countries.

NGOs and the MAI

The process of negotiating at the OECD did not initially provide for any input from organisations other than those which already had formal consultative status (though no role in actual negotiations), namely the Business and Industry Advisory Committee (BIAC) and the Trade and Industry Advisory Committee (TUAC). Other organisations, such as environmental groups which had had dealings with the OECD on environmental issues, were not consulted partly because the negotiations were seen as technical issues of investment and controlled very closely by the committee and division of the OECD secretariat which deals with investment.

A number of NGOs, especially the Third World Network in Malaysia, had been critical of investment negotiations at the OECD and of attempts to push investment negotiations prior to the December 1996 Singapore World Trade Organisation (WTO) ministerial meeting. A small number of environmental and development NGOs had expressed concern about the MAI and met informally with the chair of the OECD negotiating group in the late winter of 1996–7 but, overall, had very little opportunity to have input. This changed after the leaking of the draft text in early 1997. Concerned about accusations of a secretive process the MAI negotiators, urged on by the secretariat, approved the release of the draft text on an OECD MAI website. Apparently stung by the negative view of the MAI revealed when the chair of the negotiating group surfed the Net, the OECD decided to meet formally on 27 October 1997 with a much larger number of NGOs[5] (Sierra Club 1997). By all accounts the meeting was quite fractious and, for some negotiators, eye-opening about the extent to which domestic concern and opposition was growing in some countries, reinforced, in Canada's case, by the presence of CBC television coverage. The NGOs which had attended the meeting were able, despite differences in tactics, to formulate a common position and confront the negotiators with a demand to suspend talks. When the negotiators refused the NGOs vowed all-out opposition to any agreement (Public Citizen 1998). In many ways this signalled a turning point as the NGOs began concerted and co-ordinated efforts to mobilise domestic opposition within the OECD countries and elsewhere. It thus marks the beginning of the real politicisation of these negotiations in a number of countries. How important was the Internet in this process? How was it used as a tool that is somehow different from, or new in comparison to, the existing technologies of communications?

The Internet and civil society

The growth of the Internet has been a topic of discussion and debate in the media and popular culture and one that has been characterised much more by hype and exaggerated claims than serious analysis. There is, however, some evidence that the Internet has had an impact on the way in which information is produced and communicated. Three characteristics have been identified by a number of analysts. First, many argue, the Internet greatly enhances the speed of communication of large amounts of information, at a relatively low, and certainly declining, cost. Second, unlike the broadcast media, which is a one-way, producer–receiver process, the Internet, more analogous to the telephone (Rowland 1997), permits interactivity where participants both produce and consume information. The Internet thus creates a rather anarchic environment where information flows in a largely unmediated way, and can be shared so as to facilitate collaborative, rather than competitive, behaviour. In addition changes to standards, developments in software and hardware, and government- and industry-supported initiatives, facilitated a major growth in the Internet in the mid-1990s just as the OECD negotiating process was under way.

Because the Internet is such a rapidly changing, and in many ways anarchic, network of networks, studying its use by groups is not easy. For many political scientists interest in the way in which groups have used the Net began with observations of its use by the specialised networks in the areas of human rights and the environment (Deibert 1998; Stanbury and Vertinsky 1995) and by groups such as the Chiapas rebels, who were able to bring their message to a wider world and co-ordinate external support through the use of a website (Cleaver 1998). A second major aspect of the Internet has been its use, primarily through e-mail, listservs and news groups, to create a network of activists who can easily and quickly share information and co-ordinate strategy. To date there has been little study of how groups used this technology in the case of the MAI.

We began then by surveying the presence on the Internet of MAI websites in February and March 1999, less than three months after the cessation of negotiations on 2 December. While it may have been preferable to have done the survey during the negotiations, one characteristic of websites is that, while they can be changed easily and updated frequently, they, like the smile of the Cheshire cat, can remain for some time after the body has disappeared. Thus while many of the websites had not been updated since the winter of 1998, they were still on the Net a year later. While some may have disappeared or been transformed we feel that our survey is still broadly indicative of what citizens searching for information would have found, for example, in the winter of 1998 when public debate about the MAI was probably at its height.[6]

Our search for sites used several search engines, including Copernic and Mata Hari, and cross-referenced results, eliminating duplicates and errors. The search was conducted using the term Multilateral Agreement on Investment or its equivalent in French, Spanish and German. The linguistic choices were a function of the researchers' language skills. In each case we worked backwards from the MAI pages that came up in the search also to find the person or organisation responsible for, or the sponsor of, the website. The result was 400 MAI sites,[7] reflecting the groups and organisations that sponsored them. Those sites in English, French and German were then coded for a number of characteristics using Microsoft Access.[8] The result provides a very preliminary snapshot of what sorts of groups and organisations used websites to communicate information about the MAI. Those who are knowledgeable about the Net will recognise that our methods did not capture all of the websites which contained information about the MAI and we do not claim to have done so.[9] However, cross-referencing our findings with a number of sources suggests that we did locate most of the major groups and organisations seeking to influence the public debate about the MAI using websites.

Second, we wished to find out how many NGOs, especially those credited with playing a major role in the campaign of opposition to the MAI, specifically used the Internet in their efforts. We identified twenty-three organisations, contacted them and asked them to respond to a set of simple questions about how they had used the Internet. Responses came in the course of face-to-face or telephone interviews, or via e-mail. About half of the organisations responded, and, coupled with interviews with negotiators and OECD officials done over three years, they provide a picture of how groups used the Internet.

Who is on the Web?

The first simple question we asked was who was on the Web? We were initially interested in what types of organisations, in which countries, were using the Web to communicate on the MAI. Table 12.1 provides a breakdown by type or organisation of the 352 sites our researcher was able to code fully. It is based on locating the name and type of group or organisation sponsoring the site – not always an easy feat. The table raises one of the questions about the definition of civil society discussed above. Much of the anecdotal discussion of the Internet and the MAI suggests it was a tool of NGOs – usually conceived of in terms of non-profit groups, separate from the political process. However, although a number of advocacy NGOs, such as Public Citizen and the Council of Canadians, did play a major role in leaking the draft text and providing detailed critiques of the MAI, the surprise is the number of websites that were, in fact, sponsored by elected members of legislatures and political parties (in most cases, opposition parties). Clearly some would place parties and parliamentarians within the purview of civil society, but also in the top six types are business groups (in some cases law offices), individuals, media organisations (including both broadcast and print) and government agencies. Our interviews would suggest, however, that MAI websites came in waves and if we were able to track the timing would find that many of the media and government (departments, agencies, parliaments and even

Table 12.1 Websites by type of sponsoring organisation

Type of group sponsoring site	Number of sites	Per cent of total sites
Public Policy Advocacy	53	15.1
Political Parties and MP sites	45	12.8
Media Organisations	37	10.5
Government Agencies – all levels	35	10
Individual/Personal	30	8.5
Business Organisations (incl. law offices)	26	7.4
Broad, anti-MAI coalitions	20	5.7
Environmental Organisations	19	5.4
Trade Unions	16	4.6
International Organisations	17	4.8
Research Institutes/Centres	15	4.3
Student Groups	9	2.6
Other (unable to classify)	9	2.6
Arts/Cultural organisations	8	2.3
Church/Religious	5	1.4
Total	352	100.0

municipalities) websites followed in response to those of the advocacy, environmental and development NGOs.

We also tried to get a sense of the countries where organisations were located which were active on the Web; again, this was not always easy.[10] Clearly what we found was a function of a range of factors. As the World Bank's 1998 and a recent OECD report indicate, access to the Internet is very uneven (Hanson 1999) and largely a function of the level of wealth of an economy, the telecommunications infrastructure and cost of connection. Second, our linguistic limits led us to under-report the total number of sites, especially in Asia. However, a couple of aspects of the results are interesting. The significant number of USA sites is no surprise, but the relatively large number of Canadian sites, relative to population (over half the number in the USA) is striking and reflective of both the level of connectedness in Canada, which now approaches numbers in the USA, and the extent to which groups were active on this issue in Canada, itself a reflection of the controversy the agreement generated. A similar comment could be made about Australia, New Zealand and Austria. A surprise, however, was the small number of French sites found. Given the strong telecommunications infrastructure and the political controversy the MAI generated this clearly merits more investigation.[11] It may reflect two other factors: first, the cost of connection; and second, unlike a number of other countries, media attention to the MAI from earlier on was very high in France. Surprising, too, were the number of websites in Spanish overall, and the number in Latin America countries, which, with the exception of Mexico, were not OECD members. Brazil, Chile and Argentina were, however, major candidates for accession to the agreement and were courted by the OECD and sat

Table 12.2 Websites by country

Country	Number of websites	Per cent of total
United States	129	31.9
Canada	71	17.6
Australia	36	8.9
Germany	32	7.9
United Kingdom	17	4.2
Spain	16	4
New Zealand	14	3.5
Austria	12	3
Mexico	10	2.5
Sweden	8	2
Uruguay	6	1.5
Nicaragua	4	1
Argentina	4	1
Switzerland	4	1
South Africa	3	0.7
Norway	3	0.7
Netherlands	3	0.7
Japan	3	0.7
Denmark	3	0.7
Chile	3	0.7
Brazil	2	0.5
Singapore	2	0.5
France	2	0.5
Other Countries	15	4.5
Total	400	100.0

as observers during the negotiations. This may have spurred some attention to the issue in this region as did NAFTA, perhaps, and the upcoming Free Trade of the Americas negotiations.

How is information linked and shared on the Web? A number of commentators on the Internet have pointed to two aspects that make it an especially speedy and effective way to share and gather information – these are the use of hypertext links and the extent to which information may be reproduced and shared in a variety of websites located around the world. While this sharing of information has been a bane for copyright lawyers it has been a cheap and effective way for groups with very limited resources to have virtually instant access to the information generated by groups with more resources. According to commentators like de Brie (1998a) of *Le Monde Diplomatique* this aspect of the Internet was a key in redressing the traditional monopoly on complex, technical information which large corporations, governments and the media have, and providing citizens and groups with limited resources with quick and easy access to large amounts of complex information. As Table 12.3 indicates, virtually all of the websites (650) had links to other sites which provided information and our researcher was able to

Table 12.3 Top ten organisations appearing as links of websites

Name of organisation	Frequency	Rank
OECD	95	1
MAI Not (Flora)-OPIRG-Carleton Univ.	87	2
National Centre for Sustainability (Victoria, BC)	25	3
Appleton (law office, Toronto)	23	4
YUCC (personal site York Univ. law student)	22	5
Public Citizen (Washington, DC)	21	6
Preamble Center (Washington, DC)	21	6
Friends of the Earth-US (Washington, DC)	19	7
Multinational Monitor (US-linked to Public Cit.)	17	8
Council of Canadians	16	9
Canadian Centre for Policy Alternatives (Ottawa)	12	10
Stop MAI – Australia	12	10

track the most frequently occurring links within the websites, giving a sense then of which organisations were major sources of information.

As indicated in Table 12.3 ten organisations accounted for over half of all of the hypertext links which appeared on the 400 websites. Of these the OECD's presence at the top is accounted for by the decision in the spring of 1997 to release draft texts of the MAI. What is more striking is the extent to which virtually all of the other sites are North American, with the dominance of Canadian sites. This is indicative of the fact that the North American sites appeared earliest, and because of the leak of the draft and the analysis they provided of the MAI were turned to frequently as a source of information.

This is also reflected in an examination of the content of the websites. In many cases sites merely posted texts of information, stories, news and analysis of the MAI that had been generated elsewhere. In most cases this was clearly acknowledged. However, in the world of the Internet rules on how and when to acknowledge sources are notable by their absence, making the task of tracing sources of information challenging. Indeed the whole issue of identity on the Internet is problematic. Despite the challenge, we made an effort to roughly assess and code those sites sponsored by NGOs (i.e. excluding government, political party, business and international organisation sites) according to the originality of the information (using a threshold of 60 per cent or more of news and information generated locally) provided on the site and found again, as Table 12.4 indicates, a predominance of NGO sites with original information based in North America.

NGOs and the Internet tool

In order to take a closer look at how NGOs used the Net we asked the NGOs we contacted six simple questions about how they used the Internet, its advantages and disadvantages and their assessment of the impact it had. The NGOs were strikingly similar in the way that they used the Internet and what variation there was was often a function of their size or restrictions on their activities dictated by

Table 12.4 Number of sites with 60 per cent or more original content

Country	Number of sites
United States	20
Canada	16
Australia	8
Germany	6
United Kingdom	4
New Zealand	3
Austria	1
Costa Rica	1
Netherlands	1
South Africa	1

their funding sources. Virtually all of the organisations used a website, e-mail and a listserv as part of their anti-MAI activities. Websites were generally targeted at a broader public than just a group's main membership and were not, by and large, used to fundraise for campaigns or for more routine communications with members. Their main function was to provide a means of gathering and sharing information and mobilising those concerned about the agreement. One respondent described the process as a giant relay of obtaining and quickly passing on information. Some of the larger advocacy and environmental groups shared detailed technical and often legal, analyses of the draft MAI texts. A number of organisations used their sites to mobilise concerned citizens by providing accessible means to lobby decision-makers with draft faxes, open letters which citizens could sign and send automatically, and press releases which local groups could also use in an effort to garner more media coverage. A few groups, such as Preamble and the Canadian Centre for Policy Alternatives, were prohibited from engaging in advocacy and were limited by tax or charitable status to sharing information and research. In their own lobbying efforts, however, virtually all the groups interviewed continued to use traditional methods with their domestic legislators and officials, including phone calls and face-to-face meetings, which they regard as more personal and more effective with decision-makers.

E-mail, especially automated mailing lists, were used by all groups to maintain links with other activists and concerned citizens both within and outside their own countries. For the larger groups that played a very active role in the anti-MAI campaign, such as World Wide Fund for Nature (WWF) and Friends of the Earth (FoE), it was used to link local, national and international organisations in the campaign to share strategy and intelligence and co-ordinate activities with allied groups. E-mailing lists, in some cases, involved as many as several thousand names. Some more institutionalised groups, such as WWF, were co-ordinating meetings and consultations with OECD officials while at the same time being involved in broad anti-MAI campaigns. Some groups maintained two or more separate mailing lists, one for contacting concerned and interested groups and individuals and a smaller, closed list of key contacts and activists in other groups, with whom they shared strategy. These smaller lists were often based on previous campaigns and connections from, for example, anti-NAFTA or World Bank networks.

For most groups the key advantages of using the Internet were its speed, the capacity to move large amounts of information easily and the overall lower costs for NGOs compared with traditional methods such as mail-outs. E-mail also allowed anti-MAI strategists to quickly share intelligence and strategy and compare notes in a timely way as events unfolded. The speed, the ease and the cost made sharing complex technical information easier and provided individuals with resources they would not have otherwise had. The access to information was seen by NGOs to be both empowering for themselves and the public. Many of their views echoed Le Brie's comments cited above. In essence the Internet helped to break the information monopoly enjoyed by business, government leaders and OECD officials. Several NGOs commented on how, even though the OECD negotiations centred on complex, technical issues, conducted in secret in an exclusive organisation, by being able to access the latest intelligence and analysis of the long complicated draft texts instantaneously, as well as the state of play of the negotiations, they and their supporters were able to challenge their own government officials and OECD officials. This was especially the case when they were being given selective or misleading information. Negotiators, in a number of countries, confirm that groups and individuals often came armed with information they had obtained off the Internet, although some officials bemoaned what they saw as outdated or misleading information on some websites.

Groups were also similar in the concerns they expressed about the disadvantages of the Internet as a tool. In the main these centre on three issues. The first is the problem of uneven access. This is an important issue for all groups, but most especially those in, or dealing with, Third World organisations and citizens, or low-income groups or regions. In some cases unreliable electrical power sources, the lack of a telecommunications infrastructure, or high connection costs limit access. Even groups within very affluent societies, however, recognise that some of their members are not connected and are careful to treat them equitably in terms of providing information in order not to alienate or inadvertently marginalise them.

The second major concern is with the quality and volume of information to which the Internet provides access. Stanbury and Vertinsky (1995) have raised the question of how empowering huge volumes of meaningless information may be in a democracy. Might swamping citizens with low-quality information lead to manipulation, or, at best, anxiety and confusion? In the case of the anti-MAI campaign many NGOs reported that the volume of e-mail was a problem, required more and more resources and, while speedy and timely, carried its own difficulties. Commentators have pointed to the lack of social conventions and frameworks which, while making e-mail informal, flexible and easy, also make it intemperate, leading, as NGOs acknowledged, to misunderstanding, crises and confusion at times. With greater volume comes the problem of separating wheat from chaff and the risk of really important information slipping by.

The quality of information was also a concern for many groups. The ease of entry – anyone can create a website – and the lack of standards or rules, mean that the quality and reliability of information varies widely. In some cases, such as news groups, where anyone can post a message or respond to previous postings, discussions can lose focus and attract the more fringe, somewhat paranoid individuals who are never more than a click away. In a few cases useful anti-MAI news groups or listservs descended into discussions of Monsanto seeds or Y2K conspiracies. Some NGOs took on a conscious role in editing and screening messages to ensure the quality of information met some minimal criteria in order to preserve the utility and credibility of their information. A number of NGOs were concerned, too, that inaccurate, outdated or hysterical claims about the MAI would undermine the more serious and thoughtful critiques which they had worked hard to provide.

The management of websites and large volumes of e-mail were, especially for some smaller organisations, burdens on resources, either in staff time or the need to upgrade servers and other hardware. Some felt that the heightened expectations of ever faster and more powerful technologies created pressure to respond quickly to messages and update sites. Finally a number of groups also raised concerns about the increased reliance on Internet technology and thus more vulnerability to technology failures and security concerns, particularly given the growing tendency to share intelligence and co-ordinate strategy this way. Overall, however, NGOs saw the Internet as an important tool in their activities, despite its disadvantages. Did it ultimately, though, make any difference to the fate of the MAI? It is to this question that we now turn.

Stopping the MAI – did the Internet really matter?

How do we know that the use of the Internet had an important impact on the resulting failure of the negotiations? To determine that we need to address three questions. First, did the MAI Internet campaign have an impact, i.e. was there evidence that it affected citizens in some way? Second, if it did have an impact, how was that translated into increased domestic opposition to the agreement? Third, did the opposition to the MAI which emerged affect the attitudes of particular governments towards the agreement? While none of the NGOs we contacted felt that the Internet campaign alone was responsible for the defeat of the MAI, they all felt that they had some evidence that it had had an impact on citizens and the broader public debate, and that this, in turn, did ultimately have an impact on negotiators and OECD officials.

New technologies, spurred on by the growth in electronic commerce and marketing, now enable site sponsors on the Internet to track the accessing of websites (hits, in computer vernacular). While a few NGOs now have the capacity to track hits there has not been a lot of analysis of the MAI campaign in those terms, but most NGOs did monitor e-mail communications and other forms of public contact and activities which appeared to be connected to their websites. Many NGOs experienced increased e-mail contacts, phone calls and personal requests for information on the MAI. A number also noticed increased, or higher than expected, attendance at meetings, discussions or demonstrations which appeared to be linked, again, to interest generated by information on their web-sites. Most NGOs also noted a broader range of contacts, both national and international, as a result of their websites. The earliest North American sites noted a large amount of European contact and hits during the first part of 1997. This first wave was followed by a second wave, in late 1997 and early 1998, of new websites in Europe, especially in smaller countries like the Netherlands and Austria, as well as in Australia and New Zealand. Communication on the Web is, however, a much more random process than more targeted efforts such as mail-outs and most NGOs are now more conscious of the need to monitor and track contacts and ensure that sites are user friendly.

All of the groups contacted felt that the Internet campaign had affected the domestic and international public debate on the MAI. In particular, many pointed to the greater co-ordination of activities and the sharing of information among groups. Coupled with the limited mainstream media coverage of the negotiations in many countries, this led to a situation where NGOs, by late 1997 and early 1998, had already set the terms of the public debate. Citizens and groups that were well co-ordinated and armed with detailed information and analysis were much harder for negotiators, or OECD officials, to dismiss as uninformed, nationalist or fringe elements.

In a number of cases NGOs felt the presence of anti-MAI information on the Internet had shaped domestic media coverage and citizen opposition. In the case of Austria, even negotiators admit that media coverage and active and growing opposition to the MAI in the spring of 1998 was a result of the Internet campaign. Business representatives also ruefully admit that the NGOs had successfully, although in their view misleadingly, set the terms of the debate.[12] Some business representatives were privately critical of the inadequacy of OECD efforts to respond to the campaign. Attempts to dismiss opponents as un- or mis-informed, such as the OECD Secretary-General's speeches during a visit to Montreal and Ottawa in May 1998, only inflamed opponents and irritated state negotiators who were well aware, after lengthy conversations with ordinary citizens (such as a grandmother from Kelowna) on issues such as dispute resolution or the Ethyl case, that dismissing public concerns was an inadequate response.

The question of how this more aroused and concerned group of citizens affected the decisions and actions of negotiators at the OECD is much more difficult to assess. Had there not already been major inter-state divisions over aspects of the agreement, delays and splits within governments (e.g. France) would the Internet campaign have made a difference? This is hard to say. The ability to share large amounts of information quickly and co-ordinate positions and actions among groups and citizens via the Internet clearly enhanced the effectiveness of the effort to mobilise citizens in opposition to the MAI. Since rules on trade and investment are still largely the purview of state negotiators within international economic organisations virtually all of which, in the case of the OECD, are representative governments that must ultimately obtain domestic ratification of agreements, increasing domestic mobilisation in opposition to an agreement is not a trivial achievement. Raising the political costs of signing an MAI, which indirectly, one could argue, is what the Internet campaign helped do, made it less likely that negotiators would find enough gain in any version of the agreement to offset the domestic pain. When France withdrew it was already clear to a number of other negotiators that their governments did not have the political will to continue. They heaved a collective sigh of relief and welcomed the opportunity to let France take the blame for pulling the plug.

Conclusion

Our examination of the use the Internet by forces in civil and global society to mobilise against the MAI indicates that it is certainly premature to claim that globalisation and citizenship are incompatible. On the contrary, the growth of a global civil society facilitated by the rise of informational technologies has the potential to enhance citizenship globally and domestically. By opening public spaces and making critical aspects of politics more relevant new information technologies are revitalising democratic institutions. A quick review of how the Net was used to mobilise against the MAI will help understand what we mean.

At the outset the MAI negotiations had all the classic attributes of top-down, hierarchical, secretive, bureaucratic, technical, undemocratic, if not anti-democratic, decision-making. Few citizens even knew about the MAI. Clearly the activities of NGOs using the Net radically altered the context in which the debate took place and how it was framed. In terms of citizen activity and democratic government this was crucial. Both citizens and democratic government depend upon information and communication. Once the draft February 1997 text was posted on the Net the floodgates were opened. No longer could negotiations be hidden from the spotlight of public scrutiny. No longer could mainstream media and broadcasting continue to ignore what was happening in Paris. In brief, through adept use of the Internet those opposed to the MAI were able to open up and strengthen the public spheres which citizens depend upon for active participation in civil society. They did so by opening up public spaces in which citizens engaged in discourse and by making domestic and international institutions of governance more permeable to the dialogue within these public spaces.

Our examination of website content and interviews indicates that a vast amount of information, stories, news and analyses of the MAI were generated and disseminated by means of the Net and e-mail. Citizens and groups that were left out of the discussion could discuss among themselves the merits of the MAI utilising detailed, and heretofore unavailable, analyses of the MAI posted on websites all over the world. Stimulated by what they read, and even wrote, citizens began to contact their elected representatives. Thus, the traditional institutions of governance were now becoming permeable to the dialogue taking place in civil and global civil society. Those we interviewed emphasised the ability of activists to communicate and mobilise the grassroots. One interviewee stressed that the anti-MAI campaign gave people a sense that they could participate in their democracies again. Indeed, one outcome was to make governments more accountable. As noted previously, in a number of countries parliamentary committees began to hold public hearings and parliamentary debates occurred.

Our analysis indicates that those who engaged in activities on the Net represented a full range of participants in civil society (Tables 12.1 and 12.3). What is particularly striking is the extent to which the use of the Net levelled the playing field in terms of who could and did participate, de-centring public discussion away from government agencies and business organisations. The anti-MAI groups became particularly adept at linking horizontally to exchange information and to engage in unmediated civic communication, thus eroding the monopoly of information possessed by traditional economic, broadcast media and political hierarchies.

Furthermore, we found that in the case of the MAI the use of the Internet and its facilitation of the growth of a global civil society and global citizenship do not necessarily come at the expense of domestic civil society. Rather, one could argue, the rise of a global civil society can help revitalise domestic civil society and democracy, expand public debate over international issues and enhance public accountability of political elites.

Clearly, the campaign against the MAI poses a serious challenge to international trade negotiators and politicians. Can they carry on behind closed doors with business as usual? Probably not. How then do they incorporate groups from civil and global civil society into their negotiations? What criteria do they use? Should NGOs, for example, be required to prove that they are democratic themselves and accountable to their members and general public? Clearly not all are. Some are structured as top-down organisations themselves. Moreover, there is still a question of just how democratic participation in global civil society really is. While the Internet broadens access to debate not everyone has access to the Internet. In fact, as indicated previously, access is highly correlated with the level of wealth in a society, the telecommunications infrastructure and cost of connection. Those participating are often self-selected and tend to be middle-class white males.

It also must be emphasised that the use of the Internet is not a substitute for traditional political activity and participation. Repeatedly those we interviewed stressed that there is no substitute for face-to-face contact not only amongst activists themselves, but also with politicians and the bureaucratic elite. While the Net can broadly inform people there is a need to follow up directly with individuals and decision-makers. For example, one person representing an advocacy organisation we interviewed spoke of meetings with a government minister and a government negotiator in Paris. As soon as the meetings were over the results were disseminated on the Net around the world.

While the use of the Internet enhances the potential for citizenship in a number of respects those who we interviewed were perfectly aware of its limitations. Not all information provided is good, accurate or timely. Often there is too much information and it is impossible to analyse, digest and respond to all of it.

Furthermore, communication on the Net is not always civil. It is often intemperate and tangential to the debate.

The Net, then, is not a panacea for all that ails citizenship. It does, however, have the potential to enhance it. Can it help restore the welfare state and social citizenship that some desire? By helping make politics more relevant it underscores the fact that the struggle between markets and states is not yet over. Moreover, if some citizens don't get what they want – a viable welfare state, a clean environment, enhancement of human rights, protection of national cultures – global capitalism may not receive the political legitimacy it needs to expand and maintain itself. The biggest test of future multilateral discussions may lie in their ability to incorporate these concerns in their negotiations. Whatever occurs, multilateral negotiators now know they are in the global spotlight and will be under the scrutiny of NGOs and citizens who are well connected, well armed with information, and prepared to challenge them every step of the way.

Notes

The authors wish to acknowledge the research assistance of Leonard Stoleriu-Falchidi and the financial support of the Mission Critical Research Fund of Athabasca University. This chapter was presented as a paper at the Panel *Politics beyond Borders through the Internet: A Global Civil Society* of the Annual Meeting of the International Studies Association, Los Angeles, 17 March 2000.

1 Even this is questionable. Both Marx and Aristotle agreed that citizenship could best be realised when 'men' were freed from material necessity and possessed the leisure that would permit them to participate in public decision-making.
2 For example, Michael Waltzer, Jean Cohen and Ronnie Lipschutz all omit the economy from civil society. Roland Axtman includes the economy.
3 This definition parallels Lipschutz's except that we do not exclude the economy and the family.
4 Robert Cox (1999) has suggested such movements may have the potential to form a counterhegemony to global capital. While this debate is beyond the scope of this paper our research does suggest that new information technologies may have an important role to play in this process.
5 At the time twenty-seven NGOs signed the Joint Declaration on the Multilateral Agreement on Investment. By February 1998 the number had risen to over 600.
6 An early trial search of sites in January yielded virtually the same number of hits as our detailed research in March. Many of those in the NGOs we interviewed also indicated that they were unable to update sites frequently because of limited staff and, in some cases, even as negotiations were faltering, left anti-MAI material in place on websites because they expected negotiations to migrate to the WTO.
7 The 400 websites were the result of many more hits. Each hit with a search engine indicates a Web page containing the search term. Some larger sites contained a number of pages dealing with the MAI and thus would be recorded as several hits.
8 Time constraints did not permit the coding of the Spanish sites. A number of sites in other languages also came up during the search which we are unable as yet to code.
9 Most industry analysts claim that because of the exponential increase in sites and the way in which search engines operate, even the most thorough search will only yield 30–40 per cent of what is really out there.
10 Not all URLs contain a country code, and it is quite possible that a site which might be sponsored by a group in one country could be on a website in another.

11 The early withdrawal of France from the negotiations on 16 October which abruptly ended the public debate may mean that some sites had disappeared by the time of our analysis. This does not mean however, that the sites we did capture were unimportant. At least one did play a key role on the ground in Paris, sharing intelligence with other groups worldwide. Even groups that did not have websites often had access to information on other sites which they could use effectively, as the case of Austria, discussed below, indicates.

12 Based on interviews conducted in September 1998 in Vienna, December 1998 in Paris and February 1999 in Washington, DC.

References

'A Case of MAI Culpa' (1998) *Financial Times*, editorial (Oct. 20).

Adorno, T. and Horkheimer, M. (1973) *Dialectic of Enlightenment*. London: Allen Lane.

Albrow, Martin (1996) *The Global Age*. Cambridge: Polity Press.

—— and Washbourne, Neil (1997) 'Sociology for postmodern organisers – working the Net' in Martin Albrow (ed.), *Do Organizations Have Feelings?* London: Routledge.

Alexander, Cynthia J. and Pal, Leslie A. (1998) 'Introduction: new currents in politics and policy', in Cynthia J. Alexander and Leslie A. Pal (eds), *Digital Democracy: Politics and Policy in a Wired World*. Toronto: Oxford University Press, 1–22.

Alexander, J. (ed.) (1988) *Durkheimian Sociology: Cultural Studies*. Cambridge: Cambridge University Press.

Altschull, H. (1995) *Agents of Power*. London: Longman.

—— (1997) 'A crisis of conscience: is community journalism an answer?', in J. J. Black (ed.), *Mixed News: The Public Civic Communitarian Journalism Debate*. Hove: Lawrence Erlbaum Associates.

Amin, A. (1997) 'Placing globalization', in *Theory, Culture and Society* 14(2): 123–38.

Anderson, J. L. (1997) *Che Guevera, a Revolutionary Life*. New York: Bantam.

Archibugi, D. (1995) 'From United Nations to cosmopolitan democracy', in D. Archibugi and D. Held (eds), *Cosmopolitan Democracy*. Cambridge: Polity Press.

Atton, C. (1996) 'Anarchy on the Internet', *Anarchist Studies* 4: 115–32.

Attwood, F. (1999) 'Same old story? The tale of Diana, Princess of Wales', *Journal of Gender Studies* 8(3): 313–21.

Aufderheide, P. (1998) 'Niche-market culture, off- and online', in D. L. Borden and K. Harvey (eds), *The Electronic Grapevine: Rumour, Reputation and Reporting in the New Online Environment*. London: Lawrence Erlbaum Associates, 43–57.

Axford, Barrie and Huggins, Richard (eds) (2000) *New Media and Politics*. London: Sage.

Axtman, Roland (1996) *Liberal Democracy into the Twenty-first Century*. New York: Manchester University Press.

Barcan, R. (1997) 'Space for the feminine', in Re:Public (ed.), *Planet Diana: Cultural Studies and Global Mourning*. Kingswood, NSW: Research Centre in Intercommunal Studies, University of Western Sydney, Nepean.

Bardoel, J. (1996) 'Beyond journalism', *European Journal of Communication* 11(3): 283–302.

Baringhorst, S. (1998) *Politik als Kampaigne*. Opladen: Westdeutscher Verlag.

Barnett, A. and Bourne Taylor, J. (1999) 'Diana and the constitution: a conversation', *New Formations* 36: 47–58.

Barrett, M. (1992) *The Politics of Truth: From Marx to Foucault*. Cambridge: Polity Press.

Barry, A. (1999) 'Demonstrations: sites and sights of direct action', *Economy and Society* 28(1): 78–94.

Bauman, Z. (1992) *Intimations of Postmodernity*. London: Routledge.

—— (1999) *In Search of Politics*. Cambridge: Polity Press.

Beck, U. (1992) *Risk Society: Towards a New Modernity* London: Sage.

—— (1995) *Ecological Politics in an Age of Risk*. Cambridge: Polity Press.

—— (1998a) 'The cosmopolitan manifesto', *New Statesman*, 20 March 1998, 28–30.

—— (1998b) *Democracy without Enemies*. Cambridge: Polity Press.

Begbie, S. (1997) 'Dianaland – not a playground for the fainthearted', in Re:Public (ed.), *Planet Diana: Cultural Studies and Global Mourning*. Kingswood, NSW: Research Centre in Intercommunal Studies, University of Western Sydney, Nepean.

Beiner, Ronald (ed.) (1995) *Theorizing Citizenship*. Albany, NY: State University of New York Press.

Bell, D. (1976) *The Coming of Post-industrial Society: A Venture in Social Forecasting*. London: Peregrine Books.

Bellah, R. (1967) 'Civil religion in America', in W. G. McLoughlin and R. Bellah (eds), *Religion in America*. Boston: Houghton Mifflin.

Benton, Ted (ed.) (1996) *The Greening of Marx*. New York: Guilford.

Berkman, R. and Kitch, L. W. (1986) *Politics in the Media Age*. New York: McGraw Hill.

Bettercourt, B. Ann (1996) 'Grassroots organizations: recurrent themes and research approaches', *Journal of Social Issues* 52(1): 207–20.

Billig, M. (1995) *Banal Nationalism*. London: Sage.

Blackmann, L. (1999) 'An extraordinary life: the legacy of an ambivalence', *New Formations* 36: 111–24.

Blumler, J. and Gurevitch, M. (1995) *The Crisis of Public Communication*. London: Routledge.

Bollas, C. (1994) *Being a Character: Psychoanalysis and Self Experience*. London: Routledge.

Bonchek, M. (1995) 'Grassroots in cyberspace: recruiting members on the Internet', paper for the annual meeting of the Midwest Political Science Association, Chicago.

Brass, E. and Poklewski Koziell, S. (1997) *Gathering Force: DIY Culture – Radical Action for Those Tired of Waiting*. London: The *Big Issue* Writers.

Braudy, L. (1997) *The Frenzy of Renown: Fame and Its History*. New York: Vintage.

Brennan, T. (1997) *At Home in the World: Cosmopolitanism Now*. Cambridge, Mass.: Harvard University Press.

Brodie, Janine (1997) 'Meso-discourse, state forms and the gendering of liberal-democratic citizenship', *Citizenship Studies* 1: 1.

Brown, Phil and Masterson-Allen, Susan (1994) 'The toxic waste movement: a new type of activism', *Society and Natural Resources* 7(3): 269–87.

Bullard, Robert D. (1994) *Dumping in Dixie: Race, Class and Environmental Quality*. Boulder, Colo.: Westview Press.

Burchill, J. (1998) *Diana*. London: Orion.

Burkhalter, B. (1999) 'Reading race online: discovering racial identity in usenet discussion', in M. Smith and P. Kollock, *Communities in Cyberspace*. London: Routledge.

Burt, E. (1999) 'Information and communication technologies: reshaping voluntary organisations? Uptake and innovations', paper presented at research seminar, *ICTs: Reshaping Voluntary Organisations?* at London Voluntary Section Resource Centre, 18 Nov.

Butler, D. and Kavanagh, D. (1997) *The British General Election of 1997*. London: Macmillan, 33–44.

Butler, J. (1998) 'Merely cultural', *New Left Review* 227 (Jan./Feb.): 33–44.

Calhoun, Craig (ed.) (1992) *Habermas and the Public Sphere*. Cambridge, Mass. and London: MIT Press.

—— (1998) 'Community without propinquity revisited: communication technology and the transformation of the urban public sphere', *Sociological Inquiry* 68: 373–97.

—— (2000) ' "New social movements" of the early nineteenth century', in K. Nash (ed.), *Readings in Contemporary Political Sociology*. Blackwell: Oxford, 129–54.

Callister, T. and Burbules, N. (1998) 'Paying the piper: the educational cost of the commercialization of the Internet', *Electronic Journal of Sociology* 3(3).

Campbell, B. (1998) *Diana, Princess of Wales: How Sexual Politics Shook the Monarchy*. London: Virago.

Carey, J. W. (1995) 'The press, public opinion, and public discourse', in T. L. Glasser and S. Craft (eds), *Public Opinion and the Communication of Consent*. New York: Guilford.

Carlson, M. (1996) *Performance: A Critical Introduction*. London: Routledge.

Carracedo, J.-D. (1999) 'To what extent is the scheme of panopticism useful in the age of electronic communication to make sense of the concepts of power and surveillance?', in J. Armitage and J. Roberts (eds), *Exploring Cyber Society*. Newcastle-upon-Tyne: University of Northumbria.

Castells, Manuel (1996) *The Rise of Network Society*, vol. 1 of *The Information Age: Economy, Society and Culture*. Oxford: Blackwell.

—— (1997) *The Power of Identity*, vol. 2 of *The Information Age: Economy, Society and Culture*. Oxford: Blackwell.

—— (1998) *End of Millennium*, vol. 3 of *The Information Age: Economy, Society and Culture*. Oxford: Blackwell.

Cerny, Phillip (1995) 'Globalization and the changing logic of collective action', *International Organization* (Autumn) 49: 607.

Cerulo, Karen and Janet M. Ruane (1997) 'Reframing sociological concepts for a Brave New (Virtual?) World', *Sociological Inquiry* 67: 48–58.

—— and —— (1998) 'Coming together: new taxonomies for the analysis of social relations', *Sociological Inquiry* 68: 398–425.

Chancellor, Edward (1999) *Devil Take the Hindmost: A History of Financial Speculation*. London: Macmillan.

Chaney, D. (1994) *The Cultural Turn*. London: Routledge.

Charity, A. (1995) *Doing Public Journalism*. New York: Guilford.

Chesters, G. (2000) 'Resist to exist? Radical environmentalism at the end of the millennium', *ECOS: A Review of Conservation* 20(2): 19–25.

Chivhanga, B. (1999) 'Living it out – the Internet in Africa', in J. Armitage and J. Roberts (eds), *Exploring Cyber Society*. Newcastle-upon-Tyne: University of Northumbria.

Clark, T. N. and Hoffmann-Martinot, V. (eds) (1998) *The New Political Culture*. Boulder, Colo.: Westview.

Cleaver, Harry M. Jr (1998) 'The Zapatista effect: the Internet and the rise of an alternative political fabric', *Journal of International Affairs* 51(2) (Spring): 621–40.

Clegg, S. R. *et al.* (1996) 'Management knowledge for the future: innovation, embryos and new paradigms', in S. R. Clegg and G. Palmer (eds), *The Politics of Management Knowledge*. London: Sage.

Cohen, A. (1993) *Masquerade Politics: Explorations in the Structure of Urban Cultural Movements*. Oxford: Berg.

Cohen, Jean (1995), 'Interpreting the notion of civil society', in Michael Walzer (ed.), *Towards a Global Civil Society*. Oxford: Berghahn Books, 35–40.

Collin, M. (1997) *Altered State: The Story of Ecstasy Culture and Acid House*. London: Serpent's Tail.

Collins, R. (1988) 'The Durkheimian tradition in conflict sociology', in J. Alexander (ed.), *Durkheimian Sociology: Cultural Studies*. Cambridge: Cambridge University Press, 107–28.

Commission on Global Governance (1995) *Our Global Neighbourhood: The Report of the Commission on Global Governance*. Oxford: Oxford University Press.

Cox, D. (1999) '*Diana: Her True Story*: post-modern transgressions in identity', *Journal of Gender Studies* 8(3): 323–37.

Cox, Robert (1999) 'Civil society at the turn of the millennium: prospects for an alternative world order', *Review of International Studies* 25: 3–28.

Crewe, I. and Sarlvik, B. (1983) *Decade of Realignment: The Conservative Victory of 1979 and Electoral Trends in the 1970s*. Cambridge: Cambridge University Press.

Crook, S., Pakulski, J. and Waters, M. (1992) *Postmodernization: Change in Advanced Society*. London: Sage.

Cudmore, P. (1999) Book Reviews, *Political Quarterly* 70(1): 110–12.

Curran, J. (1998) 'Crisis of public communication: a reappraisal 1998', in T. Liebes and J. Curran (eds), *Media Ritual and Identity*. London: Routledge, 205.

Curtice, J. and Semetko, H. (1994) 'Does it matter what the papers say?', in A. Heath *et al.* (eds), *Labour's Last Chance? The 1992 Election and Beyond*. London: Dartmouth.

Cushing, P. (1996) 'Gendered conversational rituals on the Internet: an effective voice is based on more than simply what one is saying', *Anthropologica* 38: 47–80.

Dahl, R. (1956) *A Preface to Democratic Theory*. Chicago: University of Chicago Press.

—— (1985) *A Preface to Economic Democracy*. Cambridge: Polity.

—— (1991) *Modern Political Analysis*, 5th edn. London: Prentice Hall.

Dalton, Russell J. (1994) *The Green Rainbow: Environmental Groups in Western Europe*. New Haven and London: Yale University Press.

Daly, M. (1997) 'We're going to win this one: victory for Lyminge tunnellers', *Big Issue* 245 11–17 August: 5.

D'Anjou, Leo and van Male, John (1998) 'Between the old and new: social movements and cultural change', *Mobilization* 3: 207–26.

Davies, J. (1999) '*Princess*: Diana, femininity, and the royal', *New Formations* 36: 141–54.

Davis, N. Z. (1981) 'Anthropology and history in the 1980s: the possibilities of the past', *Journal of Interdisciplinary History* 11: 267–75.

Davis, R. and Owen, D. (1998) *New Media and American Politics*. Oxford: Oxford University Press.

De Brie, Christian (1998a) 'Vers le mondialisation de la résistance: comment l'AMI fut mis en pièces', *Le Monde Diplomatique,* December.

—— (1998b) 'L'Ami dans la tourmente économique et financière', lecture at the University of Geneva, 2 December.

Debord, G. (1992) [1967] *The Society of the Spectacle*, trans. D. Nicholson-Smith. New York: Zone Books.

Deibert, Ronald (1997) *Parchment, Print and Hypermedia: Communication in World Order Transformation*. New York: Columbia University Press.

—— (1998) 'Altered worlds: social forces in a hypermedia environment', in Cynthia J. Alexander and Leslie A. Pal (eds), *Digital Democracy: Politics and Policy in a Wired World*. Toronto: Oxford University Press, 23–45.

De Jonquieres, Guy (1998) 'Network guerillas', *Financial Times*, 20 April: 8.

Della Porta, Donatella (1988) 'Recruitment processes in clandestine political organisations: Italian left-wing terrorism', in B. Klandermans, K. Kriesi and S. Tarrow (eds), *From Structure to Action*. Greenwich, Conn.: JAI Press, 155–69.

—— and Diani, Mario (1999) *Social Movements: An Introduction*, Oxford: Blackwell.

Desai, Manisha (1996) 'Informal organizations as agents of change: notes from the contemporary women's movement in India', *Mobilization* 1: 159–73.

Desan, S. (1989) 'Crowds, community, and ritual in the work of E. P. Thompson and Natalie Davis', in L. Hunt (ed.), *The New Cultural History*. Berkeley: University of California Press.

De Tocqueville, Alexis (1969) *Democracy in America*. New York: Doubleday Anchor Books.

Dews, P. (1984) 'Power and subjectivity in Foucault', *New Left Review* 144: 72–95.

Diamond, E. (ed.) (1996) *Performance and Cultural Politics*. London: Routledge.

Diani, Mario (1992) 'The concept of social movement', *Sociological Review* 40(4): 1–25.

—— (1995) *Green Networks. A Structural Analysis of the Italian Environmental Movement*. Edinburgh: Edinburgh University Press.

—— (2000) 'The concept of social movement', in K. Nash (ed.), *Readings in Contemporary Political Sociology*. Oxford: Blackwell.

—— and Donati, Paolo R. (1999) 'Organizational change in western European environmental groups: a framework for analysis', *Environmental Politics* 8: 13–34.

DiMaggio, P. J. and Powell, W. W. (1991) 'The iron cage reversed: institutional isomorphism and collective rationality in organizational fields', in W. W. Powell and P. J. DiMaggio (eds), *The New Institutionalism in Organizational Analysis*. Chicago: Chicago University Press.

Dines, Nicholas (2000) 'I centri sociali', *Quaderni di Sociologia* 23: 90–111.

Doherty, B. (1997) *Direct Action against Road-building: Some Implications for the Concept of Protest Repertoires*. Political Studies Association Annual Conference, Ireland, vol. 2: 147–55.

—— (1999a) 'Change the world via e-mail', *New Statesman*, 1 Nov.: xviii–xix.

—— (1999b) 'Manufactured vulnerability: forms of protest in the radical ecology movement in Britain', *La Lettre de la Maison Française d'Oxford* 10: 5–22.

—— (1999c) 'Paving the way: the rise of direct action against road-building and the changing character of British environmentalism', *Political Studies* 47: 275–91.

Dordoy, A. and Mellor, M. (2000) 'Ecosocialism and feminism: deep materialism and the contradictions of capitalism', *Capitalism, Nature, Socialism* 11(3) September: 41–61.

Downs, A. (1957) *An Economic Theory of Democracy*. New York: Harpers and Row.

Dowse, R. and Hughes, J. (1972) *Political Sociology*. London: John Wiley and Sons.

Doyle, Timothy and McEachern, Doug (1998) *Environment and Politics*. London: Routledge.

Drohan, Madeleine (1998) 'How the Net killed the MAI', *Globe and Mail*, 3 July.

Dunleavy, P. and Husbands, C. (1985) *Democracy at the Crossroads*. London: Allen and Unwin.

Durkheim, E. (1915) *The Elementary Forms of the Religious Life*. London: George Allen and Unwin.

Dutton, W. H., Taylor, J., Bellamy, C., Raab, C. and Peltu, M. (1994) 'Electronic service delivery: themes and issues in the public sector', *Policy Research Paper* no. 29. Uxbridge: PICT, Brunel University.

Eagleton, T. (1996) *The Illusions of Postmodernism*. Oxford: Blackwell.

Electrohippies collective (2000) 'Client-side distributed denial-of-service: valid campaign tactic or terrorist act?' http://www.gn.apc.org/pmhp/ehippies/files/op1.htm.

Elliott, A. (1996) *Subject to Ourselves: Social Theory, Psychoanalysis and Postmodernity*. Cambridge: Polity Press.

Emirbayer, Mustafa and Sheller, Mimi (1999) 'Publics in History', *Theory and Society* 28: 145–97.

Epstein, B. (1997) 'The environmental justice/toxics movement: politics of race and gender', *CNS* 8(3).

Ericson, R. R. (1991) 'Mass media, crime, law, and justice: an institutional approach', *British Journal of Criminology* 31(3): 233.

Etzioni, A. (1999) *The New Golden Rule: Community and Morality in a Democratic Society*. London: Profile.

Evans, D. (1997) 'Michel Maffesoli's sociology of modernity and postmodernity: an introduction and critical assessment', *Sociological Review* 45(2): 220–43.

Evans, Peter (1997) 'The eclipse of the state? Reflections of stateness in an era of globalization', *World Politics* 50(1): 62–87.

Eyerman, R. and Jamison, A. (1991) *Social Movements: A Cognitive Approach*. Cambridge: Polity Press.

—— and —— (1998) *Music and Social Movements*. Cambridge: Cambridge University Press.

Falk, R. (1995a) 'The world order between inter-state law and the law of humanity: the role of civil society instituions', in D. Archibugi and D. Held (eds), *Cosmopolitan Democracy*. Cambridge: Polity, 163–79.

—— (1995b) *On Humane Governance: Towards a New Global Politics*. Cambridge: Polity.

Featherstone, M. (1992) 'The heroic life and everyday life', *Theory, Culture and Society* 9: 159–82.

Fisher, D. R. (1998) 'Rumouring theory and the Internet; a framework for analyzing the grass roots', *Social Science Computer Review* 16(2): 158–68.

Foucault, M. (1972) *The Archaeology of Knowledge*. London: Tavistock.

—— (1980) 'Two lectures', in C. Gordon (ed.), *Power/Knowledge: Selected Interviews and Other Writings 1972–1977*. Brighton: Harvester, 78–108.

—— (2000) 'The subject and power', in K. Nash (ed.), *Readings in Contemporary Political Sociology*. Blackwell: Oxford, 8–26.

Foweraker, Joe (1995) *Theorizing Social Movements*. London: Pluto.

Franklin, B. (1994) *Packaging Politics: Political Communications in Britain's Media Democracy*. London: Edward Arnold.

—— (1997) *Newszat and News Media*. London: Arnold.

Fraser, N. (1989) 'Foucault on modern power: empirical insights and normative confusions', in N. Fraser *Unruly Practices: Power, Discourse and Gender in Contemporary Social Theory*. Cambridge: Polity, 17–34.

Friedland, Lewis A. (1996) 'Electronic democracy and the new citizenship', *Media, Culture and Society* 18: 185–212.

Frith, S. and Street, J. (1992) 'Rock against Racism and Red Wedge: from music to politics, from politics to music', in R. Garofal (ed.), *Rockin' the Boat: Mass Music and Mass Movements*, Boston: South End Press, 67–80.

Fukuyama, F. (1992) *The End of History and the Last Man*. London, Hamish Hamilton.

Gans, H. (1998) 'What can journalists actually do for democracy?', *Press/Politics* 3(4): 6–12.

Garcia Canclini, N. (1995) *Hybrid Cultures: Strategies for Entering and Leaving Modernity*. Minneapolis: University of Minnesota Press.

Garner, C. (1997) 'Back to bronze age for Swampy's friends', *Independent*, 26 July: 8.

Garnham, N. (1986) 'The media and the public sphere', in P. Golding, G. Murdock and P. Schlesinger (eds) *Communicating Politics*, Leicester: Leicester University Press, 55–67.

—— (1992) 'The media and the public sphere', in C. Calhoun (ed.), *Habermas and the Public Sphere*. Cambridge, Mass.: MIT Press, 359–76.

Gartner, M. (1995) 'Give me old-time journalism: "democracy-enhancing" label runs counter to what media ought to be about', *Quill* 86.

Geertz, C. (1973) *The Interpretation of Cultures*. New York: Basic Books.

Genovese, E. (1976) *Roll, Jordan, Roll: The World the Slaves Made*. New York: Vintage Books.

George, P. (1999) 'McSpotlight: freedom of speech and the Internet', in Liberty (ed.), *Liberating Cyberspace: Civil Liberties, Human Rights and the Internet*. London: Pluto, ch. 14.

Geras, N. (1995) *Solidarity in the Conversation of Mankind: The Ungroundable Liberalism of Richard Rorty*. London: Verso.

Gerhards, J. and Rucht, D. (1992) 'Mesomobilization contexts: organizing and framing in two protest campaigns in West Germany', *American Journal of Sociology* 98: 555–96.

Gibson, M. (1999) 'The temporality of democracy: the long revolution and Diana, Princess of Wales', *New Formations* 36: 59–76.

Giddens, A. (1984) *The Constitution of Society: Outline of the Theory of Structuration*. Cambridge: Polity.

—— (1990) *The Consequences of Modernity*. Cambridge: Polity.

—— (1991a) *Modernity and Self-identity: Self and Society in the Late Modern Age*. Cambridge: Polity.

—— (1991b) *The Transformation of Intimacy*. Cambridge: Polity.

—— (1994) *Beyond Left and Right*. Cambridge: Polity.

—— (1998) *The Third Way: The Renewal of Social Democracy*. Cambridge: Polity.

Gilder, G. (1992) *Life after Television*. New York: Norton.

Gill, Stephen (1995) 'Globalization, market civilization and disciplinary neo-liberalism', *Millennium* 24(3): 399–423.

Ginsberg, B. and Shefter, M. (1990) *Politics by Other Means: The Declining Importance of Elections in America*. New York: Basic Books.

Gitlin, Todd (1980) *The Whole World Is Watching: Mass Media in the Making and Unmaking of the New Left*. Berkeley: University of California Press.

—— (1998) 'Public sphere or public sphericules', in T. Liebes and J. Curran (eds), *Media Ritual and Identity*. London: Routledge, 168–74.

Glasser, T. L. and Craft, S. (1998) 'Public journalism and the search for democratic ideals', in T. Liebes and J. Curran (eds), *Media Ritual and Identity*. London: Routledge, 205.

Goldman, Benjamin A. (1996) 'What is the future of environmental justice?', *Antipode* 28(2): 122–41.

Goodwin, S. (1997) 'Blue, John and Whinger dig deep to keep their Wild Wood free from a holiday village', *Independent*, 3 July: 6.

Gould, Roger V. (1995) *Insurgent Identities*. Chicago: University of Chicago Press.

Grant, David, Keenoy, Tom and Oswich, Cliff (eds) (1998) *Discourse + Organization*. London: Sage.

Gray, J. (1995a) 'The sad side of cyberspace', *Guardian*, 10 April.

—— (1995b) 'Virtual democracy', *Guardian*, 15 Sept.

—— (1997) *Endgames: Questions in Late Modern Political Thought*. Cambridge: Polity.

Greider, William (1995) *One World Ready or Not: The Manic Logic of Global Capitalism*. New York: Simon and Schuster.

Habermas, J. (1989) *The Structural Transformation of the Public Sphere*. Cambridge: Polity.

Hacker, Kenneth L. (1996) 'Missing links in the evolution of electronic democratization', *Media, Culture and Society* 18: 213–32.

Halcli, Abigail and Webster, Frank (2000) 'Inequality and mobilization in *The Information Age*', *European Journal of Social Theory* 3(1): 67–81.

Hall, John H. 'In Search of Civil Society', in John Hall (ed.) 1995, *Civil Society: Theory, History*. Cambridge: Polity Press, 1–31.

Hamelink, C. (1994) *The Politics of World Communication: A Human Rights Perspective*. London: Sage.

——— (1995) *World Communication: Disempowerment and Self-empowerment*. London: Zed Books.

Hanagan, Michael, (1998) 'Irish transnational social movements, deterritorialized migrants, and the state system: the last one hundred and forty years', *Mobilization* 3: 107–26.

Hanson, Betty (1999) 'The diffusion and distributional effects of the Internet', paper presented at the Annual Meeting of the International Studies Association, 17–20 Feb. 1999, Washington, DC.

Hardt. H. (2000) 'Conflicts of interest: news workers, media, and patronage journalism', in H. Tumber (ed.), *Media Power, Professionals and Policies*. London: Routledge.

Harpold, T. and Philip, K. (1999) 'Of bugs and rats: cyber-cleanliness, cyber-squalor, and the fantasies of globalisation', in J. Armitage and J. Roberts (eds), *Exploring Cyber Society*. Vol. 1. Newcastle-upon-Tyne: University of Northumbria.

Harris, Jose (1993), *Private Lives, Public Spirit: Britain 1870–1914*. Harmondsworth: Penguin.

Hart, R. (1994) *Seducing America: How Television Charms the Modern Voter*. New York: Oxford University Press.

Hartley, Troy W. (1995) 'Environmental justice: an environmental civil rights value acceptable to all world views' *Environmental Ethics* 17(3): 277–89.

Heiman, Michael K. (1996) 'Race, waste and class: new perspectives on environmental justice', *Antipode* 28(2): 111–21.

Held, D. (1987) *Models of Democracy*. Cambridge: Polity.

——— (1993) 'Democracy: from city-states to a cosmopolitan order?', in idem (ed.), *Prospects for Democracy*. Cambridge: Polity Press.

——— (1995) *Democracy and Global Order: From the Modern State to Cosmopolitan Governance*. Cambridge: Polity.

Heller, A. (1989) 'From hermeneutics in social science toward a hermeneutic social science', *Theory and Society* 18.

Hetherington, K. (1996) 'Identity formation, space and social centrality', *Theory, Culture and Society* 13(4): 33–52.

Hey, V. (1999) 'Be(long)ing: New Labour, New Britain and the "Dianaization" of politics', in A. Kear and D. L. Steinberg (eds), *Mourning Diana: Nation, Culture and the Performance of Grief*. London: Routledge, 60–76.

Heywood, P. (1997) 'Political corruption: problems and perspectives' *Political Studies* 45: 417–35.

Higgott, Richard and Reich, Simon (1999) 'From globalisation to glamorisation: the rise and rise of the NGO in international relations', paper presented at the Annual Meeting of the International Studies Association, Washington, DC, 16–20 Feb. 1999.

Hindess, B. (1996) *Discourses of Power: From Hobbes to Foucault*. Oxford: Blackwell.

Hirst, P. and Thompson, G. (1996) *Globalization in Question: The International Economy and the Possibilities of Governance*. Cambridge: Polity.

Hobsbawm, E. J. (1994) *Age of Extremes: The Short Twentieth Century*. London: Michael Joseph.

——— and Ranger, T. (1983) *The Invention of Tradition*. Cambridge: Cambridge University Press.

Hoffman, J. (1995) *Beyond the State*. Cambridge: Polity.

Hofrichter, Richard (1993) *Toxic Struggles*. Philadelphia: New Society Publishers.

Holmes, David (ed.) (1997) *Virtual Politics: Identity and Community in Cyberspace*. London: Sage.

hooks, bell (1991) *Yearning: Race, Gender and Cultural Politics*. London: Turnaround.

Hunt, L. (ed.) (1989) *The New Cultural History*. Berkeley: University of California Press.

Huyssen, A. (1990) 'Mapping the postmodern', in J. Alexander and S. Seidman (eds), *Culture and Society: Contemporary Debates*. Cambridge: Cambridge University Press.

Jasper, J. M. and Poulson, J. D. (1995) 'Recruiting strangers and friends: moral shocks and social networks in animal rights and anti-nuclear protests', *Social Problems* 42(4): 493–512.

Johnston, H., Larana, E. and Gusfield, J. R. (1994) 'Identities, grievances and new social movements', in E. Larana, H. Johnston and J. R. Gusfield, *New Social Movements: From Ideology to Identity*. Philadelphia: Temple University Press, 3–35.

Jones, S. (1997) *Virtual Culture: Identity and Communication in Cybersociety*. London: Sage.

Jordan, G. and Maloney, W. (1997) *The Protest Business? Mobilizing Campaign Groups*. Manchester: Manchester University Press.

Jordan, T. (1999) 'Cyberpower and the meaning of online activism', *Cybersociology Magazine* 5.

Kaldor, M. (1999) *New and Old Wars*. Cambridge: Polity Press.

Kamieniecki, Sheldon, Colman, S. Dulaine and Vos, Robert O. (1995) 'The effectiveness of radical environmentalists', in Bron Raymond Taylor (ed.), *Ecological Resistance Movements*. New York: SUNY Press.

Kant, I. (1991) 'Perpetual peace: a philosophical sketch', in H. Reiss (ed.), *Kant: Political Writing*. Cambridge: Cambridge University Press, 93–130.

Kavanagh, D. (1995) *Election Campaigning: The New Marketing of Politics*. Oxford: Blackwell.

—— (1997) 'The Labour campaign', in P. Norris and N. Gavin (eds), *Britain Votes 1997*. Oxford: Oxford University Press, 25–33.

Kear, A. and Steinberg, D. L. (eds) (1999) *Mourning Diana: Nation, Culture and the Performance of Grief*. London: Routledge.

Kellner, D. (1995) 'Intellectuals and new technologies', *Media, Culture and Society* 17: 201–17.

Kimball, P. (1994) *Downsizing the News*. Washington, DC: Woodrow Wilson Center Press.

Knudson, Jerry (1998) 'Rebellion in Chiapas: insurrection by Internet and public relations', *Media, Culture, and Society* 20: 507–18.

Kobrin, Stephen (1998a) 'Back to the future: neo-medievalism and the post-modern digital economy', *Journal of International Affairs* 51(2): 361–86.

—— (1998b) 'The MAI and the clash of globalization', *Foreign Policy* (Fall), 97–109.

Koweck, Glenn (1997) 'Internet governance and the emergence of global civil society', *IEEE Communication*, May: 52–7.

Krinks, P. (1997) 'Eco-warriors "storm" rank: West Wood protesters "occupy" leisure giant's London HQ', *Folkstone Herald*, 21 Aug.: 1.

Kumar, K. (1995) *From Post-industrial to Post-modern Society: New Theories of the Contemporary World*. Oxford: Blackwell.

Kundera, M. (1985) *The Unbearable Lightness of Being*. London: Faber and Faber.

Kurzman, Charles (1998) 'Organizational opportunity and social movement mobilization: a comparative analysis of four religious movements', *Mobilization* 3: 23–50.

Kymlika, Will and Norman, Wayne (1995) 'Return of the citizen: a survey of recent work on citizenship theory', in Ronald Beiner (ed.), *Theorizing Citizenship* Albany: State University of New York, 283–323.

Laclau, E. (1990) *New Reflections on the Revolution of Our Time*. London: Verso.

—— and Mouffe, C. (1985) *Hegemony and Socialist Strategy: Towards a Radical Democratic Politics*. London: Verso.

Lahusen, C. (1996) *The Rhetoric of Moral Protest*. Berlin: Walter de Gryler.

Lamb, R. (1996) *Promising the Earth*. London: Routledge.

Lash, S. and Urry, J. (1994) *Economies of Signs and Space*. London: Sage.

Law, John (1994) *Organizing Modernity*. Oxford: Blackwell.

Leadbeater, Charles (2000) *Living on Thin Air*. Harmondsworth: Penguin.

Lévi-Strauss, C. (1945) 'French sociology', in G. Gurvitch and W. E. Moore (eds), *Twentieth Century Sociology*. New York: The Philosophical Library, 508–37.

Lindblom, C. (1977) *Politics and Markets: The World's Political-economic Systems*. London: Basic Books.

Linklater, A. (1998) *The Transformation of Political Community*. Cambridge: Polity Press.

Lipschutz, Ronnie D. (1992) 'Reconstructing world politics: the emergence of global civil society', *Millennium* 21(3): 389–420.

—— (1998) 'Members only? Citizenship in a time of globalization', paper presented at the Annual Meeting of the International Studies Association, Minneapolis, 17–21 March.

Lloyd, J. (1999) 'Putting freedom to the torch', *Financial Times*, 13/14 March: i.

Loader, Brian D. (ed.) (1997) *The Governance of Cyberspace: Politics, Technology and Global Restructuring*. London: Routledge.

Longhurst, Richard (1995) 'Charity begins on the Net', *.net* 16–17 (March).

Low, Murray (1997) 'Representation unbound: globalization and democracy', in Kevin R. Cox (ed.), *Spaces of Globalization*. London: Guilford Press.

Lubbers, E. (1996) 'Netactivism', http://www.xs4all.nl/~evel/report.htm.

Lukes, S. (1974) *Power: A Radical View*. London: Macmillan.

—— (1975) 'Political ritual and social integration', *Sociology* 9: 289–308.

Lumley, Robert (1990) *States of Emergency*. London: Verso.

Lynch, Cecelia (1998) 'Social movements and the problems of globalization', *Alternatives* 23: 149–73.

McAdam, D. (1988) *Freedom Summer*. New York: Oxford University Press.

—— and Rucht, Dieter (1993) 'The cross-national diffusion of movement ideas', *Annals of the AAPSS* 528: 56–74.

McClure, K. (1992) 'On the subject of rights: pluralism, plurality and political identity', in C. Mouffe (ed.), *Dimensions of Radical Democracy: Pluralism, Citizenship, Community*. London: Verso, 108–27.

McCormick, J. (1991) *British Politics and the Environment*. London: Earthscan.

McCurry, M. (1998) *Correspondent – The Presidents' Scorpions*. BBC2, 31 October.

Macdonald, Laura (1994) 'Globalizing civil society: interpreting international NGOs in Central America', *Millennium* 23(2): 267–85.

McGrew, A. (1997) 'Democracy beyond borders', in idem (ed.), *The Transformation of Democracy? Globalization and Territorial Democracy*. Cambridge: Polity.

McGuigan, Jim (2000) 'British identity and the "people's princess"', *Sociological Review* 48(1): 1–18.

McKay, G. (1996) *Senseless Acts of Beauty: Cultures of Resistance since the Sixties*. London: Verso.

—— (ed.) (1998) *DiY Culture: Party and Protest in Nineties Britain*. London: Verso.

McKibbin, R. (1998a) 'Mass Observation on the Mall', in M. Merck (ed.), *After Diana – Irreverent Elegies*. London and New York: Verso.

—— (1998b) *Classes and Cultures: England 1918–1951*. Oxford: Oxford University Press.

McManus, J. H. (1994) *Market Driven News*. London: Sage.

McNay, L. (1994) *Foucault: A Critical Introduction*. Cambridge: Polity.

Maffesoli, M. (1996) *The Time of the Tribes: The Decline of Individualism in Mass Society*. London: Sage.

Malyon, T. (1998) 'Tossed in the fire and they never got burned: the Exodus Collective', in G. McKay (ed.), *DiY: Party and Protest in Nineties Britain*. London: Verso, 187–207.

Mancini, P. and Swanson, D. (1996) 'Introduction', in D. Swanson and P. Mancini (eds), *Politics, Media, and Modern Democracy*. Westport, Conn.: Praeger, 1–28.

Mansell, Robin and Silverstone, Roger (eds) (1997) *Communication by Design: The Politics of Information and Communication Technologies*. Oxford: Oxford University Press.

Marcus, G. (1989) *Lipstick Traces: A Secret History of the 20th Century*. Cambridge, Mass.: Harvard University Press.

Markovits, A. S. and Silverstein, M. (eds) (1988) *The Politics of Scandal: Power and Process in Liberal Democracies*. New York: Holmes & Meier.

Marshall, P. D. (1997) *Celebrity and Power: Fame in Contemporary Culture*. London: University of Minnesota Press.

Marshall, T. H. (1964) 'Citizenship and social class', in T. H. Marshall, *Class, Citizenship and Social Development*. New York: Doubleday.

Martin, G. (1998) 'Generational differences among New Age travellers', *Sociological Review* 46(4): 735–56.

Mathiesen, Thomas (1997) 'The viewer society: Michel Foucault's "Panopticon" revisited', *Theoretical Criminology* 1(2): 215–34.

Mattelart, A. (1999) 'Against global inevitability', *Media Development* 46(2): 3–6.

Maynard, R. (1998) 'Vision 2000', *Change Your World*: 16–17.

Mele, C. (1999) 'Cyberspace and disadvantaged communities: the Internet as a tool for collective action', in M. Smith and P. Kollock (eds), *Communities in Cyberspace*. London: Routledge.

Mellor, Mary (1992) 'Ecofeminism and ecosocialism: dilemmas of essentialism and materialism', *Capitalism, Nature, Socialism* 3(2): 43–62.

—— (1997) *Feminism and Ecology*. New York: Polity and New York University Press.

—— (2000a) 'Feminism and environmental ethics: a materialist approach', *Ethics and the Environment* 5(1): 107–23.

—— (2000b) 'Nature (re) production and power: a materialist ecofeminist perspective', in F. Gale and M. Mgonigle (eds), *Nature, Reproduction and Power*. London: Edward Elgar.

Melucci, A. (1989) *Nomads of the Present: Social Movements and Individual Needs in Contemporary Society*, ed. J. Keane and P. Mier. London: Hutchinson Radius.

—— (1994) 'A strange kind of newness: What's "new" in new social movements?', in E. Larana, H. Johnston and J. R. Gusfied (eds), *New Social Movements: From Ideology to Identity*. Philadelphia: Temple University Press, ch. 5.

—— (1996) *Challenging Codes: Collective Action in the Information Age*. Cambridge: Cambridge University Press.

Merck, M. (ed.) (1998) *After Diana – Irreverent Elegies*. London and New York: Verso.

Merrill, D. (1996) 'Missing the point', *American Journalism Review* July–August.

Merritt, D. (1995) *Public Journalism and Public Life*. Hove: Lawrence Erlbaum Associates, 1–11.

Meyrowitz, J. (1985) *No Sense of Place*. Oxford: Oxford University Press.

Michels, Robert (1962) [1915] *Political Parties: A Sociological Study of the Oligarchical Tendencies of Modern Democracy*, 2nd edn. New York: Free Press.

Miliband, R. (1969) *The State in Capitalist Society*. London: Weidenfeld and Nicolson: London.

Miller, D. (1993) 'Deliberative democracy and social choice', in D. Held (ed.), *Prospects of Democracy*. Cambridge: Polity Press.

Mills, C. W. (1956) *The Power Elite*. Oxford: Oxford University Press.

Mitchell, A. (1999) 'New Labour, new consumer', *New Media Age*, 24 June: 8.

Mouffe, C. (1993) *The Return of the Political*. London: Verso.

Mouzelis, N. (1995) *Sociological Theory: What Went Wrong?* London: Routledge.

Myers, D. J. (1994) 'Communication technology and social movements: contributions of computer networks to activism', *Social Science Computer Review* 12: 250–60.

Nash, K. (2000) *Contemporary Political Sociology: Globalization, Politics and Power*. Oxford: Blackwell.

—— (forthcoming) 'Thinking political sociology: beyond the limits of post-Marxist political theory', unpublished paper.

Negrine, R. (1994) *Politics and the Mass Media in Britain*, 2nd edn. London: Routledge.

Negroponte, N. (1994) *Being Digital*. London: Coronet Books.

Neuborne, E. (1996) 'Vigilantes stir firms' ire with cyber antics', *USA Today*, 28 Feb.

Neveu, E. (1999) 'Media and social movements', *La Lettre de la Maison Française d'Oxford* 10: 43–60.

Newsome, R. (1997) 'If you go down to the woods today . . .', *The Big Issue*, 3–9 Nov: 10–11.

Norris, P. *et al.* (1999) *On Message: Communicating the Campaign*. London: Sage.

Novotny, P. (1995) 'Where we live, work and play: reframing the cultural landscape of environmentalism in the environmental justice movement', *New Political Science* 32: 61–79.

Nunn, H. (1999) 'Violence and the sacred: the Iron Lady, the princess and the people's PM', *New Formations* 36: 92–110.

Nuthall, K. (1997) 'Eco-warriors go soft and opt for the telly', *Independent on Sunday*, 16 Nov.: 12.

—— (1999) 'ICI heads list of worst pollutors', *The Times*: 7.

O'Brien, J. (1999) 'Writing in the body: gender (re)production in online interaction', in M. Smith and P. Kollock (eds), *Communities in Cyberspace*. London: Routledge.

Offe, C. (1987) 'Challenging the boundaries of institutional politics: social movements since the 1960s', in C. S. Maier (ed.), *Changing Boundaries of the Political: Essays on the Evolving Balance between the State and Society, Public and Private in Europe*. Cambridge: Cambridge University Press, 63–107.

Oliver, Pamela and Marwell, Gerald (1992) 'Mobilizing technologies for collective action', in A. Morris and C. McClurg Mueller (eds), *Frontiers in Social Movement Theory*. New Haven: Yale University Press, 251–72.

Parry, G. (1969) *Political Elites*. London: George Allen and Unwin.

Pickerill, Jenny (2000) 'Environmentalism and the Net: pressure groups, new social movements and new ICTs', in R. Gibson and S. Ward (eds), *Reinvigorating Government? British Politics and the Internet*. Aldershot: Ashgate.

Pipes, S. (1996). 'Environmental information on the Internet', *ECOS* 17(2): 63–6.

Plant, S. (1992) *The Most Radical Gesture: The Situationist International in a Postmodern Age*. London: Routledge.

—— (1996) 'Connectionism and the post humanities', in W. Charnaik, M. Deegan and A. Gibson (eds), *Beyond the Book: Theory, Culture, and the Politics of Cyberspace*. Office for Humanities Communication Publications, no. 7.

Polletta, Francesca (1999) '"Free Spaces" in collective action', *Theory and Society* 28: 1–38.

Porter, Gareth and Welsh Brown, Janet (1991) *Global Environmental Politics*. Boulder, Colo. and London: Westview Press.

Preamble Center (1998) *MAI Bibliography, Print Media Coverage* (downloaded from website Dec. 1998).

Public Citizen (1998) 'Internet coalition launches campaign against the MAI, a new stealth agreement', press release, 12 Feb.

Pulido, Laura (1996) 'Multiracial organizing among environment justice activists in Los Angeles', in Michael J. Dear *et al.* (eds), *Rethinking Los Angeles*. London: Sage, 171–89.

Purcell, Kristen (1997) 'Towards a communication dialectic: embedded technology and the enhancement of place', *Sociological Inquiry* 67: 101–12.

Putnam, Robert (1995) 'Bowling alone: America's declining social capital', *Journal of Democracy* 6(1): 65–78.

Ramachandra, Guha and Martinez-Alier, Joan (1997) *Varieties of Environmentalism: Essays North and South*. London: Earthscan.

Rawcliffe, P. (1992). 'Swimming with the tide – environmental groups in the 1990s', *ECOS* 13(1): 2–9.

Reed, M. (1999) 'Wide open to the Web warriors', *Marketing On-line*, http://193.133.103.27/feature99/0204a/0204a.htm.

Re:Public (ed.) (1997) *Planet Diana: Cultural Studies and Global Mourning*. Kingswood, NSW: Research Centre in Intercommunal Studies, University of Western Sydney, Nepean.

Rheingold, Howard (1994) *The Virtual Community*. New York: HarperCollins.

Riché, Pascal (1998) 'Jospin: adieu l'AMI, salut les copains', *Liberation*, 15 Oct.

Ritchie, D. (1999) 'Electronic communications', *Change Your World: The Newsletter of Friends of the Earth Local Groups*, 14 (Dec.–Jan.): 11–14.

Rorty, R. (1998) 'Human rights, rationality and sentimentality', in idem, *Truth and Progress, Philosophical Papers*, vol. 3. Cambridge: Cambridge University Press, 167–85.

—— (1999) 'Pragmatism, pluralism and postmodernism', in idem, *Philosophy and Social Hope*. Harmondsworth: Penguin, 262–77.

Rose, J. (1999) 'The cult of celebrity', *New Formations* 36: 92–11.

Roseneil, Sasha (1995) *Disarming Patriarchy*. Milton Keynes: Open University Press.

Rosenstiel, T. and Kovach, B. (1999) 'The journalism that doesn't bother to check its facts', *Herald-Tribune*, 3 March: 8.

Rotherbuhler, E. W. (1988) 'The liminal fight: mass strikes as ritual and interpretation', in J. Alexander (ed.), *Durkheimian Sociology: Cultural Studies*. Cambridge: Cambridge University Press.

Rothkopf, David J. (1998) 'Cyberpolitik: the changing nature of power in the information age', *Journal of International Affairs*, Spring: 325–59.

Rothman, Franklin D. and Oliver, Pamela (1999) 'From local to global: the anti-dam movement in southern Brazil, 1979–1992,' *Mobilization* 4: 41–58.

Rowland, Wade (1997) *The Spirit of the Web: The Age of Information from Telegraph to the Internet*. Toronto: Somerville House.

Rüdig, W. (1995). 'Between moderation and marginalisation: environmental radicalism in Britain', in B. R. Taylor (ed.), *Ecological Resistance Movements*. Albany: State University of New York Press, 219–240.

Rupp, Leila and Taylor, Verta (1987) *Survival in the Doldrums: The American Women's Rights Movement, 1945 to the 1960s*. Columbus: Ohio State University Press.

Samson, A. (1996) 'The crisis at the heart of our media', *British Journalism Review* 7(3): 42–51.

Sassen, Saskia (1998a) *Globalization and its Discontents*. New York: The New Press.

—— (1998b) 'On the Internet and sovereignty', *Global Legal Studies Journal* 5: 545–59.

Scammell, M. (1995) *Designer Politics: How Elections Are Won*. London: Macmillan.

Schechner, R. (1977) *Performance Theory*. London: Routledge.

—— (1988) 'Introduction to Victor Turner's work', in V. Turner, *The Anthropology of Performance*. New York: Paj Publications.

Schofield, J. (1999) 'Searching for the perfect engine', *Guardian Online*, 15 July.

Scott, A. (1997) 'Globalization: social process or political rhetoric', in A. Scott (ed.) *The Limits of Globalization: Cases and Arguments*. Routledge: London.

Scott, J. C. (1990) *Domination and the Arts of Resistance*. New Haven: Yale University Press.

Scott, John (1994) *Poverty and Wealth: Citizenship, Deprivation and Privilege*. London: Longman.

—— (1997) *Corporate Business and Capitalist Classes*. Oxford: Oxford University Press.

Shibley, Mark A. and Prosterman, Annette (1998) 'Silent epidemic, environmental justice, or exaggerated concern?', *Organization and Environment* 11(1): 33–58.

Shields, John and Mitchell Evans, B. (1998) *Shrinking the State: Globalization and Public Administration Reform*. Halifax: Fernwood Publishing.

Shilling, C. and Mellor, P. A. (1998) 'Durkheim, morality and modernity: collective effervescence, homo duplex and the sources of moral action', *British Journal of Sociology* 49(2): 193–209.

Shils, E. and Young, M. (1953) 'The meaning of the coronation', *Sociological Review* 1: 63–81.

Sierra Club of Canada (1997) *Presentation to the House of Commons Standing Committee on Foreign Affairs and International Trade*, Subcommittee on Trade, Trade Disputes and Investment, 18 Nov. Appendix 1, Joint NGO Statement on the Multilateral Agreement on Investment.

Sikkink, Kathryn (1993) 'Human rights, principled issue-networks, and sovereignty in Latin America', *International Organization* 47: 411–41.

Simeon, Richard (1997) 'Citizens and democracy in the emerging global order', in Tom Courchene (ed.), *The Nation State in a Global Information Era: Policy Challenges*. Kingston, Ont.: John Deutsch Institute for the Study of Economic Policy, 299–314.

Simmel, G. (1950) 'The secret society', in K. H. Wolff (ed.), *The Sociology of Georg Simmel*, New York: The Free Press.

Smith, A. (1995) *Nations and Nationalism in a Global Era*. Cambridge: Polity.

Smith, Jackie (1997) 'Characteristics of the modern transnational social movement sector', in J. Smith, C. Chatfield and R. Pagnucco (eds), *Transnational Social Movements and Global Politics*. Syracuse, NY: Syracuse University Press, 42–58.

——, Chatfield, Charles and Pagnucco, Ron (eds) (1997) *Transnational Social Movements and Global Politics: Solidarity beyond the State*. Syracuse, NY: Syracuse University Press.

Smith, M. (1995) 'Pluralism', in D. Marsh and G. Stoker (eds), *Theory and Methods in Political Science*. London: Macmillan.

Smith, P. and Alexander, J. (1996) 'Review essay: Durkheim's religious revival', *American Journal of Sociology* 102(2): 585–92.

Snow, David A., Zurcher, Louis A. and Ekland-Olson, Ekland (1980) 'Social networks and social movements: a microstructural approach to differential recruitment', *American Sociological Review* 45: 787–801.

Stallabrass, J. (1996) *Gargantua: Manufactured Mass Culture*. London: Verso.

Stanbury, W. T. and Vertinsky, Ilan B. (1995) 'Assessing the impact of the new information technologies on interest group behaviour and policymaking', in Thomas Courchene (ed.), *Technology, Information and Public Policy*. Kingston, Ont.: John Deutsch Institute for the Study Economic of Policy, 293–380.

Stevenson, N. (1999) *The Transformation of the Media: Globalisation, Morality and Ethics*. London: Longman.

Strange, Susan (1996) *Retreat of the State*. Cambridge: Cambridge University Press.

Streck, J. (1998) 'Pulling the plug on electronic town meetings: participatory democracy and the reality of the usenet', in C. Toulouse and T. Luke (eds), *The Politics of Cyberspace*. New York: Routledge.

Szasz, Andrew (1994) *EcoPopulism: Toxic Waste and the Movement for Environmental Justice*. Minneapolis: University of Minnesota Press.

—— and Meuser, Michael (1997) 'Environmental inequalities: literature review and proposals for new directions in research and theory', *Current Sociology* 45(3): 99–120.

Tarrow, S. (1998a) 'Fishnets, Internets, and catnets: globalization and transnational collective action', in M. Hanagan, L. Pasge Moch and W. te Blake (eds), *Challenging Authority: The Historical Study of Contentious Politics*. Minneapolis: University of Minnesota Press, ch. 15.

—— (1998b) *Power in Movement: Social Movements and Contentious Politics*. Cambridge: Cambridge University Press.

Taylor, Bron Raymond (1995) *Ecological Resistance Movements*. New York: SUNY Press.

Taylor, C. (1991) *The Ethics of Authenticity*. Cambridge, Mass.: Harvard University Press.

Taylor, J., Bellamy, C., Raab, C., Dutton, W. H. and Peltu, M. (1996) 'Innovation in public service delivery', in W. H. Dutton (ed.), *Information and Communication Technologies*. Oxford: Oxford University Press: 265–82.

Thompson, F. M. L. (1988) *The Rise of Respectable Society: A Social History of Victorian Britain, 1830–1900*. London: Fontana.

Tilly, C. (1978) *From Mobilisation to Revolution*. Reading: Addison-Wesley.

Tiraykian, E. (1981) 'The elementary forms as revelation', in Buford Rhea (ed.), *The Future of the Sociological Classics*. London: Allen and Unwin.

—— (1988) 'From Durkheim to Managua: revolutions as religious revivals', in J. Alexander (ed.), *Durkheimian Sociology: Cultural Studies*. Cambridge: Cambridge University Press, 44–65.

Tokar, Brian (1995) 'The "Wise Use" Backlash: responding to militant anti-environmentalism', *The Ecologist* 25(4): 150–6.

Tomlinson, J. (1999) *Globalization and Culture*. Cambridge: Polity Press.

Touraine, A. (1971) *The Post-industrial Society: Tomorrow's Social History: Classes, Conflicts and Culture in the Programmed Society*, trans. L. F. X. Mayhew. London: Wildwood House.

—— (1981) *The Voice and the Eye: An Analysis of Social Movements*. Cambridge: Cambridge University Press.

Tranvik, Tommy (2000) 'Surfing together and the rise of social capital?', paper for the *Investigating Social Capital* conference, Solstrand, Norway, 18–21 May.

Tumber, H. (1993) 'Selling scandal: business and the media', *Media, Culture and Society* 15: 345–61.

—— and Bromley, M. (1998) 'Virtual soundbites: political communication in cyberspace', *Media, Culture and Society* 20(1): 159–67.

Turkle, Sherry (1997) 'Multiple subjectivity and virtual community at the end of the Freudian century', *Sociological Inquiry* 67: 72–84.

Turner, V. (1974) *Dramas, Fields and Metaphors: Symbolic Action in Human Society*. Ithaca, NY: Cornell University Press.

—— (1988) *The Anthropology of Performance*. New York: Paj Publications.

Van Dijk, Jan (1999) *The Network Society*. London: Sage.

Van Zoonen, L. (1998) 'A day at the zoo: political communication, pigs and popular culture', *Media, Culture and Society* 20(2): 183–200.

Vidal, J. (1997) *McLibel: Burger Culture on Trial*. London: Pan Books.

Virnoche, Mary and Marx, Gary (1997) '"Only Connect" – E. M. Forster in an age of electronic communication: computer-mediated association and community networks', *Sociological Inquiry* 67: 85–100.

Von Dirke, Sabine (1997) *All the Power to the Imagination! The West German Counterculture from the Student Movement to the Greens*. Lincoln, Neb. and London: University of Nebraska Press.

Wackernagel, Mathis and Rees, William (1996) *Our Ecological Footprint*. Gabriola Island, Canada: New Society Publishers.

Waisbord, S. R. (1994) 'Knocking on newsroom doors: the press and political scandals in Argentina', *Political Communication* 11: 19–33.

Walch, J. (1999) *In the Net: An Internet Guide for the Activist*. London: Zed Books.

Wall, D. (1999) *Earth First! and the Anti-roads Movement: Radical Environmentalism and Comparative Social Movements*. London: Routledge.

Walters, T. (ed.) (1999) *The Mourning of Diana*. London: Berg.

Walzer, Michael (1995) 'The concept of civil society', in idem (ed.), *Towards a Global Civil Society*. Oxford: Berghahn Books, 7–28.

Wapner, Paul (1995) 'Politics beyond the state: environmental activism and world civic politics', *World Politics* 47(2): 311–40.

Ward, K. J. (1999) 'The cyber-ethnographic (re)construction of two feminist online communities', http://www.socresonline.org.uk/socresonline/4/1/word.html.

Warf, B. and Grimes, J. (1997) 'Counterhegemonic discourses and the Internet', *Geographical Review* 87(2): 259–74.

Washbourne, N. (1999) 'Beyond iron laws: information technology and social transformation in the global environment movement', unpublished Ph.D. thesis, University of Surrey.

Wattenberg, B. J. (1991) *The First Universal Nation*. New York: Free Press.

Watts, C. (1999) 'Unworkable feeling: Diana, death and feminisation', *New Formations* 36: 34–46.

Weber, M. (1948a) 'Politics as a vocation', in H. H. Gerth and C. W. Mills (eds), *From Max Weber: Essays in Sociology*. London: Routledge and Kegan Paul, 77–128.

—— (1948b) 'Class, status and party', in H. H. Gerth and C. W. Mills (eds), *From Max Weber: Essays in Sociology*. London: Routledge and Kegan Paul, 180–95.

Webster, Frank (1997) 'Is this the information age? Towards a critique of Manuel Castells' *City* 8 (Dec.): 71–84.

—— (2000) 'Information, capitalism and uncertainty', *Information, Communication and Society* 3(1): 69–90.

Webster, Ruth (1998) 'Environmental collective action: stable patterns of cooperation and issue alliances at the European level', in J. Greenwood and M. Aspinwall (eds), *Collective Action in the European Union*. London: Routledge, 176–95.

Wellman, Barry, *et al.* (1996) 'Computer networks as social networks: collaborative work, telework, and virtual community', *Annual Review of Sociology* 22: 213–38.

Wernick, A. (1991) *Promotional Culture*. London: Sage.

Whittier, Nancy (1995) *Feminist Generations: The Persistence of the Radical Women's Movement*. Philadelphia: Temple University Press.

Wilson, E. (1997) 'The Unbearable Lightness of Diana', in M. Merck (ed.), *After Diana – Irreverent Elegies*. London and New York: Verso.

Wray, S. (1998) 'Electronic civil disobedience and the World Wide Web of hacktivism: a mapping of extraparliamentarian direct action Net politics,' http://www.nyu.edu/projects/wray/wwwhack.html, New York University: 13.

Yearley, S. (1996) *Sociology, Environmentalism, Globalization*. London: Sage.

Yelvington, S. (1999) (file://G/cd/keynote/yelving.htm).

Young, J. E. (1993) *Global Network: Computers in a Sustainable Society*, World Watch Paper 115, September, Washington, DC.

Zald, M. N. and McCarthy, J. (1987) *Social Movements in an Organizational Society*. New Brunswick, NJ: Transaction Books.

Zeitlin, M. R. (1989) *The Large Corporation and the Capitalist Class*. Cambridge: Polity.

Zizek, S. (1997) 'Multiculturalism, or the cultural logic of multinational capitalism', *New Left Review* 223: 28–51.

Zolo, D. (2000) 'The "Singapore Model": democracy, communication and globalization', in K. Nash and A. Scott (eds), *Companion to Political Sociology*. Oxford: Blackwell.

Index